LANGUAGE DEVELOPMENT:
Form and Function in Emerging Grammars

LANGUAGE DEVELOPMENT:
Form and Function in Emerging Grammars

LOIS BLOOM

 Research Monograph No. 59
THE M.I.T. PRESS
Cambridge, Massachusetts, and London, England

Set in Monophoto Times Roman. Printed and bound in the United States of America by The Colonial Press Inc.

Second printing, November 1973

ISBN 0 262 02056 4 (hardcover)

Library of Congress catalog card number: 77-107987

Foreword

This is the fifty-ninth volume in the M.I.T. Research Monograph Series published by the M.I.T. Press. The objective of this series is to contribute to the professional literature a number of significant pieces of research, larger in scope than journal articles but normally less ambitious than finished books. We believe that such studies deserve a wider circulation than can be accomplished by informal channels, and we hope that this form of publication will make them readily accessible to research organizations, libraries, and independent workers.

HOWARD W. JOHNSON

To my mother and father—
Estre and Jack Masket

Acknowledgments

The investigation reported here is part of an extended study of the language development of three children and is, essentially, my 1968 Columbia University dissertation. The greater part of this study was carried out under the direction of William Labov, and his influence is apparent in every aspect of the project. None of what follows here would have been possible without the benefit of his insight and his wisdom—he has been the *great teacher*. The actual investigation and analysis of the data are, of course, my own, and so the responsibility for the resulting interpretations and any errors is mine alone.

Throughout the study, Edward D. Mysak and Seymour Rigrodsky gave counsel, encouragement, and valued assistance in planning and procedure. I am grateful to Walter MacGinitie for his constant support and for his special insight into the nature of many of the problems along the way. I am especially indebted to Janellen Huttenlocher who provided a knowledgable perspective that led to completion of the portion of the study presented here. Her enthusiasm and support will always be warmly appreciated.

I want to thank Nancy Richardson, who made the initial playground explorations in my search for subjects, and Elena Chopek for her assistance in tabulating and counting all those words, words, words. I am particularly grateful to Courtney B. Cazden for her comments and suggestions after reading the original dissertation and portions of the revised manuscript.

My husband, Robert H. Bloom, gave his time, support, and enduring patience in the three years of the study. His searching questions, criticisms, and, more than all else, his supreme confidence are truly appreciated.

Financial support for the investigation was provided by Public Health Service Fellowship No. 5-Fl-MH-30,001-03 from the National Institute of Mental Health.

A small child learning to talk is a delight, and the delight in this task has been threefold because of Kathryn, Eric, and Gia—who let me listen in as they learned to talk—and their parents—who included me with my tape recorder in the daily course of events, so easily and so willingly.

But my greatest debt is to the many children I have known for whom learning to talk was so difficult. They gave me my first insight into the complexity of language and the enormity of the task of its acquisition.

L.B.

Contents

1 Form and Function of Children's Speech

A young child's success in learning to talk depends on his ability to perceive and organize his environment, the language that is a part of that environment, and the relation between the two. Thus, the acquisition of language is a complex process that is crucially related to the child's cognitive-perceptual growth and his interaction in an environment of objects, events, and relations. Clues to children's cognitive development have long been sought in the study of children's language. It is now a basic assumption that the specification of *what* the child learns when he learns to talk and *how* this learning takes place—knowledge of the substance and process of language development—can be a preeminent source of insight into the development of thought and the learning process.

In the last decade, inquiry into what the child learns when he learns grammar has focused attention on the formal syntax of children's speech—on descriptions of the arrangements of words in sentences uttered and understood at successive stages. These studies (which are described briefly in Table 1.1 and discussed at length in Section 1.1) were able to demonstrate that children's earliest sentences were systematic. Rules of grammar were proposed to account for the juxtaposition of words in these early syntactic utterances, but while proposing 'generative' rules of grammar, these studies were essentially taxonomic. They relied exclusively on distributional analyses—describing the form and cooccurrence of linguistic elements in children's utterances. There was no attention to linguistic function—to what the

1

utterances seemed to be saying. Yet it is precisely this kind of information which is most directly relevant for inferring something about the cognitive function underlying linguistic expression.

It is the nature of language that a linguistic fact assumes significance in relation to its "element of experience ... content or 'meaning,'" (Sapir, 1921, p. 10), and according to current linguistic theory, the grammar of a language "is a system of rules that relate sound and meaning in a particular way" (Chomsky, 1968, p. 23). This study was based upon the premise that linguistic descriptions of the form of children's speech provide only partial information about the child's intuitive knowledge of a linguistic code. The approach to analyzing children's language reported here attempted to reach the 'meaning' of children's sentences by focusing on the correlation of linguistic and contextual features—on what the child said in relation to what he was talking about and the situation and behavior that cooccurred with what he said— rather than on strictly formal considerations of language content. Relating utterance to referent provided information for interpreting the semantic intent of utterances so that inherent grammatical structure could be identified. In the linguistic theory of generative transformational grammar, the "grammatical relations that determine semantic interpretation" are defined by the phrase structure rules of grammar (Chomsky, 1965, p. 141). The linguistic analysis of the data sought to discover evidence of such rules in relation to what could be inferred about cognitive function underlying the children's linguistic expression.

The data for the study were obtained from observations, every six weeks, of three children—Kathryn, Eric, and Gia. Eric and Gia were 19 months 1 week old and Kathryn was 21 months old when first seen. The collection of samples from Eric and Gia began at linguistically earlier stages of development than the level Kathryn had reached at Time I. Gia's and Eric's earlier use of language was studied until the time when their linguistic maturity (in terms of mean length of utterance) approximated the level of Kathryn at Time I. Rules of grammar were proposed for the language of the three children when mean length of utterance was less than 1.5 morphemes: the first observation of Kathryn, the first two observations of Gia, and the first three observations of Eric.[1] Thus, the three children were studied individually and

---

[1] It should be pointed out that mean length of utterance—although valuable as a means of describing and comparing speech samples—is a superficial index of linguistic maturity. As observed by Cazden (1968), there are important differences in relative grammatical competence among children when mean length of utterance is held constant. The structural complexity of sentences may be varied without necessarily increasing length of production; "ə book," "more book," "read book," and "Mommy (subject) book (object)" are structurally different although the surface form of each consists of only two morphemes.

eventually compared at similar levels of linguistic development and not compared according to their progress in terms of chronological age. The grammatical subsystem of negation was studied further and the development of the semantics and syntax of negation was described for those samples of the children's speech with mean length of utterance less than 3.0 morphemes (during which time the three children were each less than 28 months old). Table 2.1 in Chapter 2 presents a description of the children in terms of age and mean length of utterance during the time period covered by the study reported here.

Section 1.1 discusses the psycholinguistic investigations in the last decade that have studied the emergence of grammar in children's spontaneous speech. Following this there is a discussion of interpretation of the semantic intent of children's utterances, as that notion has been used in this study. Chapter 2 describes the three children, the frame of reference used for the evaluation of speech events, and certain procedural decisions that were made for the purposes of the linguistic analysis. Chapter 2 concludes with a brief discussion of aspects of the theory, notations, and terminology of generative transformational grammar that were pertinent for the grammatical description of the children's language.

The grammars proposed to account for the children's language are discussed separately for each child: Kathryn in Chapter 3, Gia in Chapter 4, and Eric in Chapter 5. Chapter 6 presents a discussion of the linguistic rules proposed in the grammars to account for the result of the constraints that appeared to operate on length and complexity of the children's utterances. The description of the development of the syntax and semantics of negation is presented in Chapter 7. The final chapter discusses different strategies that the children appeared to use in their approaches to learning the model language and the relationship between the children's linguistic expression and development of cognition.

1.1. The Form of Children's Utterances

Several psycholinguistic studies in the last decade have used similar approaches to study the acquisition of syntax (see Table 1.1). In each of these studies a small number of children were visited in their homes soon after the emergence of their first phrases, and several hours of speech were tape-recorded at periodic intervals. In the study by Braine, the mothers of two of the children kept written records of their utterances.

Table 1. Longitudinal Psycholinguistic Studies of Language Acquisition

Principal Investigator	No. of Subjects	Age Span Studied	Sample Size and Spacing	Sample Uniformity
Braine (1963)	3 boys	19 to 24 months	2 subjects: parent's written record	"Play sessions" recorded for third subject
			1 subject: 4 hours over a 4-week period, audio record	Professional parents
Brown et al., (1963, 1964, 1969)	2 girls, 1 boy	18 to 28 months; 27 to 42 months; 27 to 48 months (Initial MLU: 1.40; 1.75; 1.84)	2 to 6 hours every month; audio record	Mother–child interaction. Parents: college or high school graduates. Firstborn
Miller and Ervin (1964, 1966)	5	From 21 or 24 months over a 3-month period	45 minutes weekly, then 4 to 5 hours every 2 months; audio record	Investigator– child interaction

Linguistic analysis was applied to these individual samples by Brown and Fraser or to a number of the samples over a period of several months by Brown and Bellugi, Miller and Ervin, and Braine. On the basis of privileges of occurrence, the words in the children's utterances were grouped into classes, and rules were derived to account for the ordering of the classes. It was significant that these studies were able to demonstrate that the earliest two-word utterances by young children are systematic and rule-governed. Moreover, the several investigators concurred in the nature of the rules with which they described children's syntactic constructions. When utterances were analyzed in terms of the form and distribution of their elements and the elements classified on the basis of their cooccurrence, there appeared to be essentially two classes of words. A small class of words occurred frequently, in relatively fixed sentence position as *pivots* in juxtaposition with a larger class of *x-words*, each of which occurred less frequently. The x-words generally provided lexical content, and pivots functioned as syntactic operators. The pivot and x-word terminology was used originally by Braine; Brown and Bellugi referred to "functors" and

"contentives" and Miller and Ervin to "operators" and "nonopera-
tors." Essentially, these two classes of words were viewed as the pre-
cursors for function and substantive classes of morphemes in the adult
model language.

The linguistic evidence presented for the rules of grammar proposed
by the Brown group and by Miller and Ervin consisted of patterns of
sentences in a subset of the children's utterances—lists of the two-word
or three-word utterances arranged according to shared features of their
surface constituents. For example, Miller and Ervin presented utterances that contained the forms "on" and "off" and all utterances that
contained the demonstratives "this," "that," "that's," "thatsa";
Brown presented all utterances with "here," "there," "Mum," and
"Dad" in his study with Fraser, and all utterances with surface features
of a noun phrase with Bellugi. Thus, the pivots—"on," "off," "this,"
"that's," "here," "there," "Mum," "Dad," the articles and modifiers
in a noun phrase, and others—were small in number, and they occurred
in relatively fixed positions, with many different words.

Two early sentence types were identified in children's language, by
Braine and by McNeill (1966; on the basis of his review of the literature
and the data collected by Brown), according to a description of the
surface constituents of utterances: constructions with pivot forms,
pivot + x-word or *x-word + pivot*; and constructions without pivot
forms, two substantive words in juxtaposition, *x-word + x-word*. It
appears that in children's speech, as in adult speech, some words (such
as pivots and function words) occur more frequently and in a greater
number of linguistic environments than do other words. Moreover, in
children's speech, it is not simply the case that any two words can occur
in any order in an utterance. However, the distributional analyses used
to obtain 'pivot grammars' ignored the linguistic function of utterances—notions of linguistic contrast, interpretation, 'meaning,' or
reference were not considered.

It can be demonstrated that the notion of 'pivot grammar' describes
children's utterances in only the most superficial way. In a sample of
speech with mean length of utterance of 1.32 morphemes from Kathryn
at age 21 months, the utterance

(1) Mommy sock.

occurred twice in two separate contexts, as follows:

(1) (i) Kathryn picked up her mother's sock;
    (ii) Mommy putting Kathryn's sock on Kathryn.

The two occurrences of the utterance would have the same structural description if classed as pivot + x-word or x-word + x-word because the surface form of each is the same.

Similarly, the negatively marked utterances that occurred at the same time in Kathryn's speech, for example,

(2) no fit.
(3) no dirty soap.
(4) no pocket.
(5) no Mommy.

would be classed together as pivot + x-word, and nothing more could be said about the structure of the sentences, which occurred in the following situations:

(2) Kathryn was unable to put a lamb into a small block;
(3) Kathryn pushing away a piece of worn soap in the bathtub, wanting to be washed with new pink soap;
(4) Kathryn unable to find a pocket in Mommy's skirt;
(5) Kathryn pulling away from someone else, not Mommy, who had offered to comb her hair.

Utterances (1) through (5) are ambiguous when presented in a list of utterances apart from the contexts in which each occurred. For example, "no dirty soap" could be interpreted in at least four ways:

(3) (i) There is no dirty soap.
     (ii) The soap isn't dirty.
     (iii) That isn't dirty soap.
     (iv) I don't want the dirty soap.

There is no formal way to describe the relationship between "no" and "dirty soap"—the inherent syntax of the sentence—so as to be able to explain its semantics and thereby resolve the ambiguity. In the child's earliest grammar (or sequence of grammars) there are no formal features such as morphological inflection or prosodic intonation and juncture that might distinguish the inherent structure of utterances (1)(i) and (ii) or (2) to (5) to justify, linguistically, the semantic contrasts they represent. The same surface structure occurs in different situations with different interpretations or functions. In the example (1) (i) and (ii), "Mommy sock," the two forms were homonymous, and the same utterance was used by Kathryn in two different contexts with apparently different semantic relationship between the constituents.

The notion of sentence structure implies a pattern of organization—

an arrangement of otherwise independent parts that is based on the relationship of the parts to each other. If there are different semantic interpretations of utterances with similar surface form, as in the two occurrences of "Mommy sock" and utterances (2) to (5) with "no," then the relationships of the elements in the utterances to each other are different. For example, "no" in (4) denies the existence of "pocket," but the relationship of "no" to the rest of the sentence in (3) is different—the soap exists, and it is 'dirty.' This would imply that Kathryn has demonstrated an awareness of some of the possibilities for combining lexical items with different relationships between them to correspond with different cognitive experiences. It appears that children may be learning more about grammar—more about the structural relationships between linguistic elements—in this early stage than just the permitted patterns of juxtaposition.

Chomsky (1964b) pointed out that "there is surely no doubt that the child's achievements in systematizing linguistic data, at every stage, go well beyond what he actually produces in normal speech," and that there no doubt exists "an underlying, fuller conception of sentence structure [which may be] unrealized in his speech." Kathryn's use of "Mommy sock" and utterances with "no" provided preliminary evidence that supported this contention. It would therefore appear to be necessary for grammars of child language to do more than just describe the surface constituents of sentences that can occur.

1.2. Underlying and Superficial Linguistic Structure

The linguistic theory of generative transformational grammar (Chomsky, 1957, 1965) has been the dominant theoretical influence on studies of children's language and language development in the last decade. However, the earliest attempts to apply generative transformational grammar in investigations of children's language ignored what have come to be two of the most significant and crucial aspects of the theory: (1) the distinction between underlying and superficial linguistic structure, and (2) the essential relevance of the semantics of a sentence for the specification of its structure (Postal, 1964; Chomsky, 1965, p. 16).

Essentially, a sentence of a language has two representations—a *surface structure* and an *underlying structure*. The surface structure is the structural specification for the actual physical and acoustic event of the sentence as it is spoken—the linear sequence of elements produced by the sender and heard by the receiver. The underlying or 'deep' structure specifies an abstract account of the 'meaning' or semantic interpretation of the sentence—as intended by the sender and understood by the receiver. The underlying structure is abstract in the sense that it represents a construct that is intrinsic to the sentence it represents but actually 'exists' only in the theoretical linguistic account of the sentence.

The basic grammatical relations within a sentence—such as sentence subject or predicate object—determine the semantics of the sentence and are specifiable only in its underlying structure. For example, the two sentences (a) "John is easy to please" and (b) "John is eager to please" have similar surface structure—"John" functions as the *grammatical* (superficial) subject of the sentence in both cases. But in the first sentence, (a) "John is easy to please," "John" is not the *logical* subject of the sentence—someone else, not John, pleases John. The semantic relationship between "John" and the rest of sentence (a) would be specified in the underlying structure where "John" does not function as subject-of-the-sentence. "John" would be the logical subject in (b) "John is eager to please," where it is John who pleases.

The two occurrences of "Mommy sock" could be said to have the same surface structure inasmuch as the sequence of elements actually produced was the same in each instance. However, semantic interpretation of the two different utterances would depend on the fact that the underlying structure of each was necessarily different. That is, the semantic-syntactic relation between "Mommy" and "sock" was necessarily specifiable for the two utterances in two different ways to account for the fact that in one instance Mommy was an actor-agent and in the other instance "Mommy" was an attribute of the sock.

The meaning or semantics of a sentence is known intuitively by the speaker-hearer of a language. It is possible to tap the intuition of an adult and obtain information about his grammatical judgment or his knowledge of semantic notions, and this kind of information serves as primary evidence for rules of generative grammar. For example, one might ask an adult to explain the ambiguity of such sentences as "Fighting lions can be dangerous," or one might question him as to whether "John is easy to please" and "John is eager to please" 'mean' the same thing. However, in attempting to describe and explain a developing language system, it is not possible to search the intuition of a 'native speaker' for grammatical judgments in the same way. One simply could not ask Kathryn to explain the ambiguity of "Mommy sock" or, indeed, to judge whether the two occurrences of the utterance were 'the same' or 'different.' The early studies of children's language that attempted to use generative transformational grammar for analyzing children's utterances recognized but failed to compensate for this lack of accessibility to the intuition of a native speaker-informant.

Generative transformational grammar could be used in a more powerful way to account for children's language than it has been if semantic information were available in order to make inferences about underlying structure. However, to obtain such evidence for constructing grammars for children's language it appears to be necessary to depend on the intuition of a native speaker of the mature language for interpreting the semantic intention of what the child says, as in the examples "Mommy sock" and utterances with "no."

1.3. The Function of Children's Utterances: Interpreting Semantic Intention

The difference in linguistic function between the two occurrences of "Mommy sock" and among utterances with "no" became apparent when the behavioral context in which the utterances occurred was known. It has often been observed that what young children say is usually related directly to what they do and see. Brown and Bellugi (1964, p. 135) took notice of the fact that children speak "very much in the here and now." Leopold (1949, Vol. III, p. 31) made extensive use of the "aid of the situation" in inferring the intended meanings of utterances. Although some utterances may be equivocal or otherwise not interpretable, it is generally not difficult to judge the relationship between what a child says and what he is talking about. When Kathryn said "Mommy sock" and Mommy was putting Kathryn's sock on Kathryn, it was clear that Mommy's relation to that sock was somehow different than when Kathryn said "Mommy sock" and picked up Mommy's sock. Adults who know children tend to know what they are saying more often than not. The child probably comes to depend on this factor of *communication* to a certain extent. Several studies that give support to this notion are cited by McCarthy (1954, pp. 588–589).

Moreover, overt behavior and features of context and situation signal the meanings of what children say in a way that is not true for what adults say. Generally, it is not possible to understand what adults mean by observing context or behavior; adults transmit information, and the exchange is essentially linguistic. If an adult or an older child mounts a bicycle, there is no need for him to inform anyone who has seen him do it that he has done it. But a young child who mounts a tricycle will often 'announce' the fact: "I ride trike!" What young children say usually relates directly to what they do and see, and what they do and see can also be seen and evaluated by a listener-observer in the environment.

For the purpose of this study, evaluation of the children's language began with the basic assumption that it was possible to reach the semantics of children's sentences by considering nonlinguistic informa-tion from context and behavior in relation to linguistic performance. This is not to say that the inherent 'meaning' or the child's actual semantic intent was obtainable for any given utterance. The semantic interpretation inherent in an utterance is part of the intuition of the child and cannot be 'known' with authority. The only claim that could be made was that evaluation of an utterance in relation to the context in which it occurred provided more information for analyzing intrinsic structure than would a simple distributional analysis of the recorded corpus.

1.3.1. 'One-Word Sentences'

Many investigators have reported that the child's single-word utter-ances, before the development of syntax, seem to function as one-word sentences (McCarthy, 1954, p. 525; Lenneberg, 1967, pp. 281–283). This has been an attractive notion, and the ability of children to under-stand more than they can express at this age gives some support to it. That such words are indeed holophrastic is open to question. Some words uttered by the child translate readily to "I see X" or "I want X" or "X is." The child has named the one aspect of the referent that has greatest salience for him—an object he wants or recognizes. His wanting the object or recognizing the object is part of his experience of the object, but there is no evidence that the experience of wanting or recognizing is part of the overt or covert linguistic behavior. His extra-linguistic behavior—reaching, pointing, or whining—accounts for the interpretation of his utterance as a direction or comment, but the interpretation cannot introduce structure. If such were the case one might want to assign structural descriptions to gestures alone.

There was evidence that the children recognized more than one aspect of the referent or recognized relationship between aspects of the referent without expressing (syntactically) either cooccurrence or relationship. Leopold (1939–1949, Vol. III, p. 20) observed this same linguistic be-havior: "two [related] one-word utterances ... said in succession" just before the emergence of the earliest two-word constructions in his daughter's speech. There were numerous examples of the children successively naming aspects of a referent in this way in the first texts obtained, when the mean length of utterance was 1.12 morphemes for Gia and 1.10 morphemes for Eric:[2]

(6) G:I (Gia picking up her mother's
    slipper)   Mommy. Mommy.

    What is that?   slipper.

    slipper.   Mommy.

(7) G:I (Gia looking at a picture of a
    boy in a toy car)   go.

    car.   car. ride.

(8) G:I (Gia looking at a picture of a
    girl in a bathtub with a toy fish)   bath.

    bath.   girl fish. fish.

    fish. Who's taking a bath?

    (Gia pointing to the fish)   fish.

    fish.   water.

(9) E:I (Eric looking out the window
    at street below; cars going by;
    children and adults walking)   car. see.

    see.   car.

    car.   boy.

The order in which the forms occurred when the child successively named aspects of the referent in this way was variable. However, as will be discussed in Chapter 3, when the child produced a construction such as "girl fish" in (8) above, and in Eric's earliest construction, *see X*, the consistency with which the surface word order corresponded to the inherent grammatical relation within the utterance was impressive. In this example, "girl fish" could be a conjunction (expressing simple cooccurrence of two referents), or it could be an expression of the inherent relationship between girl (subject) and fish (object).

[2] Examples of speech events are numbered consecutively within each chapter; the source is identified by the child's initial (K, Kathryn; E, Eric; G, Gia) and the roman numeral that identifies the speech sample. Description of context is contained in parentheses and appears on the left, along with utterances spoken by someone other than the child. The utterance spoken by the child appears on the right. For further explanation, see the Note, Table 3.2, p. 42, and the Glossary of Terms and Notations.

The following example also occurred at Time I :

> (10) G : I (Gia picked up the plastic disc
> that had covered her toy watch,   button.
> calling it a button)   button. button. button.
>
> Oh, button. You found the button
> again. Did you find the button
> again?   pocket. pocket.
>
> (Gia struggling to put the disc
> into her pocket, but unable to do
> so because she was sitting on the
> pocket)   . . . . .
>
> Where is the button? Where are
> you putting the button?
>
> (Gia holding the disc out to the
> investigator; struggling with the
> utterance; wanting the investigator −bɑi↑/ /bəp/ /bə́bə̀/
> to put the disc into her pocket)   /bɑi/ ------

In this exchange it was evident that Gia 'knew' the 'names' for the two objects—"button" and "pocket." It was also evident that she wanted *the button in her pocket.* When she was unable to put the button in her pocket she could not express the relationship between the two objects, even though she 'knew the words.' It might be argued that the child's linguistic competence was being interfered with—that the struggle with the small button and the inaccessible pocket operated to restrict somehow her linguistic performance. However, all that can be said in this example is that Gia knows what she wants and that she cannot express the relationship she wants to exist between the two objects she can name separately without difficulty. There is evidence that Gia cannot 'use' the syntax. There is no evidence that she 'knows' the syntax.

The example (9) above, which is closer to the original example of the child's earlier one-word utterances translating to "I see X," occurred at a time when Eric had barely begun to express the predicate *see X* (discussed in Chapter 5). The following also occurred at this time:

> (11) E : I (Eric watching the tape re-
> corder reels through the window in
> the tape recorder lid)

Window.	see. ↑
See.	window.
Window. Close it up. Close it up. (Investigator trying to cover tape recorder lid)	------ ------ ------ ------
hm? What? (Eric looking at tape recorder reels through window in lid)	------ ------ see. ↑
See.	see ↑ · window.
Window.	

This expansion of an utterance by the child was an early example of what subsequently became frequent linguistic behavior for all three children. These examples of syntactic process—the child's connecting two aspects of the referent after naming them singly—provided evidence for assuming that the child appreciated the underlying relationship that existed for the elements as he used them. The sentence status of "see window" in (11) is strong, and the holophrastic status of "see" and "window" as they occurred in (11) is tenable. However, there is no evidence that "see" and "car" and "boy" in (9) or "button" and "pocket" in (10) have the same holophrastic status.

1.3.2. Syntactic Constructions

Overinterpreting is a stronger tendency when children begin to combine words to form constructions. There is more evidence available for interpreting what is said, but there is also more room for giving the child's linguistic competence greater credit than is deserved. Brown and Bellugi (1964) observed that it is very natural for adults to respond to the child with an expansion of his utterance. It is tempting indeed to 'fill in the blanks' in the child's sentences. It is this type of expansion that needs to be distinguished from the notion of assigning a semantic interpretation to what the child says, as that notion has been used in this analysis.

Expanding the utterance "Mommy sock" would consist of supplying missing, but predictable, elements in a linear sequence and could conceivably continue indefinitely:

(i) *Mommy* puts on my *sock*,
(ii) *Mommy* is putting on my *sock* now,
(iii) I see that *Mommy* is putting on my *sock*. . . .

In contrast, imposing a semantic interpretation on the utterance would seek to account for only as much of the relationship between the elements of the utterance that actually occur, that is, between "Mommy" and "sock," as can be justified by what is known about the referent—that *Mommy* is the agent and *sock* the single object goal of an ongoing event. The grammatical relationship that holds between "Mommy" and "sock" in this case is that of subject-object, with a dummy element having features specifying the temporal immediacy of the event linking the two in the abstract underlying representation of the sentence.

Thus, notions of underlying structure were postulated on the basis of interpretation of the semantic intention of utterances as inferred from information relating to behavior and context in the larger structural units—the *speech events*—in which the utterances occurred. The data used as 'input' to the grammars included evidence from the children's linguistic performance and intuitive judgments of the meanings of sentences by a speaker of the adult model of the language.

The mentalistic nature of the secondary data (the primary data being the children's linguistic expression) may be seen as a limitation in the study. Chomsky has answered critics of mentalism in linguistics as follows: "Mentalistic linguistics is simply theoretical linguistics that uses performance as data (along with other data, for example, the data provided by introspection) for the determination of competence, the latter being taken as the primary object of its investigation" (Chomsky, 1965, p. 193). To be sure, the "introspection" spoken of is the introspection by a native speaker of the language being analyzed. The intuition that was the source of the secondary data in this study was literally removed from the "mental reality underlying [the] actual behavior" (Chomsky, 1965, p. 4) being studied. However, the assumptions that were made about semantic intention were based on extralinguistic data that related directly to the children's linguistic performance. The fact of the child's utterance is only one part of a larger, complex reality. The utterance occurs within situations that can be characterized in terms of behavior, other participants, and context—factors that need to be apprehended by the child learning to use the language and by the listener seeking to understand what the child says as he uses language.

2 Description of the Study

Three children—Kathryn, Eric, and Gia—were seen individually in their homes, for approximately eight hours over a three- or four-day period, every six weeks. The tape-recorded observations of approximately eight hours of activity formed the individual speech *samples* that were used for analysis. The first speech samples were obtained from Eric and Gia when each was 19 months 1 week old and from Kathryn when she was 21 months old. Table 2.1 presents a description

Table 2.1. Description of the Children for Each of the Individual Speech Samples

	Kathryn			Eric			Gia	
	MLU	Age		MLU	Age		MLU	Age
I	1.32	21,0	I	1.10	19,1	I	1.12	19,1
II	1.92	22,3	II	1.19	20,2	II	1.34	20,2
III	2.83	24,2	III	1.42	22,0	III	1.58	22,1
			IV	1.69	23,2	IV	1.79	23,3
			V	2.63	25,1	V	2.30	25,2
			VI	2.84	26,3	VI	2.75	27,1

Note: In order to identify the individual speech samples in the discussion and presentation of data, the samples are numbered with roman numerals. The numbering of the samples is individual and consecutive for each child, so there is no relation between Kathryn I, Eric I, and Gia I except that each is the first sample collected. Age is given here in months and weeks.

of the three children in terms of mean length of utterance (MLU)[1] and age for the samples that were used in the analyses reported here.

Each sample consisted of the child's speech (1) while playing with a group of toys and books (described in Appendix A.2) that all three children knew only in the observation situations, (2) during eating, dressing, and toileting activities, and (3) during play with a peer. The planned activities accounted for roughly one-half to two-thirds of each session.

With a few brief exceptions, the investigator, who was well known to the children, was present in the observation sessions and interacted freely with the child. The mothers were present less than one-third of the time and the fathers only occasionally. The investigator's participation was necessary for noting features of behavior and environment in order to transcribe the tape recordings subsequently, and for maintaining the relative uniformity of the sessions for the three children. The samples were less than 'naturalistic' to this extent.

Each observation was recorded using a Uher 4000 Report-L battery-operated tape recorder at $3\frac{3}{4}$ ips, with 1.0-mil polyester Scotch magnetic tape, No. 150. Two dynamic microphones were used: the RCA BK-12A or the RCA BK-6B. The microphone, with a 15-foot cord, was mounted on a portable stand because lavaliere placement caused excessive noise and the wire interfered with freedom of movement. The ready portability of the tape recorder and the microphone made it possible to follow the children quickly from room to room. The microphone was most often within three feet of the child. The children accepted the presence of the recording equipment as a natural extension of the investigator and they were unaware of its purpose.

The tape recordings were transcribed by the investigator, usually within less than two weeks, so that taping and transcribing different subjects did not overlap. All of the child's utterances and everything said to him were transcribed along with information about the nonlinguistic context as it was recalled and understood from linguistic and nonlinguistic cues recorded on the tape. Although identification of the utterance and situation recorded on the tape was sometimes indeterminable, in the course of the eight-hour sample these unidentified utterances represented a small minority of the total number of utterances available for analysis.[2]

[1] Mean length of utterance was computed according to the directions supplied by Roger Brown in Slobin, 1967, p. 19, with the exception that immediate utterance repetitions were not counted.

[2] For a more detailed description of the children and discussion of the procedures used in collecting and transcribing the tape recordings, see Appendix A.1.

2.1. Procedures for Analyzing Obtained Utterances

The *corpus* of utterances selected for grammatical analysis consisted of constructions of more than one tentative morpheme that occurred in the course of a speech sample. Tentative morpheme identity was ascribed initially to forms with morpheme status in the adult model or forms that were not in the adult model but were productive in the child's lexicon. Subsequent analysis often revealed that certain forms were not contrastive—for example, inflectional suffixes, "-ing" and "-s," or "here" in the utterance "here Mommy" produced by Gia at Time II, when (1) "here" did not occur elsewhere and (2) "here Mommy" accompanied Gia's giving objects to people other than Mommy.

Duplications, with or without reduction, of something said to the child; immediate repetitions of the same utterance by the child; fragments of songs, rhymes, or stories; and utterances that were wholly or partially unintelligible were not included in the analysis.

2.1.1. Linguistic Productivity

Rather than account for all of the obtained utterances, it was necessary to establish criteria for 'well-formedness.' An attempt was made to determine regularities of performance that could be used as evidence for inferring the most productive and stable components of underlying competence. This involved defining a standard of *productivity* and accounting for those structures that were productive in the child's linguistic system at a given time. Productivity of a structure was judged on the basis of its use in the corpus with different formatives in different situations, and the frequency and consistency with which it was used in linguistic and nonlinguistic contexts where it had occurred before and might therefore have been expected to occur again. Generally, a structure was *unique* if it occurred only once in the corpus of a speech sample, *marginal* if it occurred fewer than five times with different formatives in different situations, and *productive* if it occurred five times or more.

The goal of accounting for the structural description of every unique sentence in the child's output would be not only formidable but a superfluous requirement for a grammar of his language. There were two sources of unique sentences in the texts. First, the factors of "memory limitations, distractions, shifts of attention and interest, and errors," which interact with the competence of the adult speaker and so affect his performance (Chomsky, 1965, p. 3), also affect the performance of the child, whose competence is presumably more tenuous than the well-learned, automatically operating system of the adult. There is strong evidence that the child's language is systematic, but the system is in a state of flux, and violations occur.

Second, the isolated or occasional occurrence of a structure is not sufficient evidence for crediting the child with the pertinent rule-operating behavior. In this respect, children's performance often belies competence. As examples of this, Eric produced the unique negative sentence "ə don't want baby" and dropped a doll he was holding at Time II, when in all other expressions of negation, he produced one pattern—"no more" plus a noun. Six weeks later, he had begun to differentiate the form of the negative element—the forms "no more" and "no" occurred syntactically in complementary distribution. At this time he also produced the unique negative sentence "ə want any shoes" when he did not want to wear his shoes.

Unique utterances from either of the above sources were excluded and not accounted for by rules of grammar. However, these un-accounted-for utterances are presented and described in the discussion of the children's grammars in Chapters 3, 4, and 5.

Utterances were entered sequentially on the Analysis Form, Appendix B.1. The entries consisted of transferring the utterance and coding the nonlinguistic information obtained from the original transcriptions. The nonlinguistic context was entered on the Form in terms of the *factors* and *functions* of *speech events*, using the notations in Appendix B.2. Preceding language and pertinent responses from someone else to what the child said were recorded in full. The factors and functions of speech events were identified and described in order to infer (1) semantic interpretations of utterances and (2) the structural descriptions that would account for semantic interpretation.

2.1.2. Speech Events

To provide a framework for examining the relationship between utterance and referent, utterances produced by the child were considered within the larger structural units of "speech events," as suggested originally by Jakobson and subsequently elaborated by Hymes (1964, pp. 215 ff.). "A speech event implies a set of constitutive factors and functions." Hymes proposed a set of major types of factors of speech events as a "heuristic starting-point" in the "study of speech as part of behavior."

Factors of Speech Events

Hymes distinguished seven types of factors of speech events: message-form, code, channel, sender, receiver, topic, and context, with further distinctions possible for each. In this study, the *message-form* was the variable being investigated in an effort to determine the *code* being used by the child. Certain of the other factors were constant factors in the data obtained: the *channel* used was the voice; the *sender* was the child being observed.

Others of the factors distinguished by Hymes were functionally more relevant to analyzing the child's use of language and contributed to interpreting the semantic intent of utterances. Whether or not utterances were actually 'directed' to a listener in the environment, the *receiver* was the investigator or the mother most often and thus was a relatively constant factor, although other children, younger siblings, fathers, and toys were also receivers.

The *topic* or theme of an utterance was what the child was talking about; generally, the children talked about events, persons, and objects. The topic was usually inferable from the utterance content and corresponding salient features of the context. When Kathryn said "Mommy sock" and picked up Mommy's sock, the topic was *sock*; when she said "Mommy sock," and Mommy was putting on her sock, the topic was the *event*; when she said "cat raisin," wanting the cat to have raisins, the topic was either *cat*, or *raisin*, or possibly the *event*: *cat(subject)*, *raisin(object)*; when she said "ə sit down now" and then sat down, the topic was the *event*. The topic identified the referent; put another way, the referent was the element of the environment that corresponded to the topic of the utterance.

The most important component that contributed to interpreting the utterance was the *context* in which it occurred. Broadly conceived, the context included the factors of sender and receiver and provided evidence for inferring the topic. More specifically, the context could be described in terms of (1) aspects of the referent—spatial immediacy and number of persons and objects, and initiation, control, and agents of events; (2) temporal immediacy of events in relation to occurrence of the utterance; and (3) prior linguistic expression (by the child or someone else).

Spatial immediacy of objects and persons—the distance between the referent and the child—was specified as proximal, distal, or removed. *Proximal* and *distal* described the referent as manifest—existent within the visible or audible environment. *Proximal* further implied nearness to the child, within his immediate presence. *Distal* implied distance from the child—visible or audible to him, but reachable only by a change in position, or unreachable. *Removed* indicated that the referent was not manifest within the environment.

Number of objects or persons was specified as singular, dual, or plural. Dual and plural were distinguished in order to determine distinctions in the use of "more" and "another." The use of these forms to refer to 'another instance of' or 'more than one' occurred in the data before plural noun inflection.

Initiation of events was attributed to the child, to another, or to no other (events that occurred spontaneously—for example, a bridge falling). The initiator of an event was not necessarily the agent or actor. The child may have initiated an event by requesting a bridge, although someone else did the building. The child's *control* of events initiated by the child was described in terms of his being able or unable to effect action as the agent.

The *agent* of an event was the child, the receiver, or another.

Temporal immediacy of events—the interval between the occurrence of the event and the occurrence of the utterance—was described relatively as occurrence of the event (1) during the utterance, (2) immediately subsequent to the utterance, (3) immediately previous to the utterance, or (4) previous to or during the utterance and repetitive. Two further subdivisions extended the time continuum in both directions to include events that did not occur within the environment: events that occurred remotely previous to the utterance and events that were remotely subsequent to the utterance.

The importance of *linguistic* features of the context was a variable influence on the occurrence of utterances in the course of development. For example, except for imitations, the children responded infrequently to something said to them in the earliest observations, and it was observed that, with maturation, prior utterances to the child increased in influence on the occurrence of subsequent utterances by the child. There was also an increase in occurrence of consecutive utterances. In the early samples, speech events characteristically included only a single child utterance. However, in the subsequent samples, there was a successive increase in consecutive utterances as one spontaneous child utterance appeared to lead to another, within the boundaries of a single speech event.

As participation in discourse developed, there was a progressive increase in the number of responsive utterances that could be included within the boundaries of a speech event, that is, utterances with shared features of topic, context, receiver, and sender. The utterances occurring within such a 'shared' speech event may have differed from one another only in message-form, and previous linguistic expression often influenced message-form directly. For example, message-form varies in adult response to questions as opposed to response to comments or a response to something seen or heard. The adult coming upon a found object might announce "I found a penny"; but in response to the question "What did you find?" the elliptical utterance "a penny" would be acceptable.

The influence of a prior linguistic fact on a subsequent utterance of the child could be determined on the basis of the "relative occurrence" of the elements in the discourse. Discourse depends on the "inter-dependence" of sentences "spoken . . . in succession by one or more persons in a single situation" (Harris, 1964, p. 357). Where subsequent utterances of the child shared elements with a prior utterance, there was evidence for considering the child's subsequent utterance as a response to the prior utterance. Utterances occurred as response to discourse— a comment, question, or direction from someone in the environment— or were related to a previous utterance of the child as an association, expansion, or repetition. It could not be known whether or not the child's utterances would have occurred had the prior utterance not occurred.

There was less evidence for determining whether nonlinguistic events operated to occasion the occurrence of the child's utterance. If a bridge collapsed and the child requested "another bridge," there was no way of knowing whether the child would have made the request had the bridge not fallen. But the fact that the bridge fell and the child subsequently made the request was evidence for establishing at least a tentative relation between the two events.

Thus, the framework for analysis of the relationship between referent and utterance included certain constitutive factors of speech events that were variable factors in the data obtained. Of the seven factors suggested by Hymes—sender, receiver, channel, message-form, code, topic, and context—several contributed to the analysis in a functional way: the factors of message-form, topic, and context most particularly, and receiver less directly. Channel and sender were constant factors, and the code was the unknown factor being investigated.

Functions of Speech Events
The data that were obtained suggested a categorization of the functions of speech events as comments, reports, directions, or questions.

Comments occurred when the referent was manifest and functioned to name or point out objects, persons, or events. Comments frequently accompanied ongoing behavior or announced the child's immediately subsequent behavior. They were either directed to a receiver or not, but did not attempt to influence the behavior of the receiver.

Reports occurred in the absence of a referent and were informative utterances directed to a receiver. They did not attempt to influence the behavior of the receiver.

Directions were characterized by the child's seeking a change in the context, which he was unable or unwilling to effect himself, involving the behavior of someone else.

Questions were characterized by the child's seeking information or confirmation and were directed to a receiver.

Certain utterances seemed to serve a *paralinguistic* or *metalinguistic* function as the child practiced attractive or selected linguistic forms. For example:

(1) E:V (Eric trying to
      stand a wire figure with
      large leaden shoes,
      without success)   man ə good boy. man ə good boy.
                                 /tu/. /tu/ shoe.
                                 man ə good boy /tu/.
                                 /tu/ shoes.

(2) K:II (Kathryn wanted
      all the wheels for the
      slide and took the one
      the investigator wanted
      to play with)   my have ə this. this mys.
                                 this my. . . .
                                 this ə mine. my this.
                                 this ə my this.

Sometimes strings of sounds or sequences of sounds seemed to serve no other function than that talking was great fun. For example:

(3) E:V (Eric giving the
      investigator the broken
      slide)   fix it.

     (The investigator fixing
      the slide)   /bá bù/ /tʃú tʃù/ /bí bì/ /tú tù/.

and again :

(4) E : VI (Eric picking up
the box of puppets,
which he had not seen
in six weeks)   that the puppets.
that the puppets ↓ · from last night!
that's that the cat ↓ · from last night!

2.2. Generative Transformational Grammar and Analysis of Child Language

Because the theory of generative transformational grammar provided the model for linguistic analysis in this study, the following sections discuss those aspects of the theory that are of special importance for the analysis of children's language that follows. Although it is no doubt true that other linguistic theories (for example, tagmemic grammar or stratificational grammar) are applicable to the study of children's language, generative transformational grammar has had particular appeal for several reasons.

The linguistic goals of the theory involve notions that are familiar and attractive to psychologists. In addition to specifying the need for a linguistic theory to *describe* language, it is also required that the theory be *explanatory*. Most significantly, it is necessary for a theory of language to explain the notion of linguistic creativity: the ability of a native speaker of a language to speak and understand an infinite number of sentences, given a finite set of linguistic facts. This is precisely what needs to be accounted for in a theory of language acquisition. Clearly, learning language could not depend on the child's hearing and somehow remembering all the possible sentences in his language. A child's linguistic experience is limited to only those sentences spoken in his environment. Nevertheless, he eventually comes to understand and speak sentences that he has never heard before—new and different sentences that are not only grammatical but also situationally appropriate.

The means by which the infinite number of possible sentences of the language is specified is finite and, in generative transformational theory, formulated as a system of process or sequence of operations. This generative notion has probably been the most attractive aspect of the theory for the psycholinguistic study of child language because of the implicit assumption of underlying cognitive function.

Finally, the attraction between the study of child language and the linguistic theory of generative grammar has been a mutual one.

Chomsky has proposed an expository analogy between the linguist who seeks to describe and explain the grammatical system of a language, on the one hand, and the child who seeks to learn that system. Both the linguist and the child are presented with a sample of the possible sentences of the language, and although the capabilities of each differ in a nontrivial way, both the linguist and the child are faced with the task of discovering the grammar of the language.

2.2.1. The Components of a Grammar

A grammar accounts for both underlying and superficial structural representations of sentences through the functioning of three interrelated components: the *syntactic component*, the *semantic component*, and the *phonological component*.

The syntactic component specifies both the underlying structure and the surface structure for each sentence. By specifying an underlying structure of a sentence, the syntactic component specifies the system of grammatical relations in the sentence—for example, *subject of the sentence, object of the verb*, and the speaker's choice of such meaningful elements as negation and number. The syntactic component provides this information as input to the semantic component so that the semantic component can represent, in some way, the semantic interpretation or intended meaning of the sentence.

The surface structure is derived from the deep structure by a series of transformational rules. By specifying the surface structure of the sentence, the syntactic component provides information to the phonological component so that the phonological component can determine the sequence of phonetic signals for the produced sentence.

Thus, the phonological and semantic components 'interpret' information provided to them by the syntactic component. The phonological component uses the syntactic information to determine the phonetic signals—the sequence of sounds that is the sentence that is spoken. The semantic component uses the syntactic information to determine the semantic interpretation of the sentence (Chomsky, 1965, pp. 16–17).

The linguistic analysis in this study was concerned with representing only the syntactic components of grammars; there was no attempt to say anything about the operation of the semantic and phonological components in the children's grammars. The goal was to provide an account of how underlying structures are specified and then mapped into the surface structures of the obtained sentences.

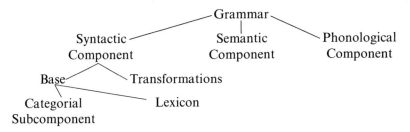

Figure 2.1. A schematic representation of the components of a generative grammar.

The *syntactic component* contains two components: a *base* component and a *transformational* component. In the base there are two sub-
components—a categorial subcomponent and a lexicon (Chomsky,
1965, p. 141). Figure 2.1 is a schematic representation of these components.

The underlying structure of a sentence is specified by the *phrase
structure rules* that operate in the categorial subcomponent in the base.
The surface structure of a sentence is determined by an ordered set of
rules, *transformations*, that map deep structures into surface structures
through processes of deletion, permutation, and addition of elements.

The phrase structure rules in the categorial subcomponent of the base
are an unordered sequence of 'context-free' rewriting rules of the form

$X \rightarrow Y,$

which is read "X *is rewritten* as Y." The rewriting rules are arranged in
a linear sequence. Given the following fragment of a set of such rules:

1. $S \rightarrow NP + VP$
2. $VP \rightarrow V (NP)$
3. $NP \rightarrow \begin{Bmatrix} a \\ the \end{Bmatrix} N$

S is *sentence*, NP is the category symbol *noun phrase*, VP is the category
symbol *verb phrase*, V is *verb*, and N is *noun*. The first rule specifies that
the sentence is rewritten as a noun phrase plus a verb phrase. Rule 2
rewrites the verb phrase as a verb and a noun phrase that may or may
not occur. Symbols enclosed in parentheses, such as the NP in Rule 2,
are *optional* choices in the string. All other symbols are *obligatory* and
must occur, so that a VP must contain a V. Rule 3 rewrites the NP as
either *a* or *the* and a noun. Either *a* or *the* may occur, but one or the
other must occur. The choice of mutually exclusive elements is indicated

by the use of braces, { }. The concatenation of elements in a string can be indicated by a plus, +, or a dash, –. The concatenation symbols are implied when parentheses or braces are used and are omitted.

The successive application of the rules, rewriting one symbol at a time, results in the generation of a *derivation* of a sentence:

1.   S → # NP + VP #, where # represents sentence boundary,
2.   # NP + V + NP #
3.   # the + N + V + NP #
3.   # the + N + V + a + N #.

The lines of a derivation are numbered to correspond with the number of the rule applied on that line. Because only one symbol can be re-written at a time, in the above derivation Rule 3 is applied to the first noun phrase and then reapplied to the second noun phrase in the string.

The derivation of a sentence can be represented schematically by a branching *tree-diagram* which is specified as its *phrase-marker* (Fig. 2.2).

A phrase-marker specifies a unique structure that represents only one semantic interpretation and is the underlying structure of the sentence. Ambiguous sentences having the same surface structure will have more than one phrase-marker corresponding to the number of possibly different interpretations of the sentence.

In the phrase-marker it is said that the node N *is dominated by* the node NP from which it is immediately derived. The nodes VP and NP are *major category* symbols, which dominate, in turn, *category* symbols, N and V, from which lexical terms are ultimately derived.

The last line of a derivation and the preterminal string of a phrase-marker are composed of *terminal* symbols only. N, V, *a*, and *the* are terminal symbols. Nonterminal symbols are NP, VP, and S—representing nodes that dominate, in turn, other category symbols and can be rewritten further.

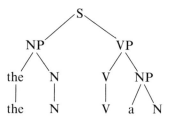

Figure 2.2. A branching tree-diagram or phrase-marker.

The notions of noun phrase or verb phrase designate *grammatical categories*. The notions of subject of the sentence, direct object of the verb, and predicate of the sentence designate *grammatical functions*. Grammatical functions are inherent notions of the relations that hold between categories in a sentence. Definitions of grammatical function do not refer to the relationships in the surface structure of actual sentences. The significant grammatical relations of a sentence are defined in the underlying structure of the sentence only (Chomsky, 1965, pp. 68–70). For example, in the structural derivation just presented with its phrase-marker, the subject of the sentence is defined as the first node NP, which is directly dominated by S, and the direct object is defined as the node NP, which is dominated by VP. Given the sentence "The ball was hit by the boy," the logical subject of the sentence, "the boy," would be derived from the first NP directly dominated by S in the underlying structure.

The categorial subcomponent of the base functions to define the system of grammatical relations in a sentence that determine its semantic interpretation, and to determine the ordering of elements in underlying structure on which the transformational rules may operate (Chomsky, 1965, p. 141).

The *lexicon* or dictionary consists of items (words) that, through the operation of a substitution transformation, are substituted as lexical items for the terminal symbols in strings generated by the categorial subcomponent.

Each lexical entry contains two representations—a phonological matrix (the phonetic shape or spelling of the word), and a *complex symbol*, which consists of a set of *inherent* and *contextual* features that specify the semantic and syntactic features of the lexical items, respectively.

For example, the inherent features of the lexicon item "sincerity" include the facts that it is a noun, [+N]; that it is an abstract noun [+abstract]; and that it is not animate, [–animate]. The inherent features of the lexical item "boy" include the facts that it is a noun, [+N], and that it is [–abstract] but [+animate] and [+human].

Contextual features specify the syntactic contexts in which the lexical items can occur in relation to other category symbols or *grammatical formatives*. Contextual features for a noun would include its occurrence or nonoccurrence after the Determiner ("a" or "the"), which is a grammatical formative. Contextual features for the verb "frighten" would allow its occurrence in the context after an inanimate, abstract noun (such as "sincerity") as a subject and before an animate nonabstract noun (such as "boy") as direct object. In this way, the lexical rules allow the sentence "Sincerity frightens the boy," but not "The boy frightens sincerity" (Chomsky, 1965, pp. 84–86, 122).

The *transformational component* contains a sequence of ordered rules —some of which are optional and others obligatory—that are applied sequentially to derive the specification for the surface structure of a sentence. Each transformation is defined by (1) a structural description (S.D.), which specifies the base string of elements (category symbols and grammatical formatives) and (2) a structural change (S.C.), which specifies the reordering, deletion, or addition of elements in the original string. For example, the passive transformation would operate on the structure underlying "The boy hit the ball" to reorder the two NP constituents and add the grammatical formative "be + en" (which in the phonological component specifies the derivation of the participle form "is hit" from the indicative "hit"). Such transformations as the passive, or Wh question are optional choices for any string. Certain other transformations, such as those involving affixation or the specification of "do" support for the auxiliary, operate obligatorily under certain conditions specified in the structural description.

In summary, the syntactic component of a grammar of a language specifies the operation of three kinds of rules—phrase structure or rewrite rules, lexical rules, and transformations. The categorial subcomponent of the base consists of a sequence of *rewrite rules* that specifies the underlying order of the elements in a sentence and the grammatical relations that hold among them. The lexicon, in the base, specifies the *inherent* (semantic) features and *contextual* (syntactic) features of lexical entries and the rules that provide for their substitution as terminal, lexical items in the last (preterminal) string of a sentence derivation. The *terminal strings* of derivations and of phrase-markers consist, then, of the lexical items and grammatical formatives (such as "a" and "the," or the auxiliary of a verb phrase).

The transformational component operates on the derivation or phrase-marker of a sentence. The transformational component can also operate on the phrase-markers of two or more sentences to combine them. Through a series of ordered *transformational rules* that reorder, add, or delete elements, the basis of the sentence is mapped into its surface structure.

2.3. Grammatical Categories in Children's Language

In order to account for the syntactic component of the child's grammar, it is necessary (1) to identify the major grammatical categories that concatenate according to the rewrite rules in the base, and (2) to determine the criteria with respect to which items in the lexicon are marked as members of major categories.

2.3.1. Rationale for Defining Categories

Inasmuch as inflectional processes do not begin to operate until the development of syntax is well under way, there are no inflectional criteria for identifying major categories. For example, in the adult model of English there are inflectional processes that distinguish parts of speech in a productive way: nouns are marked as a class that adds the suffix -*s* to form plurals; adjectives are marked as a class that adds the suffix -*ness* to form nouns.

The grammatical categories in early child language are selectional rather than inflected. They can only be marked by patterns of order and selection so that membership in categories cannot be reliably determined until lexical items occur in syntactic constructions.

In the pregrammar stage, before a child uses notions of syntax to produce constructions, his lexicon usually contains a high proportion of words that can be classed as nouns in the adult model. Although the nounness of the forms might be precarious initially (for example, they are not formally marked as *definite* or *indefinite, singular* or *plural*), such forms represented a large proportion of the words in the earliest lexicons of Kathryn, Eric, and Gia. Further, the new or different forms—adjectives, verbs, prepositions, and other nouns—that these children added to their lexicons, were just those forms that could be selected to combine with the noun forms already acquired. Emerging notions of syntax appeared to have been influenced by the potentialities for combination (1) of the forms already learned—with each other; and (2) of new forms—with existing items in the lexicon.

Because the noun forms were the most abundant in the lexicons, and because the children's emerging notions of syntax had to do with their combination—with one another and with new forms—one approach to determining the categorial, contextual features of lexical items is in terms of their occurrence as constituents with noun forms.

The notion that the child selects or chooses to learn those verbs, adjectives, and prepositions that combine most functionally with the nouns already in his lexicon compares with the specification of these forms in generative transformational theory. The rules in a base component of a generative transformational grammar that specify verbs and adjectives are based on an analysis of these forms in terms of their syntactic selection with nouns (Chomsky, 1965, p. 115). The rule

$$VB \rightarrow CS/[\alpha] \cdots \underline{\quad} \cdots [\beta]$$

analyzes a verb as a complex symbol (CS), which represents a set of syntactic and inherent features, occurring in a syntactic environment where the feature $[\alpha]$ and the feature $[\beta]$ are nouns. The rule

$$\text{``}A \rightarrow CS/[\alpha] \cdots \underline{\quad} \cdots [\beta]\text{''}$$

(Chomsky, 1965, p. 155) asserts that a lexical item A 'is rewritten as' a complex symbol with a specified environment. The "/" is read "*in the environment,*" and the "__" indicates the placement of A in the environment, in this case between the features $[\alpha]$ and $[\beta]$, which may be specified, that is, as nouns, or which may be null, so long as one or the other is nonnull.

Chomsky (1965, p. 156) subsequently gives the form of the rule for specifying a verb in terms of its occurrence with nouns:

$$\text{``}[+V] \rightarrow CS/[+N] \cdots \underline{\quad} (\cdots [+N]).\text{''}$$

This rule asserts that a lexical item with the feature $[+V]$, a verb, is a complex symbol, occurring in the environment where a preceding lexical item has the feature $[+N]$ as a noun, and where a following lexical item with the feature $[+N]$ may or may not occur.

Verb entries in the lexicon are assigned selectional features that specify the kinds of nouns with which they can occur. An example used by Chomsky (1965, p. 107) is the feature $[+[+\text{abstract}] \underline{\quad} [+\text{animate}]]$ in the lexicon entry for "frighten." This specifies the permitted occurrence of "frighten" in the context after an abstract noun and before an animate noun. This feature would allow the sentence "Sincerity frightens the boy," but not the sentence "The boy frightens sincerity."

2.3.2. Procedure for Determining Categories

A lexicon was prepared for each speech sample. The primary entries consisted of all the morphemes that occurred in at least two constructions or occurred in only one construction but also occurred elsewhere in the text as a single-word utterance. The lexical entries represented each of the syntactic occurrences of the morpheme. Secondary entries in the lexicon consisted of all forms that occurred singly and their frequencies of occurrence in the text.

Nouns represented a 'given' category and the feature $[+N]$ was assigned to all lexical items that have noun status in the adult model.

All lexical items, including nouns, were charted according to their occurrence in environments with nouns: preceding nouns, [__N] or [__ ··· N]; following nouns, [N__]; or occurring both before and after nouns, [__N, N__]. In this notation, N represents the category symbol *noun*, and "__" is read "in the environment" (of a preceding or following noun). There were four major syntactic classes determined in this way—three classes of lexical items that occurred in syntactic environments with nouns and one class of items that never occurred with nouns. Each of the four classes was subdivided into noun forms and nonnoun forms.

The categories of nonnoun forms were derived according to (1) the occurrence of the forms in syntactic contexts with nouns, and (2) inherent functional differences between forms that occurred in like environments.

Lexical items were included in a category of *verbs* if they occurred previous to a noun or following a noun, or both, (1) with a *predicatory grammatical* relationship to preceding nouns (indicating that the forms were derived from two different nodes, N and V, which were each dominated by S in a phrase-marker), or (2) a *directive objective* relationship to following nouns (indicating that the forms were derived from the same node, VP, which was dominated by S). The verbs were subdivided according to whether or not they occurred previous to a noun, and a tentative classification of transitive and intransitive forms was thereby established. A third group of forms with verb status in the adult model and no instance of occurrence with nouns was classed separately.

Lexical items were included in a category of *adjectives* if they occurred previous to a noun with an attributive, *specifying* relationship to the noun in context (indicating that both terms were dominated by the same node, NP). Several noun forms were included in this category— for example, a *bear* book, specifying a book about bears; a *girl* book, specifying a book with a picture of a girl on its cover; a *party* hat, specifying a hat for parties.

Finally, the occurrence of those forms that did not occur in immediate constituent environments with nouns was determined in syntactic contexts with the 'derived categories.'

Generally, the classes of verb and adjective included items with the same status in the adult model, but there were several exceptions and a few problems. In addition to noun forms that were also specified as adjectives (with two corresponding entries in the lexicon for each), there were several items with specialized occurrence. For example, in the lexicon for Kathryn at Time I, the word "busy" in "Mommy busy" and "baby busy" was classed as a verb with the feature [− [__N]]. "Busy" represented a predicate in its occurrence and never occurred in attributive position with a noun (as did all adjective forms).

There were a few forms that were not classed in the above categories. These included /ə/, which will be discussed subsequently in Chapter 3, and several forms that were classed as *pivots*: "Hi" and "O.K." in Kathryn's grammar; "Hi," " 'nother," "no more," "here(s)," "there(s)," and "more" in Eric's grammars. Pivots were identified as forms that occurred in linear and invariant semantic-syntactic relation to the other forms with which they occurred.

2.4. The Tentative Nature of Grammars of Early Child Language

Within the framework of generative transformational grammar there is no prescribed methodology for arriving at grammars: ". . . it is unfortunately the case that no adequate formalizable techniques are known for obtaining reliable information concerning the facts of linguistic structure." The goals of accounting for the obtained grammatical utterances and for the deviations from grammaticalness of other utterances in testing the adequacy of the grammar that is contructed depend on the accessibility of the intuition of a native speaker for judgments of grammaticalness or well-formedness (Chomsky, 1965, p. 19).

As has been stated, the intuition of the native speaker is inaccessible in an investigation of children's language, and the problem of testing the adequacy of a theory or grammar of children's language is difficult if, indeed, such a test of adequacy is possible at all. Thus, the difficulty of the task of constructing grammars for children's language is compounded by the difficulty in testing the adequacy of the grammars. Any such attempt cannot be regarded as a solution to such problems, but must be seen as a tentative proposal for accounting for the child's use of language.

The grammars that are presented here represent an attempt to account for the children's sentences by specifying the relationship of the surface structure of obtained utterances to inferred underlying structure. An important limitation in this approach has to do with the linguistic theory of generative transformational grammar, which has continued to evolve, in a dynamic way, since its introduction by Chomsky in 1957. There is no consensus among linguists today as to the nature of the underlying or 'deep' structure—whether or not there is a level distinct from semantics is an issue now being argued. However, the distinction between surface and underlying structure, far from being questioned, is more apparent than ever (see Bach and Harms, 1968; Chomsky, 1969).

Attempts to describe and explain the child's developing linguistic competence must take this distinction into account in order to determine what children learn when they learn grammar.

3 Kathryn's Language at Time I

At the time of the first observation of Kathryn, she was 21 months old; mean length of utterance was 1.32 morphemes. Six weeks later, at Time II, mean length of utterance was still less than two morphemes (1.92 morphemes). Although this second text has not been fully analyzed for the purposes of this investigation, it will be useful to look ahead to the text of Kathryn II before presenting the grammar for Kathryn I, in order to explore the potentiality for describing the early texts in terms of a pivot grammar.

3.1. Kathryn II

The sample at Time II totaled nine hours; the number of nonimitated utterances that occurred at that time was approximately 2,760 (excluding repetitions). Of that total, approximately 1,490 utterances consisted of more than one morpheme.[1]

There were utterances in the text which were similar in form to those in the data reported by Brown and Fraser (1963), and by Miller and Ervin (1964). Table 3.1 presents examples of one of the most frequent constructions that occurred at Kathryn II—the demonstrative pronouns "that," "this," and their variants before nominal forms. This construction was also tabulated (for only the two-word utterances in

---

[1] Estimates of total numbers of utterances were based on the number of utterances recorded on the first 10 pages of 121 pages of transcribed text.

Table 3.1. Examples of Utterances with Demonstrative Pronouns, Where X
is a Nominal Form

Examples of Construction	Frequency of Occurrence
(1) This ___X___ .	16
e.g., This house, This mine, This my	
(2) This ə ___X___ .	36
e.g., This ə my, This ə slide, This ə much	
(3) This ___X...___ .	9
e.g., This tiger book, This my tiger book	
(4) This ə ___X...___ .	16
e.g., This ə tiger books, This ə Mommy celery	
(5) That ___X___ .	38
e.g., That dogs, That 'chine, That cleanings	
(6) That ə ___X___ .	31
e.g., That ə boys, That ə baby	
(7) That ___X...___ .	21
e.g., That bear book, That Kathryn hair	
(8) That ə ___X...___ .	13
e.g., That ə bear book, That ə my Lois	
(9) That's ___X___ .	19
e.g., That's car	
(10) /ðæ$^{(t)}$s/ ə ___X___ .	43
e.g., That's ə train, Thas ə beanbag	
(11) That's ___X...___ .	9
e.g., That's mine toy, That's Kathryn my book	
(12) /ðæ$^{(t)}$s/ ə ___X...___ .	15
e.g., Thas ə 'chine in there, That's ə on the table	
(13) This is puppy book.	1
(14) This is sister.	1
(15) These ___X___ .	8
e.g., These my, These mines	
(16) These ___X...___ .	2
e.g., These my Kathryn's	
(17) That this.	1
(18) This my this.	1
(19) This ə my this.	1

their data) by Miller and Ervin. There were 308 occurrences of this sentence type in the text at Kathryn II.

The utterances with "this" and "that" have simply been counted, and examples of each of the variants and constructions in which they occurred have been presented in Table 3.1 out of context, for the purpose of the discussion. However, in all occurrences of the form, the referent of the predicate nominative was present in the environment, and

Kathryn either looked at it, pointed to it, or picked it up. This is to say that Kathryn never used the construction when the object she referred to was not manifest. In 142 instances, there was a preceding, related utterance from someone else: 67 utterances occurred after a Wh question; 39 utterances occurred after a yes-no question; and 36 utterances occurred after a statement that included a demonstrative pronoun.

In addition, "this" occurred 38 times and "that" occurred once as pronoun forms in sentence-object position ("Kathryn do this," "read this"), and "this" occurred 23 times and "that" occurred twice as subject pronouns ("this ǝ go in there," "this ǝ sit down"). The structure also appeared in 9 verb phrase constructions as object complements ("getting this ǝ girl," "ǝ want this bib"), and as subject noun phrases 11 times ("this lamb ǝ go in there," "this ǝ man go rides").

There were also 15 unique sentences that did not fit any of the above patterns—for example, "ǝ more this happen this," "I mys this," "this stand up pretty girl__lady," "ǝ Kathryn celery this," "Kathryn's that," and "made this sit down." "This one" occurred 33 times in isolation and 6 times in constructions.

It seems reasonable to conclude that the sentence type

$$\left\{ \begin{array}{l} \text{This} \\ \text{That(s)} \end{array} \right\} \text{(ǝ)} \quad \text{Predicate Nominative,}$$

where the predicate nominative may consist of a phrase fragment, was productive in Kathryn's grammar at Time II, and, further, that the form could be described as *pivotal*—"this" or "that(s)" occurred frequently, in relatively fixed position, as syntactic operators in juxtaposition with a variety of other forms. There were other apparently pivotal constructions at Kathryn II—for example, constructions with "no," "here," and "there." The special case of negation is discussed in Chapter 7 in the presentation of the syntactic and semantic development of negation in the three children. "Here" and "there" were productive, but occurred fewer than 50 times in the entire corpus. The example of $\left\{ \begin{array}{l} \text{this} \\ \text{that(s)} \end{array} \right\}$ was the most frequent pivotal construction at Kathryn II.

However, other lexical items also occurred frequently in the corpus. For example, there were 72 sentences with "go," 50 sentences with "read," and 42 sentences with "make."[2]

---

[2] All the utterances that included the form "make" were extracted from the Kathryn II text and are presented in Table 6.1, Chapter 6. There are three utterances in Table 6.1 in which "make" does not appear. These were included for the purpose of the discussion in Chapter 6.

If the Kathryn II grammar were a pivot grammar, with a sentence rewrite rule of the form

S → Pivot + X,

it would account for the sentences in Table 3.1 with "this" and "that(s)" (and also sentences with "here" and "there"). The forms "go," "read," and "make" might be considered pivots inasmuch as they occurred frequently before a large open class of different forms. However, in addition to their occurrence *before* complement forms, "go," "read," and "make" also occurred *after* a smaller class of different forms (which included "Mommy" and "Kathryn"), and there were sentences in which they occurred both *before and after* other constituents—for example, "Lois ə make ə bridge."

Thus, "go," "read," and "make"—although they occurred frequently with different formatives—did not occur in fixed sentence positions. One explanation for the distribution of these forms in the text is simply that they varied freely—that "read," "go," and "make" were members of a class of forms with privileges of occurrence in any sentence position. However, this explanation contradicts the basic view of children's language as systematic rule-governed behavior.

The alternative explanation for the variation in surface position is that the forms entered into complex constructions with other forms—constructions that were hierarchical in their underlying structure—and that syntactic position was motivated by the grammatical relations within the sentence. In the phrase-marker representing the derivation of the sentence "Lois ə make ə bridge," the node from which "make" is derived is dominated by a node VP (which also dominates an N, "bridge"), which does not dominate the node from which "Lois" is derived:

Hierarchical structure cannot be accounted for by a pivot grammar, since in a pivot grammar both constituents, Pivot and X, are dominated by the same node, S, and the relationship between them is linear:

```
      S
    /   \
Pivot    X
```

A pivot grammar account would describe the structure of sentences in which "read," "make," and "go" (and other forms) occurred in sentence-initial position *before* complement forms—where structure was not hierarchical:

But the same rule could not account for all the other occurrences of the same forms.

A more elaborate distributional analysis of the Kathryn II corpus would reveal the frequent occurrence of other forms as well; "Kathryn" and "Mommy" each occurred in over 100 utterances. Moreover, these two forms occurred almost exclusively in the sentence-initial position. On the basis of their frequency of occurrence with different formatives in relatively fixed sentence position, these forms could conceivably be described as pivots (as "Mum" and "Dad" in the Brown and Fraser (1963) data tabulation).

Describing "Mommy" and "Kathryn" as pivots would be largely vacuous, however, in that the description would ignore the semantic relations between the forms and the constituents with which they occurred in the text. "Mommy" and "Kathryn" occurred alternately with verbs as sentence-subjects ("Mommy read"), and with noun forms in equative relation ("Kathryn good girl"), in genitive relation ("Mommy piano"), and in predicate object relation—without expression of an intervening verb form ("Kathryn cheese"). The semantic relations that hold between constituents are accounted for by the inherent structural relationships in a sentence. If a grammar of the Kathryn corpus were a pivot grammar—which would specify only one possible structure—then the inherent alternative structures of these sentences with "Mommy" and "Kathryn" could not be accounted for.

The conclusion to be drawn from this brief exploration of the Kathryn II corpus is that pivot constructions occurred at Time II, but the notion of 'pivot grammar' could not account for sentences that occurred at the same time with (1) hierarchical structure—constituents derived from more than one phrase-marker node—or (2) apparent different semantic relations between constituents.

One explanation for the failure of a pivot grammar to account for the majority of sentences in the Kathryn II corpus might be that Kathryn had 'outgrown' a pivot grammar, or alternatively, that an original pivot grammar was included at Time II in a structurally more elaborate grammar—that her development of syntax had advanced beyond the pivot grammar stage and approached the adult model.

An alternative to specifying the constituents "read," "make," "go," "Mommy," "Kathryn" as pivots in constructions with an open class of x-words would be the inclusion of these forms in the x-word class and the specification of a rule of grammar that would rewrite $S \rightarrow X + X$. This is the rule proposed by Braine (1963) and discussed by McNeill (1966) in his analysis of the data collected by Brown. Braine reported that sentences in his data with the structural description $X + X$ occurred subsequently to pivot constructions—that the two sentence types were sequentially ordered. According to McNeill, both sentence types occurred in the earliest samples in the data collected by Brown.

The objection to the $X + X$ description is similar to the criticism of a pivotal description for the same sentences. The phrase-marker that represents an $X + X$ sentence would specify only one possible structure:

and alternative or hierarchical relationships between x-words would not be specified.

The explanation that Kathryn had possibly 'outgrown' a pivot grammar at Time II appears to hold when Kathryn's utterances at Time II are compared with the data reported by Braine. The Braine data collection began before the children he studied had produced their first syntactic constructions, and many of Kathryn's utterances at Time II were linguistically more mature than those reported by Braine.

However, the Kathryn II utterances are linguistically similar to the earliest utterances reported by Miller and Ervin and by Brown and Fraser, Brown and Bellugi, and McNeill (for the same subjects). All but one of the children in the early studies by Brown and his associates were older than Kathryn was at Time II, and mean length of utterance was similar. Although Miller and Ervin did not report mean length of utterance, their subjects were approximately the same age or older than Kathryn. It appears that Kathryn, at Time II, was similar to the subjects of these other studies in terms of chronological age and, more pertinently, the mean length of utterance and observed complexity of linguistic expression at the time when their grammars were described as pivotal. However, at Time II, Kathryn appeared to be linguistically more mature than the children in the Braine study. In order to explore the hypothesis that Kathryn had, at Time II, 'outgrown' a pivot grammar or that a pivot grammar was included in a more complex grammar, it is possible to examine the corpus obtained from Kathryn at Time I, six weeks earlier.

3.2. Kathryn I

At Time I, Kathryn was 21 months old; mean length of utterance was 1.32 morphemes. The sample totaled $7\frac{1}{2}$ hours, and the number of non-imitated utterances that occurred was approximately 1,225 (excluding immediate repetitions). Of that total, exactly 397 utterances consisted of more than one morpheme.[3]

3.2.1. Pivot Constructions

As at Time II, a small number of words occurred frequently in comparison with a larger number of words that occurred less often. Forms included in the smaller class of frequently occurring words were "Hi," "this," "thats," "more," "'nother," "no," "make," "Mommy," "Kathryn," "baby," "raisin," "toy," "sock."

The five instances of "Hi" (or "Hello") in juxtaposition with a noun occurred as follows:

(20) (Kathryn walking past the reflection of
the sun on the living room floor)   Hi shadow.

(21) (Kathryn looking at a picture of Hunky
Dory in a book)   Hi Hunky Dory.

(22) (Kathryn looking at a picture of children
in a book)   Hi children.

(23) (Kathryn looking at a picture of children
in a book)   Hello children.

(24) (Kathryn looking at spoon on her feeding table during lunch)   Hi spoon.

It is interesting to note, in terms of the function of this form, that it was not salutatory—Kathryn never used the form in greeting, for example,

[3] In comparison, there were approximately 2,760 utterances at Time II, of which approximately 1,490 were longer than one morpheme.

when Mommy or someone else entered the scene. Its use can best be described as *taking notice* and is similar to Eric's frequent use of "see" in similar contexts (a form that Kathryn did not use in the same way at Time I).

All utterances that Kathryn produced with "this" and "thats" are presented in Table 3.2; all utterances with "more" are presented in Table 3.3, and all utterances with "nother" are presented in Table 3.4.

Table 3.2. All Utterances with Demonstrative Pronouns "this" and "thats" at Kathryn I

Description of Speech Event	Kathryn's Utterance
(25) (K wearing lavaliere microphone, looking into a mirror) See the necklace? . . . . . What do you see?	> *this* necklace.
(26) (K putting man into car)	> this rides.
(27) Let's go find a book to read. (K picking up a book about babies)	> this baby book.
(28) (K trying to screw together plastic nut and bolt that do not fit) Let's try this one. (K taking bolt L offers her) (K screwing nut and bolt together)	turn. > this turn. ⎡ fit. ⎤ | turn. | ⎣ > thats turn. ⎦
(29) (K trying to screw together nut and bolt that do not fit) Shall I try it? Where is the one for this? (K trying another one that fits) Does it fit? (K turning nut and bolt)	no turn. no. > this turn.
(30) (K giving L her second slipper after L put her first one on)	> this slipper.
(31) (K picking up book)	> this book.
(32) (M trimming K's fingernails)	> this hand now.
(33) (K helping M to dress her doll; K pulling at snap fasteners on bunting)	> this button.

Description of Speech Event	Kathryn's Utterance
(34) (M putting slipper on K)	> this slipper.
(35) (K picking up another sock) That sock. Oh that's not a dirty one. That just has a big hole in it. It has a big hole in it.	> this sock. dirty. hole. no dirty.
(36) (Continuation of (35)) I know. It's not dirty. (K picking up dirty sock) That's dirty.	/ɪk/. no. > this dirty.
(37) (K holding a lamb) Is the sheep fuzzy? (K picking up second lamb) ⋮ (K holding second lamb)	sheep ə fuzzy. two sheep. $\begin{bmatrix} \text{fuzzy.} \\ > \text{this fuzzy.} \end{bmatrix}$
(38) (K putting second lamb into a block)	> this window.
(39) (K 'scrubbing' the wall in the bathtub)	> this cleaning.
(40) (K standing at balcony door; looking out at cold winter day)	> thats cold

Note: In the abbreviated descriptions of the speech events in the tables, K is Kathryn, G is Gia, E is Eric, M is Mommy, D is Daddy, and L is Lois (the investigator). Present progressive verb tense indicates that the utterance occurred during the activity; past tense indicates that the utterance occurred immediately after the activity. Utterances enclosed in brackets occurred consecutively. The utterances that are the pertinent examples are marked with >. Other utterances, not so marked, are included as aspects of the speech event that contains the utterance example. Five horizontal periods (.....) indicate lapse of time. Three vertical periods indicate lapse of time with intervening utterances or activity. Other notations are explained in the Glossary of Terms and Notations.

These 47 utterances with "this," "thats," "more," "'nother," "Hi," and the 22 utterances with "no" (presented in Table 6.2, Chapter 6) represent the productive pivot constructions in the Kathryn I corpus. That is, they occurred frequently, in fixed position, with a larger number of different words, and could be described as having the surface structure *pivot + x-word*. These 69 utterances constituted 17 percent of the total number of constructions that occurred.

Functions of Pivot Forms
Kathryn's use of the demonstrative pronouns "this" and "thats" appeared to indicate a *particular instance* of the referent she named

Table 3.3. All Utterances with "more" at Kathryn I

Description of Speech Event	Kathryn's Utterance
(41) (K looking at a picture of cereal, after seeing the same picture previously)	> more cereal.
(42) (K looking for hairnet with elastic in it that she had been playing with a few minutes previously)	> more rubber band.
(43) (K going to bag of toys after playing with wire man)	> more toy.
(44) (K taking out second wire man, after (43))	> more toy.
(45) (K had been 'feeding cereal' to the lambs; missed one, which L pointed out on the sofa) Up there on the sofa. (K looking at the sofa; looking for lamb) ⋮ (K going after lamb) He didn't get any cereal. (K going to sofa for lamb) (K subsequently 'fed' lamb)	ə sofa. > more so__ cereal.
(46) (K picking up another haircurler)	> more hair curl.
(47) (K asking M for more meat) More meat? O.K. O.K. There's some meat. (K pointing to toy cat that M had just brought in to join K at lunch; cat had no meat yet)	⎡> Mommy æ more meat.⎤ ⎣> more meat. ⎦ cat meat.
(48) Does cat need some meat?	> cat more meat.
(49) (K asking M for more meat) More meat? More meat? You're gonna get fat.	> more meat ate meat.
(50) (K eating raisins; M eating cottage cheese; K didn't persist and M didn't give her cottage cheese) mHmm. mHmm. Mommy's cottage cheese.	> more cottage cheese. Mommy cottage cheese.
(51) (K asking for more milk) You want some more milk? You thirsty? (M gave her milk)	> ə more milk. > more milk.

Description of Speech Event	Kathryn's Utterance
(52) (K finished eating nuts) More nuts?	> ə more nuts. ate nuts.
(53) (after (52)) You ate all the nuts, Honey.	> more nuts.
(54) (after (53)) You ate all the nuts. The nuts are all gone. You want some more raisins?	> more raisin.
(55) (K asking for more raisins)	> more raisin.
(56) (K asking for more raisins) More? More?	$\begin{bmatrix} \text{> more raisin.} \\ \text{> more raisin more.} \end{bmatrix}$ /eitʃ/ > more raisin.
(57) (K asking for more raisins)	> more raisin.
(58) (K asking for more raisins) You won't be able to eat dinner, Honey. I'll give you some more apple. ⋮ You want to take a nap?	> ə more raisin. > more raisin. O.K.
(59) (After (58)) You're tired.	əⁿ tire. > ə wə more raisin.
(60) (M washing K in bathtub, had just put soap on K's hand so K could soap herself; K holding out her hands for more soap) More hand? More *soap* on the hand.	> more hand.
(61) (After (60)) (M giving her soap) There	> Mommy↑ ə more hand.
(62) (M soaping K; K playing with pail in water) Take the pail. Fill it up with water? More soap? Soap's floating, Honey. (M rinsed soap off K)	> more soap.

and was not strictly deictic in the sense of pointing out the referent directly—for the sake of pointing it out. In every instance in which she used the construction, the referent named was manifest and Kathryn either looked at it or picked it up, or, in the case of events, carried out the particular action she named (for example, "this turn," "this cleaning"). The forms occurred in sentence-initial position only,

Table 3.4. All Utterances with "'nother" at Kathryn I

Description of Speech Event	Kathryn's Utterance
(63) (K stacking blocks; picking up third block)	> 'nother block.
(64) (K taking toy from box)	toy.
(Taking second toy)	> 'nother toy.
(65) (K picking up another haircurler after (46))	> 'nother hair curl.
(66) (K asking M to pin second paper sock around her foot after M pinned the first one; M wrapping second paper sock on K's foot) There's the other one. There now.------	> 'nother pin.

before noun forms ("this window," "this baby book"), verbs ("this turn"), and adjectives ("this fuzzy").

The form "more" occurred before noun forms only ("more toy," "more cereal") and indicated a comment on or request for *another instance* of the referent named or *recurrence* (after previous occurrence). The exceptions to this interpretation were "cat more meat" (the cat had not had meat as yet) and "more cottage cheese" (Kathryn was not eating cottage cheese and did not persist in asking for it). Constructions with "more" also occurred marginally in larger, more complex constructions ("Mommy æ more meat"). The form "more" was pivotal in the sense of its occurring in juxtaposition with different noun forms, but it occurred with specific semantic intent and signaled *recurrence*. "More" did not differ syntactically from the class of adjectives that also occurred (for example, "dirty," "funny," "tiny")—all occurred in attributive position before nouns and after /ə/ ("ə funny man," "ə tiny balls," "ə more milk").

The marginal form "'nother" did not contrast with "more"—both occurred with the same semantic intent (recurrence) and two of the four instances of "'nother" were identical to utterances with "more": "'nother toy," "more toy"; "'nother hair curl," "more hair curl." There was little evidence that Kathryn distinguished use of the two forms "more" and "'nother" in terms of noun categories—both forms occurred with singular count nouns. "More" occurred with noncount nouns ("milk," "cereal," "meat"), whereas "'nother" did not, but "more" appeared to be the preferred form and occurred with greater frequency.

3.2.2. Substantive Constructions: Noun + Noun

There were substantive words that also occurred frequently, in relatively fixed positions, with a large number of different forms. There were 12 occurrences of "baby" (Kathryn frequently referred to herself as "Baby"—for example, "Baby stretch," which she said while Mommy diapered her); 12 occurrences of "Kathryn"; and 32 occurrences of "Mommy." Constructions with these forms were not considered strictly pivotal constructions by Braine (1963), who originated the pivot–x-word distinction, or by McNeill (1966). They described these utterances as the juxtaposition of two x-words or 'open class' forms, respectively.

Table 3.5 presents all utterances that included "Mommy" at Kathryn I.

Table 3.5. All Utterances with "Mommy" at Kathryn I

Description of Speech Event.	Kathryn's Utterance
(67) (M put rubber band on K's finger; K shaking her hand, trying to shake it off)	⎡ throw away. ⎤ ⎣ > Mommy throw it away. ⎦
(68) (M in kitchen preparing lunch; K going into the kitchen) Hi. I'm busy. That's right.	> Mommy busy.
(69) (M and K putting pieces into puzzle; K trying to put piece in) Push. Push. Push hard. (K giving up)	push. > Mommy push.
(70) (M and K putting hat on doll) Now we'll tie. (K taking ribbon) You pull. Pull. There. We mustn't pull too hard or we'll hurt the baby, Honey. (M tying hat) uh huh. That's right.	ə pull. ə pull hat. pull. > Mommy pull.
(71) (M bouncing K on bed)	> Mommy bounce.
(72) (K trying to put lamb into block through round hole)	

Description of Speech Event	Kathryn's Utterance
Give him a push. Push hard. (K giving it to M to push) He's stuck.	push. push. > Mommy push.
(73) (K helping M to pull her diaper off) You can do it.	⌈ > Mommy do it. ⌉ ⌊ Baby do it. ⌋
(74) (L preparing to leave M and K in the kitchen; K looking at tape recorder) What are you going to do? (K coming toward L in doorway) (M laughed, explained to L that this was routine when K said good-bye)	> Mommy kiss. O.K. Lois kiss.
(75) (L and K playing in the living room; M ironing in the kitchen) Mommy iron. Mommy iron. Hot. Iron's hot. What?	> Mommy iron. Mommy. hot. hot. ------ shirts. ⌈ shirts. ⌉ ⌊ Daddy. ⌋
(76) (L and K looking out of the window; M not at home) Mommy busy? Kathryn's busy. Is Kathryn busy? Lois is coming? I brought the machine to play with you.	⌈ > Mommy busy. Mommy ⌉ ⌊ busy. Mommy busy. ⌋ ⌈ Lois. ⌉ ⌊ Lois coming. ⌋ 'chine. toys.
(77) (in sequence with (76)) Toys.	⌈ > Mommy busy. busy. ⌉ Baby busy. ⌊ ------ busy. ⌋
(78) (K reaching for M's slipper)	> Mommy slipper.
(79) (M holding M's sock) Here's Mommy's dirty socks. Wash. We'll do the laundry and we'll wash 'em. We do the laundry on Thursday too. You help me to do the laundry? (K pointing to M's socks) Yes. They're all dirty. I know.	 ------ > Mommy sock. də dirty.

Description of Speech Event	Kathryn's Utterance
(80) (K picked up another one of M's haircurlers) (K putting it in her hair) In your hair. Mommy. (L had interpreted "more" as "Mommy")	more hair curl. > Mommy hair curl.
(81) (M giving some of M's apple to K) There's some apple.	> Mommy apple.
(82) (M eating cottage cheese; K eating raisins)	> Mommy cottage cheese.
(83) (M setting out her lunch after giving K lunch) Mommy's hungry. Salad. Milk. Mommy's milk. Baby's milk. Mommy's milk. (K touching M's milk glass) Baby's milk. You touch the milk?	> Mommy milk. > Mommy's milk. > /bei__/Mommy milk. Baby milk. touch milk.
(84) (M trimming K's nails) I'll let you do mine after I do yours. Do you want to do Mommy's nails? There. There. All finished. We'll do the toes. (M trimmed K's toenails)	 > Mommy hangnail.
(85) (M and K eating; context is not clear) What's the matter? Vegetables. Where are your vegetables? There's some over here.	Oh! ------ vegetable! > Mommy vegetable. ------ vegetable. ------ vegetable.
(86) (K had just found a rubber band; M talking to L; K on M's lap, pushing her hair up toward M)	> Mommy pigtail.
(87) (Same event as (61); K had asked M for more soap on her hand) (M giving her soap) There.	 > Mommy↑ ə more hand.
(88) (M putting K's sock on K) There. That's not Mommy's sock. That's your sock. There.	> Mommy sock. > Mommy sock. Kathryn sock.
(89) (M folding diaper, preparing to put it on K)	⎡ diaper. > Mommy diaper. ⎣ fold up.

Description of Speech Event	Kathryn's Utterance
(90) (M putting K's shoe on K) Kathryn's shoes.	> Mommy shoe. Kathryn shoes.
(91) (M had sung "The Muffin Man" song and then four other songs) Muffin Man? (K apparently asking M to sing song; M didn't sing it and K didn't persist)	------ ------/ən æn/. > Mommy ə Muffin Man.
(92) (M preparing lunch; taking vegetables from refrigerator) Yes, vegetables.	> Mommy vegetable.
(93) (Same event as (47); K asking M for more meat)	> Mommy æ more meat.
(94) (in sequence after (75)) Mommy iron Daddy's shirts?	> Mommy shirts hot.
(95) (K wearing boots, going toward M in kitchen) Where are you going? See Mommy? Are you going to show Mommy the boots? (K passing reflection of sun on the floor; pointing to it) Oh a shadow. What makes the shadow? (K going toward M in kitchen)	 Mommy. shadow. > Mommy shadow.
(96) (K taking car to M in kitchen)	> me show Mommy.
(97) (M and K dressing doll) There. You're helping. You do that one, Honey. ------ have to do this. You gonna help Mommy? (K helping) There. There. There.	 > helping Mommy.
(98) (K pulling away from L, who had offered to comb her hair)	> no Mommy.

"Mommy" appeared to be pivotal in that it occurred in sentence-initial position 29 times,[4] and it occurred with a number of different formatives. Also, its occurrence was generally mutually exclusive with the other pivots—except for the utterances "no Mommy," "Mommy æ

[4] There were two instances where "Mommy" occurred as sentence-object ("me show Mommy" and "helping Mommy").

more meat," and "Mommy↑ ə more hand," "Mommy" did not occur in constructions with other pivots. However, "Mommy" did share contexts with other pivots: "Mommy" and "Hi" occurred before "shadow"; "Mommy," "more," and "'nother" occurred before "haircurl"; "Mommy" and "this" occurred before "slipper" and before "sock."

There were five possible approaches to determining structural descriptions for these sentences with "Mommy."

1. The first approach was the linguistic test of substitutability or sentence *patterning*. If two constituents, such as "Mommy sock," can occur in the same syntactic environment as one of the original two—for example, "sock"—without a change in meaning, then the one is an *expansion* of the other and they belong to the same structural form class (Wells, 1963). That is, the two utterances, "sock" and "Mommy sock," are different in form but *pattern alike* in that they would have the same external function (as noun forms) if both could occur in the same frames—for example, "find __" or "this __."

This test failed immediately because (1) the constructions in Table 3.5 did not occur in larger syntactic environments as similar constructions did at Kathryn II—for example, "This ə Mommy celery"; and (2) one could not ask Kathryn if occurrence in larger syntactic environments was 'permitted.' "Mommy sock," "this sock," and "heavy sock" occurred, but *"this Mommy sock," or *"this heavy sock," or *"this Mommy heavy sock" did not.

2. The linear order in which the elements occurred in production was also a weak criterion for determining structural description, because differences in grammatical relationship—the difference between "baby book" (a book about babies) and "Baby book" (the baby's book)—are not signalled by differences in surface order. The impressive consistency with which "Mommy" occurred in the sentence-initial position did not signal one interpretation of these sentences in preference to another.

McNeill (1966), from his observations of the Brown data, concluded that such Noun + Noun constructions as are in Table 3.5 are usually "telegraphic versions of the possessive." Certainly the order of the constituents would allow this interpretation, but the order alone would allow other interpretations as well. "As soon as two or more radical concepts are put before the human mind in immediate sequence it strives to bind them together with connecting values of some sort" (Sapir, 1921, p. 62). Interpreting these syntactic patterns as possessive constructions is an intuitively attractive notion, because, in the adult model, the occurrence of two such nouns as immediate constituents most often signals possession. But, as will be discussed, it may not be the case that two nouns juxtaposed in the same sentence produced by the child, are, indeed, immediate constituents.

3. A linguistic behavior test, suggested by Braine (1965), involved the observation of "replacement sequences"—in which a construction occurred in the corpus and was subsequently expanded by the child into a more complex construction. Braine observed that when utterances were viewed within their linguistic environments in the context of the corpus, rather than as members of an unordered list, such fragments as in Table 3.5 were often part of a "replacement sequence" in which the fragment was subsequently expanded or replaced by a more structurally complete "transform." An example given was the sequence "man/car # man/in car." Braine also reported that he was able to elicit such sequences by asking the child to repeat as though he had not been understood.

The type of replacement described by Braine was not prevalent in the texts of Kathryn, Eric, and Gia in these early stages; when asked to repeat, the children tended to duplicate or to reduce the original utterance. The kind of expansion that did occur with great frequency is demonstrated in example (70), the sequence: "pull. Mommy pull"— where two constituents were joined in construction after one or both were named singly. However, Braine made the important observation that fundamental grammatical distinctions are often contained in such sentence fragments.

4. A related linguistic behavior test that was available in the data at this stage was the successive occurrence of constructions with expansion or addition of one constituent and simultaneous deletion of another, for example:

(83) (Mommy setting out her lunch)
Mommy's hungry. Salad. Milk.   Mommy milk.

Mommy's milk.   Mommy's milk.

Baby's milk.   /bei__/ Mommy milk.

Mommy's milk.

(Kathryn touching Mommy's
milk glass)   > Baby milk.

Baby's milk.   > touch milk.

You touch the milk?

The occurrence of "touch milk" immediately after "Baby milk" provided strong support for interpreting "Baby" as subject and "milk" as direct object in assigning the structural description *subject-object* to the utterance "Baby milk." This example provided further insight into the child's struggle with sentence constructing. Mommy had provided a more complete possessive construction model, which Kathryn had duplicated—"Mommy's milk"; Mommy's subsequent utterance, "Baby's milk," was part of a frequent routine (as reproduced by Kathryn in (73) "Mommy do it. Baby do it") which Kathryn almost repeated but expanded instead. That is, it was *Mommy's milk* which *Baby* was intent on *touching*. This kind of subsequent expansion with reduction in consecutive utterances will be discussed at greater length in Chapter 6; it proved to be the most powerful linguistic behavior test available for interpreting sentences and determining their structural description.

5. Finally, in most instances, it was the nonlinguistic behavior and context that made possible the semantic interpretation of what the children said. As discussed in Chapter 1, overt behavior and features of context and situation often signal the meanings of what children say in a way that is not usual for adult utterances. What young children say usually relates directly to what they do and see—as demonstrated by virtually all the children's utterances being discussed.

Using the nonlinguistic contexts of these speech events to infer the semantic interpretation of the utterances in Table 3.5, it appeared that there were a number of possible structural descriptions that might account for the different sentences.

One possible interpretation of these sentences was *conjunction*—that Kathryn had simply named two aspects of a referent, or two referents, within the bounds of a single utterance (for example, "Mommy" and "vegetable" or "Mommy" and "iron"), without connection or with any possible connection between them. However, if this interpretation were plausible for all the sentences in Table 3.5, one could reasonably expect the constituents to be named in variable order; if Kathryn simply named any two aspects that would pertain to a referent, there would be no motivation for naming them in a particular order. But the occurrence of "Mommy" in sentence-initial position 29 times in the 32 utterances that included "Mommy" was evidence that motivation for the order of the constituents was strong.

In each of the first seven utterances in Table 3.5, (67) through (73)—for example, "Mommy push" and "Mommy busy"—"Mommy" occurred before a verb form within speech events where Mommy was the actor-agent of an event, which would indicate a *subject-predicate* relation between the two constituents. In (74) "Mommy kiss" and (75) "Mommy iron," the relationship between the constituents was equivocal,[5] because the homonymous forms "kiss" and "iron" are interpretable as action verbs and also object nouns—either of the relations *subject-object* or *subject-verb* would hold. Although "diaper" in (89) "Mommy diaper. fold up," is also a homonymous form, the fact that Mommy was folding the diaper and Kathryn produced the appropriate verb form immediately after "Mommy diaper" provided evidence for interpreting "diaper" as a noun.

The context did not permit interpretation of utterances (76) and (77) "Mommy busy"—Mommy was not at home. It is arguable that Mommy's being unavailable was somehow equivalent for Kathryn to Mommy's being busy. Kathryn's subsequent utterances in these speech events appeared to be part of a routine that Mommy might have used earlier to 'prepare' Kathryn for the events of the day: Mommy would be busy; Lois would be coming to play with Kathryn and would bring her machine and her toys. However, the context does not support a *subject-verb* interpretation in these examples as strongly as in (68) "Mommy busy," where Mommy was, indeed, busy. "Busy" was categorized as a verb because of its exclusive occurrence in predicate relation, in syntactic contexts after a noun.

The utterances (78) through (95) presented "Mommy" in syntactic contexts with another noun. In the utterances

(78) Mommy slipper.
(79) Mommy sock.
(80) Mommy hair curl.

it is clear that a *genitive* relation holds between "Mommy" and "slipper," between "Mommy" and "sock," and between "Mommy" and "hair curl," although in (80), the previous utterance "Mommy" may

[5] In the discussion of those utterances that presented interpretation problems, the terms *ambiguous, equivocal, indeterminate,* and *anomalous* have been used with specific connotation. *Ambiguous* refers to a form having two (or more) possible interpretations that can be distinguished or resolved—for example, "Mommy sock" meaning "Mommy's sock" or, alternatively, "Mommy (verb) sock." *Equivocal* describes a form having two (or more) possible interpretations that cannot be distinguished—either one or the other interpretation being acceptable in the particular situation, for example, "Mommy iron." *Indeterminate* refers to a form for which an interpretation cannot be made, most often because of insufficient evidence. *Anomalous* describes a form that appears to have no interpretation—the occurrence of an utterance in a situation to which the linguistic expression bears no apparent relation—for example, Gia eating peaches and saying "no more."

have influenced its occurrence. However, Kathryn was holding Mommy's hair curler.

Each of the utterances

    (81) Mommy apple.
    (82) Mommy cottage cheese.
    (83) Mommy milk.
    (84) Mommy hangnail.

presents a structural ambiguity with equivocal interpretation: in each instance Mommy was the actor-agent of an event—for example, Mommy was giving a piece of apple to Kathryn in (81) and Mommy was eating cottage cheese in (82). But a genitive interpretation was possible as well: it was Mommy's apple in (81) and Mommy's cottage cheese in (82). In (84) "Mommy hangnail," Mommy was trimming Kathryn's nails, but she had also commented on "Mommy's nails" previously, and Kathryn's utterance may have been related to the ongoing event (Mommy trimming Kathryn's hangnail) or to Mommy's previous utterance "Mommy's nails." Kathryn did not persist in her request to trim Mommy's hangnail, if it was indeed a request. The utterance (85) "Mommy vegetable" could not be interpreted—both Mommy and Kathryn were eating vegetables, and Kathryn still had some on her plate.

Interpretation of the remaining Noun + Noun constructions presents a different structural description. Out of the context of the speech event in which it occurred, (86) "Mommy pigtail" could be interpreted

    (86) (i) Mommy has a pigtail.
          (ii) Mommy's pigtail.
          (iii) Mommy, make me a pigtail.
          (iv) Mommy is making a pigtail.

However, knowing in this situation that (1) Mommy does not have a pigtail; (2) Kathryn does not have a pigtail; (3) Mommy can make pigtails; (4) Kathryn has just found a rubber band; and (5) Kathryn was pushing her hair up toward Mommy as she spoke would eliminate most of the 'out of context' interpretations. It was evident that Kathryn wanted Mommy to make her a pigtail, and the function of "Mommy" in the sentence is sentence-subject, of either an immediate future event or a direction.[6]

---

[6] Directions, or the imperative form, were not syntactically distinguished from immediate future events at Time I.

The same interpretation of "Mommy" as sentence-subject in juxtaposition with a predicate-object holds for the utterances

    (87) Mommy↑ ə more hand.
    (88) Mommy sock.
    (89) Mommy diaper.
    (90) Mommy shoe
    (91) Mommy ə Muffin Man.
    (92) Mommy vegetable.
    (93) Mommy æ more meat.

Mommy put soap on Kathryn's hands; Mommy gave Kathryn more meat; Mommy sang "The Muffin Man." "Mommy" might be interpreted alternatively as a vocative—for example (86) (iii) "Mommy, make me a pigtail." But the prosodic contour of the vocative did not occur—there was not a pause after "Mommy."

The utterance (94) "Mommy shirts hot" is discussed subsequently as one of the utterances not generated by the Kathryn I grammar, although it does present "Mommy" as sentence-subject in relation to "shirts" as predicate-object. The interpretation of (95) "Mommy shadow" was indeterminate: it was not really clear what Kathryn meant by "Mommy shadow." Considering just the linguistic aspects of the event, Kathryn may have answered the question "What makes the shadow?" but the fact that Kathryn was on her way to see Mommy may have influenced the utterance as well. In (96) "me show Mommy" and (97) "helping Mommy," "Mommy" is the object of a verb. The utterance (98) "no Mommy" is discussed in Chapter 6 in the discussion of all the utterances with "no."

It should be observed that Noun + Noun constructions could be ambiguous in context as they occurred—notice that Mommy interpreted (88) "Mommy sock" as a 'mistake' on Kathryn's part, which Kathryn subsequently 'corrected.' Mistakes are certainly plausible, but not likely in this instance. The occurrence of the homonymous form in (79) "Mommy sock" and the remainder of the Noun + Noun sentences provided strong evidence that Kathryn recognized the difference in syntactic relationship in these different situations. Moreover, Kathryn seemed to have learned the possessive relationship between people and objects—she never said "Kathryn cottage cheese" or "Kathryn slipper" when looking at Mommy's cottage cheese, or Mommy's slipper.

It appears that a semantic interpretation could be made for most of the sentences in Table 3.5 with "Mommy," or else the relationship between constituents was equivocal—more than one interpretation could apply. In each of the utterances (86) through (94), "Mommy" occurred as a sentence-subject in relation to a predicate-object. Otherwise, "Mommy" occurred as the possessor-noun in a genitive construction or as the subject or object of verbs—or interpretation was equivocal. The first possible interpretation of these sentences that was discussed—that Kathryn simply named two referents in conjunction—appeared to be the weakest interpretation of the sentences with "Mommy."

There were 37 other Noun + Noun constructions in the Kathryn I text; these are presented in Table 3.6. Again, there were a number of possible structural descriptions for these sentences, and there were a number of structurally ambiguous sentences among them.

Table 3.6. All Remaining Utterances with the Surface Description Noun + Noun at Kathryn I

Description of Speech Event	Kathryn's Utterance
(99) (M bringing K's umbrella and boots to where K is sitting)	> umbrella boot.
(100) (K looking at a magazine picture of a flower on the toe of a bare foot)	> foots flower.
(101) (K's feet tangled in tape recorder wire)	> 'chine foot.
(102) (K and M looking at a picture of a girl wearing a dress) See the girl. What's that?	> girl dress.
(103) (K looking at letter from Grandma on stationery with flowers on it)	> Grandma flower.
(104) (M drying K's hands; L had just left with toys after playing with K all morning)	> Lois toy.
(105) (K holding one of M's pins)	> jewelry pin.
(106) (K picking up a party hat)	> party hat.
(107) (Same event as (27)) Let's go find a book to read. (K picking up a book about babies)	> this baby book.
(108) (K looking at a bread cookbook on kitchen counter) uh hm. cookbook. cookbook.	book. ə book.

Description of Speech Event	Kathryn's Utterance
(M looking through the book) Let's see what else. What else. Bread book. You want some bread?	> bread book. bread.
(109) (M opening the refrigerator for lunch) We have some good things to eat. Milk. (M taking out milk) (K looking into refrigerator) Coffee cake! You had coffee cake this morning.	> coffee cake.↑
(110) (after (109); M taking noodles from refrigerator) Oh look what I found. Noodles.	> coffee noodles. ⎡ > coffee cake.↑ ⎤ ⎣ noodles. ⎦
(111) (K carrying her sweater to living room chair) (put it on the chair)	> sweater chair.
(112) (M and K eating lunch; Wendy had visited a few days previously) Elevator? mmhmm. Did Wendy come on the elevator?	elevator. elevator. > Wendy elevator. > Wendy elevator. > Wendy elevator.
(113) (Beanbag doll fell off the horse, where K had put it)	> beanbag horse.
(114) (K showing L tail which had come off her toy tiger) A doggie's tail. Let me see the doggie's tail.	- - - - tail. > tiger tail.
(115) (K trying to turn plastic nut and bolt; not clear whether tiger tail was still around; utterance occurred 20 minutes after (114))	> ə tiger tail.
(116) (K holding one of the lambs) Nice. That's a sheep. (K pointing to its protruding ear)	sheep. sheep. horsie. > sheep ear.
(117) (In (88)) That's not Mommy's sock, that's your sock.	> Kathryn sock.

Table 3.6. Continued

Description of Speech Event	Kathryn's Utterance

(118) (K holding a doll with long black hair;
      Wendy also had long black hair)

> ⎡   black hair.   ⎤
> ⎣ > Wendy hair. ⎦

(119) (K and M eating lunch)
      You have a big appetite.

> > Kathryn appetite.

(120) (K and M eating lunch; in sequence
      immediately after (127))

> ⎡   book.   ⎤
> ⎣ > Wendy book ⎦

      Wendy book.

(121) (K asking for more raisins after M told
      her there were no more nuts)

>   more raisin.

      You want some more raisins?

>   Kathryn want raisin.

      The cat has your raisin.

(122) (M giving K raisins)

> ⎡ > bear raisin. ⎤
> ⎣ > Baby raisin. ⎦

(123) Baby's raisins. (K eating
(124) raisins)

> ⎡ > Kathryn raisin. ⎤
> ⎣ > Kathryn ə raisin. ⎦

(125) (K eating raisins)

> > Oh Kathryn raisin!

(126) (M giving raisin to toy cat who joined K
      at lunch)
      All right. There's a raisin for the cat. There.
      (K giving raisin to the toy bear)

>   > Kathryn ə bear.

      What's that?

>   ə bear.

      Bear have a raisin too? O.K.

>   O.K.

(127) (Jocelyn, K's friend, had bruised her
      cheek on the playground several days
      previously; K and M eating lunch)
      Jocelyn!

>   Jocelyn.

      What happened to Jocelyn's cheek?

>   Jocelyn cheek.

      Did Jocelyn cry? Jocelyn hurt her cheek.

>   ə cry.

(128) (K's doll 'cried')
      What happened to the baby doll?
      Is she crying?

>   > /ɑ/ baby cheek.

(129) (M taking cottage cheese from the
      refrigerator)
      Did Wendy eat cottage cheese?

>   > Wendy cottage cheese.

      What else did Wendy eat?
      (K picked up M's letter)

Description of Speech Event	Kathryn's Utterance
(130) (M putting cottage cheese on plate) Wendy's cottage cheese? That's Kathryn's cottage cheese. There you are.	> Wendy cottage cheese. /ɑ : m :/
(131) (K eating cottage cheese; singing) (132) That's the baby's cottage cheese. (133) mm Hmm.	⎡⎡ > Wendy cottage cheese. ⎤⎤ ⎣ > Baby cottage cheese. ⎦ ⎣ > cat cottage cheese. ⎦
(134) (Same as (48); M had brought toy cat in to join K at lunch; M had just given meat to K; cat had no meat yet) (135) Does cat need more meat? (M gave meat to cat)	⎡ > cat meat. ⎤ ⎣ > cat more meat. ⎦

The first potential structural description that was discussed in relation to the sentences with "Mommy" in Table 3.5 was the possibility that they may have represented Kathryn's naming simultaneous aspects of a referent (or naming two referents) within the bounds of a single utterance without connection between them except for their cooccurrence— a *conjunction*. The subsequent discussion revealed that none of the utterances with "Mommy" could be included in this classification—all appeared to present constituents with an inherent relationship between them, although in some instances the relationship was equivocal. The prevailing occurrence of "Mommy" in sentence-initial position presented further evidence of an underlying motivation for grammatical word order that would argue against the designation of *conjunction*, where word order would presumably be variable.

Several utterances in Table 3.6 do not appear to have occurred with interpretable relationship between the constituents; (99) "umbrella boot" and (100) "foots flower" were the clearest examples of *conjunction*, although a genitive relation could conceivably be postulated for "foots flower."

Other utterances that could be interpreted as *conjunctions* would permit other interpretations as well:

(101) 'chine foot. (103) Grandma flower.
(102) girl dress. (104) Lois toy.

It was possible that "'chine," in "'chine foot" (where Kathryn was entangled in the tape recorder wire) was perceived by Kathryn as the agent of an event—an attractive notion. It was unclear, in "girl dress," whether Kathryn was referring to the dress in relation to the girl—the girl's *dress*; or the girl in relation to the dress—the *girl* has (or wears) a dress. In "Grandma flower," Grandma sent the 'flowers' and it was also Grandma's letter (with flowers on it). In "Lois toy," Lois and her toys had been there; Lois took away the toys; Kathryn had played with Lois's toys. The utterances (101) through (104) were equivocal.

In the sentences

> (105) jewelry pin.
> (106) party hat.
> (107) this baby book.
> (108) bread book.
> (109) coffee cake.
> (110) coffee noodles.

the noun in initial position specified an attribute of the second-position noun: for example, Kathryn was picking up a hat for parties; the book in (108) was a cookbook for baking bread. These sentences have been classified as *attributive* constructions.

The occurrence of "coffee noodles" was no doubt influenced linguistically by the prior occurrence of "coffee cake"; there did not appear to be an inherent relationship between the two constituents "coffee" and "noodles." "Coffee noodles" was a 'pivot' construction—in the literal sense of the term. In the immediately subsequent utterances, "coffee cake. noodles," Kathryn appeared to correct her previous utterance. The interpretation of "baby book" in (107) "this baby book" gained linguistic support as an attributive phrase from the larger linguistic context in which it occurred.

In each of the sentences

> (111) sweater chair.
> (112) Wendy elevator.
> (113) beanbag horse.

the initial position noun was the subject of a locative prediction, and these sentences were categorized as having the structural description *subject-locative.*

The three structural descriptions that have been specified so far for the sentences in Table 3.6—*conjunction, attributive,* and *subject-locative*—did not apply to the sentences with "Mommy" in Table 3.5.

However, interpretation of the remaining sentences in Table 3.6 resulted in the same classification of structures as was obtained for the utterances with "Mommy" having the surface description Noun + Noun in Table 3.5: *genitive* or *subject-object* strings, with certain utterances occurring equivocally so that both interpretations were possible.

In the four *genitive* strings,

    (114) tiger tail.
    (115) ə tiger tail.
    (116) sheep ear.
    (117) Kathryn sock.

Kathryn referred to the tiger's tail (or a tiger-kind-of-tail), the sheep's ear, and Kathryn's sock (as pointed out to her by Mommy).

The equivocal utterances

    (118) Wendy hair.
    (119) Kathryn appetite.
    (120) Wendy book.
    (121) bear raisin.
    (122) Baby raisin.
    (123) Kathryn raisin.
    (124) Kathryn ə raisin.
    (125) Oh Kathryn raisin!

could be interpreted as having the *genitive* structural description or the structural description *subject-object*, which is related transformationally to the genitive in the adult model, for example:

    Baby has raisin. ⇒ Baby's raisin.

In the following utterances in Table 3.6,

    (126) Kathryn ə bear.
    (127) Jocelyn cheek.
    (128) /ɑ/ baby cheek.
    (129)–(131) Wendy cottage cheese. (3 occurrences)
    (132) Baby cottage cheese.
    (133) cat cottage cheese.
    (134) cat meat.
    (135) cat more meat.

the noun in initial position occurred as sentence-subject in relation to the second noun as predicate-object. The utterances "Wendy cottage cheese" did not relate to the situational contexts in which they occurred —according to Mommy, Kathryn referred to Wendy's having eaten cottage cheese in a previous situation in the first instance of the utterance. But the subsequent instances of the utterance (as well as the other utterances with "cottage cheese") may have occurred because Kathryn enjoyed the pattern (which may also apply to occurrences of the utterances with "raisin" as well).

3.2.3. Structural Description of Noun + Noun Constructions

Thus, there were five possible structural descriptions that could explain the semantic relationship between constituents in utterances with the surface description Noun + Noun at Kathryn I: (1) *Conjunction*, where the two constituents named simultaneous aspects of the same referent or two referents within the bounds of a single utterance, with no connection between them, as in "umbrella boot." (2) *Attributive* construction, where the initial-position noun was an attribute of a matrix noun that occurred in second position, as in "party hat." (3) *Genitive* string, where the initial-position noun was a possessor-noun and the second-position noun was a possessed-object-noun, as in "Kathryn sock." (4) *Subject-locative* string, where the initial noun was the subject of a locative predication and the second-position noun was the relational locative constituent, as in "sweater chair." (5) *Subject-object* string, where the initial-position noun related to the whole string as sentence-subject, and the subsequent noun represented the predicate of the subject—a direct object.

It was not the case, however, that two nouns in juxtaposition could occur with any possible relationship between them. Sentences with "Mommy" were either *genitive* strings, *subject-object* strings, or otherwise equivocal. There were no instances of *conjunction* (such as *"Mommy Kathryn"), no instances of *attributive* construction (such as *"Mommy bear"), and no instances of *locative* construction (such as *"Mommy chair"). None of the Noun + Noun constructions in Tables 3.5 and 3.6 expressed *equation* or *identity*, for example, *"Mommy lady" or *"bear toy," and none expressed *disjunction*—an either-or relationship—and none represented *direct-indirect object*. Thus, grammatical relationship appeared to be an inherent factor of utterances and not dependent on extralinguistic context—giving evidence of the productivity of an underlying cognitive-linguistic rule system.

Utterances with the surface designation Noun + Noun occurred in the data reported by other investigators as well. Their occurrence was accounted for by the linear "sentence-generating" rules reported by Ervin (1966), where the last "optional class," in a string of optional classes, consists of nouns and is identical to the "required class" in sentence-final position.

Braine (1963) described the occurrence of pivot constructions and Noun + Noun constructions in his data as occurring in developmental sequence—the latter construction appearing as a subsequent stage after the pivot grammars. He described this subsequent stage as one in which there was "the appearance of an increasing number of utterances in which an x-word (e.g., an English noun) occupies both utterance positions. . . . These are not pivotal constructions, but seem rather to exemplify a primitive sentence form."

McNeill (1966) suggested the rule "(6) S → N + N," which was "highly productive" in the Brown data—"indeed, Brown's early records contain many more sentences produced by Rule (6) than by Rule (1) ["S → P + N," where P is "pivot"]." McNeill goes on to say: "Rule (6), even though it is not a pivot-open construction, is identical to [the pivot rules] in one respect; all are sequential and lack any sort of hierarchical structure."

The rules proposed by Ervin, Braine, and McNeill to account for the Noun + Noun constructions in their data were noncomplex, linear rules. What rules of grammar would account for the Noun + Noun constructions that occurred at Kathryn I? The first possibility, that any two nouns could cooccur, can be accounted for by the rule:

(i)   S → N + N

proposed by McNeill and, in a different form, by Ervin. Sentences derived from Rule (i) could be represented by two alternative phrase-markers with free variability in the order of the constituents:

(i)

But Rule (i) is weak, precisely because it would not account for the invariable order of the constituents as they actually occurred— "Mommy" always occurred in sentence-initial position. Moreover, the nouns in sentence-initial position in the remaining Noun + Noun utterances, Table 3.6, were, except in *attributives* and *conjunctions*, the names of people or, except for "sweater" in "sweater chair," 'animate' objects. A stronger rule would account for the prevailing order of the two different classes of forms that occurred in sentence-initial and sentence-final positions.

An alternative to Rule (i), $S \rightarrow N + N$, would specify the ordered relationship of two noun classes: N_i ("bear," "Mommy," "Wendy," "cat"...), a first-position class and N_j ("cottage cheese," "raisin," "elevator," "slipper"...), the second-position class. The alternative rule:

(ii) $S \rightarrow N_i + N_j$

would describe the sentences in Tables 3.5 and 3.6, except for the *attributive* and *conjunction* constructions. Sentences in which the two restricted classes, N_i and N_j, occur would be represented by the single phrase-marker:

(ii)

Rule (ii), which is similar to the rules for ordered classes proposed by Brown and Fraser (1963), would describe most of the sentences that occurred in Tables 3.5 and 3.6. At first glance, it could be taken to represent Kathryn's linguistic competence—that this, possibly, was all that Kathryn knew about sentence constructing at this time. The consistency of the surface word order in *attributive, genitive, locative,* and *subject-object* constructions was impressive; that is, the attribute noun preceded the matrix noun, the possessing noun preceded the possessed noun, and the sentence-subject preceded the locative constituent or the sentence-object.

However, three principal objections can be raised against Rule (ii)— aside from the fact that *conjunction* and *attributive* constructions (where both constituents are from the class N_j) could not be specified:[7] (1) The rule cannot explain the differences in underlying semantic relationship between the constituents—that different combinations of noun forms 'mean' different things. (2) The rule is superficial in that it describes the surface structure of the sentences only—it cannot distinguish among the different structural descriptions that underlie the obtained surface order. (3) The rule will allow sentences that did not occur, for which there was no evidence that occurrence was possible—*locative* and *attributive* constructions with "Mommy," and Noun + Noun constructions that signal *identity, disjunction,* or *indirect object.*

---

[7] Actually, the occurrence of noun forms in attributive position before other nouns would be accounted for in the lexicon where these forms would have the feature [+ADJECTIVE]—as described in the discussion of grammatical categories in Chapter 2. The occurrence of two nouns in *conjunction* could be accounted for by some sort of conjoining transformation.

If the structure of a sentence depends on the inherent relationship between its constituents, and that relationship appears to be expressed linguistically by the obtained order of the constituents, then the rule of grammar that accounts for the sentence should account for the inherent relationship that specifies the order of the constituents. Alternative rules of grammar that would specify the structural descriptions under- lying the different semantic relations that could hold between two nouns in a construction would result in a more complex model. Such rules would generate phrase-marker representations in which two noun con- stituents would be dominated by different nodes:

(iii)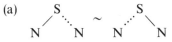

The relationship between the constituents in a sentence can be defined in terms of the major categories from which the constituents are derived in the underlying structure. Representing the five structural descrip- tions—*conjunction, attributive, subject-object, genitive,* and *locative*—in terms of hypothetical underlying phrase-markers will serve to illustrate the structural differences among them.

A *conjunction* could be represented by the alternant phrase-markers generated by Rule (i), $S \rightarrow N + N$, where the order of the constituents is variable,

(a)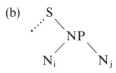

and the structural relationship between the constituents is linear—both nouns are derived from the same node, S. Further, there is no inter- pretable semantic relationship between the nodes.

An *attributive* construction also specifies a linear relationship between constituents, with the further specification of subordination— the first-position noun is subordinate to the matrix constituent or head noun, so that the two are ordered:

(b)
$$\begin{array}{c} S \\ \diagdown \\ NP \\ \diagup \quad \diagdown \\ N_i \qquad N_j \end{array}$$

Further, the constituents have structural unity as immediate con- stituents—both are dominated by a major category node, NP, which, in turn, is dominated by S and accounts for the semantic interpretation of the construction.

In actuality, those nouns that occurred in attributive relation to other nouns were included in the Kathryn I lexicon as adjectives, so that both nouns were derived from the major category NP, which dominated the constituents from which ADJ and N were derived.

A *subject-object* string would be represented by a complex phrase-marker in which the second-position noun is derived from a node VP, which also dominates another node—the unspecified immediate constituent of the second-position noun:

(c)

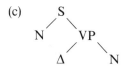

Thus, the two noun forms would be derived from different category nodes, and the semantic interpretation of the construction would depend on the derivation of the second-position noun from a VP node.

The semantic interpretation of a *genitive* construction would depend on the derivation of the second-position noun from an NP node that does not also dominate the first position noun

(d)

but that does dominate an as yet unspecified intervening constituent. The phrase-marker (d) is distinguished from the attributive phrase-marker (b) in that the first-position noun is not subordinate to the second-position noun but is instead derived from the same node as is the first-position noun in phrase-marker (c), the representation of *subject-object* construction. Alternatively, the node NP may be derived from a Predicate Phrase node, which would dominate the unspecified constituent.

The phrase-marker underlying the *locative* construction is less clearly defined by the data. The construction was marginal in that it occurred only three times, so that it was not accounted for by the grammar. The second-position noun in "Wendy elevator" and "bean-bag horse" could be derived from a node labeled PrepP (but such a node was not represented in the grammar):

(e₁)

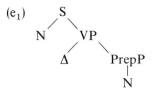

An alternative phrase-marker, which would represent "sweater chair" (where Kathryn was the actor-agent, putting the sweater on the chair), would specify the derivation of both nouns from nodes dominated by VP:

(e₂)

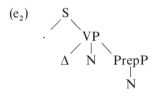

In the distribution of Noun + Noun sentences according to structural description, *subject-object* constructions (18 sentences) occurred most frequently; *locative* constructions (3 sentences) and *conjunctions* (2 sentences) occurred least frequently. There were 6 *attributive* constructions, 7 *genitive* constructions, 13 equivocal (*genitive* or *subject-object*) constructions and 10 indeterminate constructions. There were no instances of *identity, disjunction,* or *indirect object.*

Inasmuch as children's early linguistic behavior is often described as 'naming' behavior, it was significant that Kathryn did not use these early Noun + Noun constructions simply to 'name' two referents. Rather, when she produced two forms in juxtaposition there was most often an interpretable semantic relation between them.

A grammar for the Kathryn I text would have to account for (1) the differences in underlying structure of those Noun + Noun constructions with different semantic relations between constituents, and (2) the hierarchical as well as linear structure of such sentences. In short, a pivot grammar would describe the Kathryn I utterances with "Mommy" and "no" and the utterances in Tables 3.2, 3.3, and 3.4, but could not explain the differences in the semantic interpretation of constructions that were superficially the same.

The syntactic component of a tentative grammar for the text of Kathryn I, presented in the following section, consists of (1) the phrase structure, (2) lexicon feature rules, and (3) transformations. The Kathryn I lexicon is presented in Appendix C.

3.2.4. Kathryn I Grammar

Phrase structure:

1. $S_1 \rightarrow$ Nom (Ng) $\begin{Bmatrix} NP \\ VP \end{Bmatrix}$

2. $S_2 \rightarrow$ Pivot $+$ N

3. $VP \rightarrow V \begin{pmatrix} NP \\ Part \end{pmatrix}$

4. $NP \rightarrow$ (ə) (ADJ) N

5. Nom $\rightarrow \begin{Bmatrix} N \\ Dem \end{Bmatrix}$

Lexicon feature rules:[8]

- i.   N $\rightarrow$ [+N, ±animate, ±Nom]
- ii. [+animate] $\rightarrow$ +[__VB], −[Nom__], −[ADJ__]
- iii. [+N] $\rightarrow$ [±Pron]
- iv. [+Pron] $\rightarrow$ [±Nom]
- v.   [+Nom, +Pron] $\rightarrow$ [±Dem]
- vi. [+Dem] $\rightarrow$ this, that(s)
- vii. [−Dem] $\rightarrow$ I
- viii. [−Nom, +Pron] $\rightarrow$ it
- ix. [+N] $\rightarrow$ ±[Prep__]
- x.   [+Prep] $\rightarrow$ on, off, up
- xi. Ng $\rightarrow$ no
- xii. Part $\rightarrow$ [+particle]
- xiii. [+particle] $\rightarrow$ now, here, outside, away, later, right
- xiv. V $\rightarrow$ [+ V]
- xv. [+ V] $\rightarrow$ ±[__NP], ±[__Part]
- xvi. ə $\rightarrow$ −[Ng__]
- xvii. Pivot $\rightarrow$ Hi, Oh, O.K., thank you
- xviii. ADJ [+ADJ]
- xix. [+ADJ] +[__N]

Transformations:

(1) $T_{\text{Placement}}$ S.D.: $\begin{Bmatrix} ADJ \\ Prep \end{Bmatrix}$ N
$\quad$ (optional)

$\qquad\qquad$ S.C.: $x_1 - x_2 \Rightarrow x_2 - x_1$

---

[8] There does not appear to be a consensus regarding the form for rules that introduce lexical features into grammars. The form used was adopted because it appears to provide the necessary information.

(2) $T_{Reduction}$
(obligatory)

    (a) S.D.: $X - Ng - Y$

        S.C.: $x_1 - x_2 - x_3 \Rightarrow x_2 - x_3$

    (b) S.D.: $\# - X - Y - Z$, where X, Y, Z are category symbols[9]

        S.C.: $\# - x_1 - x_2 - x_3 \Rightarrow \# - x_i - x_j$,

                          where $0 \leqslant i < j \leqslant 3$

(3) $T_{/ə/\ Placement}$
(optional)

    S.D.: $X - VP$, where X may be Ng or null

    S.C.: $x_1 - x_2 \Rightarrow ə - x_1 - x_2$

The least complex phrase structure in the Kathryn I corpus was the predicate noun phrase[10]

    4. $ə + N$

which occurred in 36 construction types, with multiple occurrences of these. The full predicate noun phrase

    4. $ə + ADJ + N$

occurred 13 times—for example, "ə funny man," "ə tire baby," "ə more raisin."

Including the possessor-noun in the noun phrase rewrite rule 4 would have introduced complications into the base that would have required a series of ad hoc rules, such as redundancy deletion transformations, to resolve. Such a rule as

$$*4. \quad NP \rightarrow \binom{N}{(ə)\,(ADJ)} N$$

would allow strings of the form *"N + N + N" that were not grammatically motivated by the data. It appears best, for the present, for the distinction between *genitive* strings and *subject-object* strings to be distinguished in terms of the major categories from which the second noun in the string is derived as discussed earlier.

The pivot forms "this" and "thats" were derived from the category constituent Dem (rather than rewritten as constituents of the noun

[9] Category symbols are those symbols in underlying strings from which lexical items are derived. Thus, the constituents NP, VP, N, and V are deletable, but such elements as /ə/, "Mommy," and "fit" are not.

[10] The numbers of phrase structures or construction types discussed in the text that follows refer to the number of the phrase structure rule in the base component from which the structures were derived.

phrase) because of occurrence in the same syntactic environments as N in subject position. As discussed earlier, the pivot forms "more" and "'nother" were included as adjective forms in the lexicon. The pivot form "no" was derived from the negative operator in the sentence rewrite rule; its function in the grammar is discussed in Chapters 6 and 7.

The pivot forms not included in the categorial grammar were "Hi," which was productive (discussed earlier), and the following non-productive pivot forms in juxtaposition with nouns:

(136) (Kathryn seeing a picture of a baby)   > oh baby!

(137) (Mommy giving Kathryn the bear's
       raisins)   > thank you bear.

(138) (Kathryn putting lamb on the chair)   > O.K. lamb.

(139) (Kathryn asked Mommy for more
       "raisin")
       Want some raisin?   O.K.

       O.K.?   > O.K. raisin.

These nine utterances with "Hi" or nonproductive pivot forms were accounted for by the secondary sentence rewrite rule:

2. $S_2 \rightarrow$ Pivot + N

The one pivot not accounted for was "all," which occurred in the phrases "all through," "all dirty," and "all little children."

The frequency of occurrence of sentence types with two major category constituents expressed in performance was as follows: 18 subject-verb strings, 31 subject-object strings, and 39 verb-object strings. The utterances counted as *subject-object* strings included the 13 utterances that were equivocal—allowing interpretation as *subject-object* or *genitive* strings in the discussion of Noun + Noun constructions.

3.2.5. The Reduction Transformation
There were only four occurrences of three-term strings, including "Kathryn want raisin" in (121).

(140) (Kathryn taking car to Mommy in
       the kitchen)   me show Mommy.

(141) (Kathryn looking at the tape recorder; probably referring to feed-
back she had heard previous day)　　　'chine make noise.

(142) (Kathryn carrying a bus with figures
in it to show to Lois)　　　man ride ə bus.

There were two occurrences of "I comb pigtail" said by Kathryn as she 'combed' her hair and then 'combed' Mommy's hair. The first person pronoun was a marginal form at Kathryn I; these utterances contrast with utterance (86) "Mommy pigtail." The "I" in this context was considered a variant of the preverbal /ə/ and not vulnerable to deletion as a major category constituent, as discussed subsequently. Three-term strings representing major category constituents were not productive at Kathryn I.

However, Kathryn appeared to have learned the subject-verb-object order of English sentences (as evidenced by the productive occurrence of subject-verb, verb-object, and subject-object strings); that this order is important for the meanings of sentences; and that there are lexical constraints that influence the occurrence of lexical items in the three sentence positions. Most significantly, although the order of major categories with respect to grammatical function was well learned, there was an overriding constraint on the extent to which these major categories could be represented as constituents within the bounds of a single utterance. This is probably the most important feature of the Kathryn I grammar—that the underlying structure that accounted for the interpretation of sentences was more complex than the surface form of these utterances.

To account for the difference between underlying and surface structure, a reduction transformation was postulated that operated to delete category constituents that dominated forms that were not expressed in surface structure—for example, the V or Δ symbol postulated as an intervening constituent in *subject-object* strings. Kathryn was able to say "Mommy pull" and "pull hat," and although "Mommy hat" did not actually occur, its occurrence could be predicted from the occurrence of such sentences as "Mommy sock," "Mommy diaper." The three sentences "me show Mommy," "'chine make noise," and "man ride bus" could not be accounted for by the Kathryn I grammar, because they would violate the reduction transformation:

(2) $T_{\text{Reduction}}$ (b) S.D.: $\# - X - Y - Z$, where X, Y, Z are
(obligatory)　　　　　　　　　　　　　category symbols

S.C.: $\# - x_1 - x_2 - x_3 \Rightarrow \# - x_i - x_j,$

$$\text{where } 0 \leqslant i < j \leqslant 3$$

The mechanics of the operation of the reduction rules are discussed in the section that follows, and a full discussion of the concept of reduction in relation to the constraints on length and form of children's sentences is presented in Chapter 6.

The Form of the Rules

The problem that existed was the specification of phrase structure rules that would account for the fact that Kathryn produced reduced sentences and the pattern of reduction was variable—that is, she did not produce only subject-verb strings or verb-object strings or only pivot constructions. Moreover, the semantic interpretation of these utterances required the existence of categories in underlying strings that were not represented by constituents in production.

One approach to accounting for the facts of children's sentences would involve listing all possible sentence types or permitted combinations of forms. This appears to have been the actual result of pivot grammars—the specification of two classes of forms and their permitted patterns of combination.

An alternative model of grammatical description would specify an underlying form that is related to the actual derived form by a system of rules. The rules describe the choice of formatives that represent the result of grammatical process, and formatives can be derived from constituents represented as either *optional* or *obligatory but deletable*—to account for their nonoccurrence in actual sentences.

The specification of all categories in base strings as optional elements enclosed in parentheses would indicate that one or more or all constituents in the string may occur. The strongest objection to this notation is that designating the elements as 'optional' implies the potentiality for exercising all options in generating strings and attributes this ability to the child's linguistic competence. Further, the semantic interpretation of utterances in which elements that were not immediate constituents were juxtaposed in production (such as subject-object strings and certain negative sentences discussed in Chapters 6 and 7) would postulate intervening constituents that could not be structurally accounted for. The occurrence of the Noun + Noun sentences with structural description *subject-object* implied the designation of a dummy element linking the two categories in an underlying representation. The relational nature of the grammatical function *direct object* depends on the existence of another constituent also dominated by the same syntactic node, VP.

The postulation that the underlying structure of the sentences that occurred at Kathryn I was structurally more complete than the surface structure has been accounted for by the representation of the major categories with the functions *subject of the sentence, predicate of the sentence* as obligatory in the rewrite rules in the Kathryn I phrase structure. The nonoccurrence of obligatory major category constituents in obtained sentences was accounted for by the operation of the reduction rules in the transformational component. Using deletable elements in the phrase structure rules (1) allowed the specification of major categories in the underlying structure and their relationship, which determined the semantic interpretation of an utterance; and (2) provided insight into the nature of the child's linguistic competence by specifying the occurrence of the phrase structures that underlie produced strings.

Thus, at Kathryn I, two major category constituents have been postulated in the phrase structure: a category with the grammatical function *subject of the sentence*, and a category with the grammatical function *predicate of the sentence*. The effects on obtained sentences of (1) cooccurrence of major categories; or (2) the expansion of a major category, for example, the inclusion of the predicate complement; or (3) the selection of the negative element, in the phrase structure, are discussed at length in Chapter 6.

Briefly, the first effect is a linear reduction—the deletion of one major category if the other (which was also dominated by S) occurred or was expanded. An example was the deletion of the demonstrative pronoun with expansion of the predicate noun phrase to include the adjective, or deletion of the sentence-subject with inclusion of the complement in the verb phrase. Linear reduction involved the deletion of major category nodes in the phrase-marker representation, where $\emptyset$ is zero (deleted):

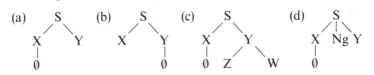

It may have been that (a) and (b) represented an earlier effect and (c) and (d) occurred at subsequent levels, but all four operated at Kathryn I.

The second effect was hierarchical reduction, which reflected lower level constraint, with reduction within a major category when another category was expanded—for example, the deletion of the verb or object-noun, with inclusion of sentence-subject. Hierarchical reduction involved deletion within major category nodes in phrase-marker representations:

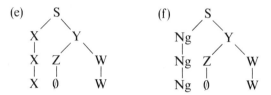

Looking ahead to Kathryn II, it appeared that in the course of development the effects of reduction were regressive and passed from *obligatory* to *optional* operation, depending on sentence complexity and the introduction of more complex structure.

Placement of Schwa

The most productive sentence types expressed were those with two major category constituents, and the immediate constituents verb-object were the most productive of these. Verb-object strings also occurred with preceding /ə/—"ə + V + N"; and /ə/ occurred as well before verbs only—"ə + V." Preverbal occurrence of /ə/ was provided for by a transformation:

(3) $T/ə/_{Placement}$ S.D.: X − VP, where X may be Ng or null
(optional)
                    S.C.: $x_1 − x_2 \Rightarrow ə − x_1 − x_2$

The transformation for placing the /ə/ in preverbal position accounted for the 31 occurrences of /ə/ before verbs—for example, "ə try," "ə see ball"—and for the fact that the schwa was not affected by the operation of the reduction transformation. The preverbal occurrence of /ə/ was observed in the texts of all three children and deserves consideration—particularly since such occurrence precluded the specification of /ə/ in the texts as an article or determiner exclusively.

The problem of ordering the /ə/ placement transformation in relation to the reduction rules has not been solved satisfactorily. The order in which they appear in the grammar was chosen because /ə/ was not affected by reduction; that is, it was not deleted with increased complexity within the sentence, and its occurrence did not appear to operate to reduce the string in the way that a preverbal noun (as sentence-subject) did. This order is attractive because /ə/ can be viewed as 'standing in' for the deleted element and appears to justify the /ə/ as a grammatical place holder. But if viewed as 'standing in' for the deleted sentence-subject at Kathryn I, its preverbal placement with inclusion of sentence-subject at Kathryn II (for example, "Mommy ə read book"), and marginally at Kathryn I ("Lois ə coming"), presents further interpretive problems. An alternative is the interpretation of /ə/ as the primitive form of verbal auxiliary or copula, but there were not sufficient data to support that conclusion.

It is important to point out that the /ə/ was not the phonological 'filler' that occurs without grammatical motivation in adult production. This kind of junctural /ə/ did not occur in the children's utterances until later. Rather, the occurrence of /ə/ appeared to be grammatically predictable in the early stages—at Kathryn I in sentence-initial positions before the negative element and before verbs and nouns, but rarely before a sentence-subject.

With the alternative order—the /ə/ placement transformation operating before the reduction transformation—the reduction transformation would not operate on /ə/ because it is not a category symbol, but its role in the phrase structure would be more difficult to specify. Including the /ə/ in the sentence rewrite rule (Rule 1 in the phrase structure) in the prepredicate position (before Ng) would preclude rewriting the predicate noun phrase and complement noun phrase simultaneously in the same rule 4—the effect of which would be a reduplication of the /ə/ before the predicate noun phrase: "ə want ə raisin," but also *"ə ə raisin" or *"this ə ə raisin."

3.2.6. Utterances Not Accounted For by the Kathryn I Grammar
The remaining utterances, which were not generated by the proposed grammar, include the following:

1. The marginal occurrence of *conjunction*, where two nouns were produced in juxtaposition without an inherent semantic relationship between them: "umbrella boot," "foots flower."
2. Structures that were not productive in that they occurred only once and appeared to be unanalyzed, 'stereotype' sentences:[11]

    (143) Kathryn looking through
           book for "Little Miss Muf-
           fet" and spider)   > Where the spider?

[11] Leopold (1961, p. 357) has described such sentences as "learned by mechanical phonetic imitation as units. The use of such stereotype phrases has nothing to do with the child's learning to put words together in an original sentence."

(144) (Kathryn looking at pictures in animal book)

$$\left[\begin{array}{l} > \text{Who has that book.}\uparrow \\ > \text{Kathryn has that book.}\downarrow \end{array}\right]$$

(145) (Kathryn eating lunch)   ə take ə nap.

You'll take a nap after a while, Honey.   > I'm busy now.

We're busy now. Yes.

(146) (Kathryn standing lamb on end)   > make him sit down.

(147) (Mommy clipping Kathryn's nails; Kathryn not offering her other hand)   > this hand now.

3. Structures that were more complex than allowed by the phrase structure rules, but nonproductive—two occurrences of a catenative verb with a main verb:

(148) (Kathryn looking for marshmallow in her pudding)   > ə want see.

(149) (Kathryn in bathtub squeezing washcloth; Mommy watching)

Squish. That's a girl.

Squish.   > helping squish.

three occurrences of fragments of a noun phrase as sentence-subject:

(150) (Kathryn picking up second lamb, after placing first lamb on chair)

$$\left[\begin{array}{l} > \text{two sit down.} \\ > \text{two sheep sit down.} \end{array}\right]$$

(151) He's looking out the window.

(Kathryn putting second lamb into block with first lamb)   > two window.

one occurrence of a noun phrase with an adverb form:

(152) (Kathryn unable to find a
pocket in Mommy's skirt)
$$\left[\begin{array}{l} \text{no pocket} \\ > \text{no pocket in there.} \end{array}\right]$$

4. Fourteen utterances with indeterminate interpretation— utterances that were not interpretable from the information available or utterances with unique form that were influenced in form by occurrence of a preceding model utterance while not being an imitation, for example:

(153) (Kathryn trying to make the
wire man sit; man fell flat)
Oh he's tired. He's lying down   lie down tire.

(154) (Kathryn holding her doll)
Oh look at the dolly's
pretty eyes.   dolly eye↑ pretty eye.↓

(155) (Kathryn and Mommy at lunch)
You want some pudding?   Kathryn want
                                            pudding.

(156) (Mommy ironing in the
kitchen; Lois and Kathryn
playing in the living room)   Mommy iron.
Mommy iron.   Mommy.
Mommy iron.   hot. hot.
Hot. Iron's hot.   - - - - shirts.
What?   shirts. Daddy.
Mommy iron Daddy's shirts?   > Mommy shirts hot.

Generally, 'unaccounted for' sentences at Kathryn I were of two kinds: (1) production 'errors' that were unique in form—for example, "bei__/ Mommy milk"; and (2) sentences that were more complex than the phrase structure would allow and seemed to be (a) influenced in form by an immediately preceding model utterance, (b) unanalyzed stereotype sentences that appeared to be 'imitations' of familiar sentences, considerably removed in time from their models, or (c) marginal forms that anticipated structures that became productive at subsequent stages.

3.2.7. Differences Between the Kathryn I Grammar and a Grammar for the Adult Model

The Kathryn I grammar has no provision for recursion: the grammar will generate only a finite number of strings, and each potential string is finite in length. That is, there is no provision in Kathryn's grammar for such features of the adult grammar as sentence embedding, which allow for the recursive properties of English sentences.

The subject-noun is not equivalent in structure or in lexical representation to the predicate nominative—both cannot be rewritten by the same rules as in the adult model. The same lexical items did not occur in both positions; only animate nouns occurred as sentence-subjects, and object-nouns were most often inanimate nouns. This represented the first inherent feature distinction for nouns in the lexicon —animate and inanimate—that was related to the syntactic restrictions of the forms.

The adjective was placed in the attributive position in the phrase structure rather than in the predicative position. The ADJ is identified in the lexicon feature rules as a complex symbol occurring in environments before nouns. This representation of adjectives differs from the lexical rule described by Chomsky (1965, p. 156):

"Adjective $\rightarrow$ CS/[+ N] $\cdots$ —," where [+ N] is a noun.

The reason for specifying adjectives in the attributive position with respect to nouns was, quite simply, that only two adjectives occurred in predicative positions and these occurred also in attributive positions, for example, "baby tire" and "tire baby." Occurrence of these adjectives in predicative position was provided for by the reordering transformation: $T_{Placement}$. Otherwise, all adjectives occurred in attributive position. The reduction transformation accounted for the occurrence of such sentences as "this dirty" and "this fuzzy," with deletion of the predicate nominative—"ə dirty sock" and "fuzzy hat" also occurred; reordering was not specified in the derivation of these sentences because "this" was never a sentence-final constituent.

Otherwise, the Kathryn I grammar is distinguished by its omissions— there is no provision for the determiner, noun inflection, personal pronouns, sentence adverbials (time, place, or manner), or number and tense of verbs. The syntactic component of the Kathryn I grammar does not include a verbal auxiliary or the copula—unless, possibly, /ə/ represented a rudimentary form of one or the other.

The grammar that has been proposed to account for the language sample obtained from Kathryn at Time 1 is not a pivot grammar, although superficial pivot constructions occurred, as they did subsequently at Time II. The earlier question—whether or not Kathryn had 'outgrown' a pivot grammar—remains. Kathryn's sentences at Time I appeared to be linguistically less mature than the data reported by Brown and Fraser (1963), Brown and Bellugi (1964), and Miller and Ervin (1964). The level of linguistic development at Kathryn I appeared to approximate the later portion of the "first phase" described by Braine (1963).

Language samples were collected from Gia and from Eric at linguistically earlier levels than the level represented by Kathryn I, so the discussion of the accountability of pivot grammars in relation to stages of syntax acquisition can be continued with discussion of the Gia texts.

4. Gia's Language at I and II

4.1. Gia I

The first sample was obtained from Gia when she was 19 months, 1 week old, and mean length of utterance was 1.12 morphemes. The sample totaled seven hours and consisted of approximately 1,015 utterances, of which exactly 141 utterances were phonologically longer than one morpheme.

Following are the phrase structure and lexicon feature rules that account for the productive constructions that occurred at Gia I. The lexicon of the Gia I text is presented in Appendix D.

4.1.1. Gia I Grammar

Phrase structure:

$$S \rightarrow \begin{pmatrix} \vartheta \\ Q \\ Hi \\ N \end{pmatrix} \begin{pmatrix} V \\ N \end{pmatrix}$$

Lexicon feature rules:

i. $N \rightarrow [+N, \pm\text{animate}]$

ii. $[+\text{animate}] \rightarrow +[\_N]$

iii. $V \rightarrow -[Hi\_]$

iv. $Q \rightarrow [+\text{quantifier}]$

v. $[+\text{quantifier}] \rightarrow \text{more, 'nother}$

The Gia I grammar is quite simple, and only a finite number of phrase structures can be generated. The most frequent utterance type contained /ə/ in sentence-initial position, where /ə/ represents an unidentified phonetic element with occasional variants such as /e/ or /i/:

(i) $S \rightarrow ə + \begin{Bmatrix} V \\ N \end{Bmatrix}$

There were 29 occurrences of a noun form with a preceding phonological element, which was /ə/ most often. Examples included:

(1) (Gia taking a box of tape from
Lois's bag)   ə /bɑk/.

(2) (Gia holding a pen)   ə pen.

(3) (Gia reaching for boxes of crackers
and cookies on kitchen counter,
looking at Lois; Mommy not at
home)

$$\begin{bmatrix} \text{crackers.} \\ > \text{/e/ crackers.} \\ \text{crackers.} \\ \text{Mommy.} \\ > \text{/e/ more. ə more.} \end{bmatrix}$$

(4) (Gia holding car, picking up driver)   ə car.

(5) (Gia watching Mommy go toward
bedroom door)   /ɛ/ Mommy.

(6) (Gia pointing to a picture of a bug)   ə bugug.

There were six occurrences of a verb form preceded by /ə/, including:

(7) (Gia scribbling on paper)   ə write.

(8) (Gia pointing to a picture of a bus) $\begin{bmatrix} \text{bus.} \\ > ə \text{ ride.} \end{bmatrix}$

(9) (Gia looking around the living
room, possibly looking for a pencil)   /e/ write.

There did not appear to be a meaningful difference in the contexts in which /ə/ occurred as opposed to the contexts of the phonological variants. Schwa did not signal a particular contrastive meaning and its interpretation was indeterminate. As will be seen, there was frequent occurrence of similar forms at Eric I and II. Although there were several possible sources for the form (the pronoun "I" or the article "a"), "ə + X" was probably not syntactic in the early Gia and Eric grammars; rather, it appeared to represent the child's attempt to extend phonologically the limits of one-word utterances.

In the lexicon feature rules, Q is rewritten as a Quantifier, either "more" or " 'nother" signifying *recurrence*, and all sentences with this form are presented in Table 4.1, where

(ii) $S \rightarrow Q \left\{ \begin{matrix} V \\ N \end{matrix} \right\}$

Table 4.1. All Utterances with "more" and " 'nother" at Gia I

Description of Speech Event	Gia's Utterance
(10) (G looking through a book for picture of a rabbit, after seeing one)	more rabbit.
(11) (L rocking clown)	
Look at the clown dance.	
(G takes clown, tries to rock it and it falls over)	more clown.
(12) (G had been scribbling on L's book; L took book away; G wanted to scribble on it)	more write.
(13) (G scribbling after she had scribbled before)	more write.
(14) (G showing L a photograph of M and G at the park)	go byebye.
(G showing L another photo of M and G at the park)	> more byebye.
(15) (G picking up another lamb)	'nother /bǽbɔ̀/.
(16) (G sitting on window ledge and kicking ledge repeatedly)	'nother bang.

The first three utterances in Table 4.1 referred to an object, (10) "more rabbit," or an event, (11) "more clown" and (12) "more write," which Gia had experienced previously and wanted to recur. In each case, the referent had been present, was no longer present, and Gia sought to reinstate it.

Utterances

   (13) more write
   (14) more byebye
   (15) 'nother /bǽbə̀/

referred to the recurrence of the referent, and (16) " 'nother bang" referred to multiple instances of a referent. Gia appeared to have learned something about the concept of *recurrence* and used "more" or " 'nother" as a syntactic operator to comment on the event of *recurrence* in (13) through (16), or to request *recurrence* in (10) through (12). Although there were only seven examples of this construction at Time I, they were important because the form "more" increased in use as a syntactic operator at Gia II and was similar semantically to Eric's and Kathryn's use of the same form. The occurrence of "more" represented the earliest use of a syntactic operator to signal a semantic contrast in the texts of both Gia and Eric. "More" also occurred in isolation as a form of request and occasionally in contexts where *recurrence* was not implied.

Both Q and /ə/ had the same distribution, in sentence-initial position before nouns and verbs, and an alternative representation of this node might be *Pivot*, with the phrase structure rule revised as follows:

$$S \rightarrow \binom{P}{N}\binom{V}{N}, \text{ where P is more, 'nother, ə}$$

There were ten occurrences of "Hi + Noun," for example:

   (17) (Gia and Lois looking out
        the window at the children
        on the playground below;
        Gia did not know Jocelyn
        or Eric)

        I see Jocelyn.

        (Gia waving)   Hi Jocelyn.

        I see Eric.

        (Gia waving)   Hi Eric.

        I see a tree.

(Gia waving)	Hi tree. Hi tree.
(turning to Lois)	/ɑ :/ tree.↑
(Gia waving again)	Hi Eric.

All these examples were said as Gia looked out the window and waved. In eight instances the utterance occurred after Lois said "I see X." As observed with Kathryn, "Hi" never occurred as a salutation when someone entered the scene. "Hi" appeared to be a pivot in constructions with nouns only, and the rule could be further revised to include the form with

$$P \rightarrow \text{more, 'nother, ə, Hi}$$

and a syntactic restriction in the lexicon permitting occurrence of "Hi" in contexts with nouns only.

Aside from utterances with /ə/, which probably were not syntactic constructions, the most productive constructions to occur at Gia I were utterances that consisted of two nouns:

(iii) $S \rightarrow N_i + N_j$,   where N_i has the feature $[+\text{animate}]$

All these utterances are presented in Table 4.2.

Table 4.2. All Noun + Noun Constructions at Gia I

Description of Speech Event	Gia's Utterance
(18) (G and L looking at a picture of a dog running alongside a boy in a toy car; the boy in the car is the dominant feature of the picture)	
What's that?	ə wowwow.
What?	
That's a car. A car.	> wowwow car.
(19) (G reaching for her doll, which is named "Blueyes") (20)	⎡ > Gia eyes. ⎤ ⎣ > Gia Blueyes. ⎦
(21) (L pointing to ear on the lamb)	
What's this?	> lamb ear.
(22) (G looking at a picture of a girl in a bathtub with a toy fish)	⎡ bath. ⎤ ⎣ > girl fish. fish. ⎦

Description of Speech Event	Gia's Utterance
Who's taking a bath?	
(G pointing to the fish)	fish.
(23) (G turning wheels on the underside of the car)	> truck wheel.
(24) (G looking at a picture of a girl bouncing a ball)	> girl ball.
(25) (G watching L putting the blocks back into the bag)	> block bag.
(26) (G seeing a fly settle on a block)	> fly block.
(27) (G watching the fly on her blanket)	
What's that?	> fly blanket.
(28) (G seeing the fly settle on the blanket again)	> fly blanket.

Because there were only 11 occurrences of this construction, as compared with 59 at Kathryn I and 66 at Gia II, classification according to interpretation and inferences about underlying structure were necessarily tentative. However, there did appear to be a prevailing order of constituents in these 11 utterances that precluded their being classed simply as *conjunctions*—where order would be unmotivated.

The utterance (18) "wowwow car" appeared to be a conjunction, where Gia included a word she had just heard in expanding (while also reducing) her original utterance. In (19) "Gia eyes" and (20) "Gia Blueyes," Gia was reaching for her doll and these, along with (21) "lamb ear" may be interpreted as *genitive* strings. An alternative interpretation, *subject-object*, would class

(19) Gia eyes.
(20) Gia Blueyes.
(21) lamb ear.
(22) girl fish.
(23) truck wheel.
(24) girl ball.

as two nouns with an inherent stative relationship between them, such as would be expressed by "have" or "want" in the adult model. However, there were no stative verbs in Gia's lexicon, and attributing their nonoccurrence in (19) through (24) to a reduction process would be difficult to defend. It appears that these six utterances can, at best, be characterized as equivocal subject-object strings. Utterances

(25) block bag.
(26) fly block.
(27) fly blanket.
(28) fly blanket.

signaled *locative* relation—the initial position noun being specified in terms of location: block (in) bag, fly (on) block. It might be observed that if (23) had occurred with reversed order, that is, "wheel truck," it could have been classed with (25) through (28) as a *locative* relational phrase.

Although the interpretation of these Noun + Noun sentences was tentative, the first-position noun was a 'movable' object and, in most cases, could be characterized as an 'animate' noun (exceptions were "truck wheel" and "block bag"). However, the occurrence of nouns in relation to verbs in the Gia I corpus introduced a problem for the specification of the derivation of noun forms in terms of grammatical function in the phrase structure rules. All the Gia I constructions with verbs, except occurrences of verbs with /ə/ and verbs with particles (for example, "lean back," "go byebye") are presented in Table 4.3.

In (35) "out Daddy" and (36) "go Mommy," Gia's utterances appear to have been influenced in their occurrence by prior utterances—by Daddy in (35) and by the preceding vocative by Gia in (36). These two examples are not provided for by the phrase structure rules because of their status as marginal forms.

Otherwise, the occurrence of nouns with verbs was infrequent, but the order of the constituents (except for "out Daddy" and "go Mommy") was Noun + Verb—regardless of the relationship between the constituents. In

(29) girl write.
(30) Mommy back.
(31) Mommy back.

the noun occurred in sentence-subject position as sentence-subject, but (30) and (31) were the same, and (29) occurred after a model utterance in the form of a question.

In

(32) slide go.
(33) balloon throw.
(34) block 'way.

Table 4.3. All Constructions with Verbs at Gia I

Description of Speech Event	Gia's Utterance
(29) (G looking at a picture of a girl drawing with crayons)	
What's the little girl doing?	> girl write.
(30) (G looking at the front door; waiting for M)	> Mommy back.
(31) (M coming in front door)	> Mommy back.
(32) (G putting keys on slide)	> slide go.
(33) (G picked up a balloon)	
Oho! What's that?	throw.
balloon	
(G dropped the balloon, as though she were throwing it)	> balloon throw.
(34) (G dragging L's bag to L, who is gathering blocks together, preparing to leave)	⎡ > block 'way. ⎤ ⎣ 'way away. ⎦
(35) (G pulling D to the door to go byebye; D wasn't feeling well)	byebye.
Maybe you can go out later for a walk with Mommy.	> out Daddy.
(36) (G pulling M to her stroller, wanting to go outside)	⎡ go byebye. go byebye. ⎤ ⎢ Mommy.↑ ⎥ ⎢ > go Mommy. ⎥ ⎣ go byebye. go. ⎦

the noun that occurred in sentence-initial position was an object
noun—and yet object nouns always occurred in sentence-final position
in constructions with other nouns. One explanation may be that Gia
had learned something about the subject-object order of English
sentence constituents but had not yet learned the relational or syntactic
features of verb forms with respect to nouns.

An alternative explanation which might apply to (32) through (34) and also to (22) through (28) in Table 4.2,

(32) slide go.
(33) balloon throw.
(34) block 'way.
(22) girl fish.
(23) truck wheel.
(24) girl ball.
(25) block bag.
(26) fly block.
(27) fly blanket.
(28) fly blanket.

would be a structural description of the surface constituents in terms of Topic + Comment as the "basic grammatical relation of [the] surface structure" of these sentences (Chomsky, 1965, p. 221). In this analysis, the Topic of the sentence was the element that was stated first—perhaps in order of importance—and the rest of the sentence is interpretable as Comment. An example of Topic + Comment construction in the adult model would be

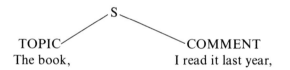

where "it" represents the Topic in a construction as the underlying sentence-object.

Reconsidering the Noun + Noun constructions in Table 4.2, it appears that the first-position noun in sentences (22) through (28) may be describable as the Topic of an utterance—for example:

(27) The *fly*, it is on the *blanket*,

where "it" represents an underlying sentence-subject. This interpretation of these sentences would allow the classification of all first-position nouns—the leftmost constituent noun in Rule (iii)—as Topics occurring before nouns or verbs that represent the Comment constituents; for example:

(33) The *balloon*, I *throw* it,

where "it" represents an underlying sentence-object.

The Topic + Comment designation would thus describe only the surface structure of the utterances, and underlying relationship—the grammatical functions *subject of the sentence* or *object of the verb*— would not be specified. Inasmuch as Gia's use of verbs was primitive, it may be that awareness of grammatical function was as primitive and her syntactic constructions could best be described in terms of surface structure at this stage.

In a study of the speech of one child between the ages of 26 and 29 months, Gruber (1967) concluded that an intermediate stage in language acquisition (after pivot constructions and "subjectless predicates" but before the child's sentences manifest subject-predicate relations) is one in which sentences can be characterized as Topic + Comment constructions. From the examples of utterances that were given ("what does the truck?," "why it go?," "do I make this way?," "he take the wheels, fire engine," "dump truck all fixed"), it is apparent that this child's linguistic development was considerably more advanced than either Kathryn's or Gia's at the stages so far discussed. Gia, at Time I, was at the stage where pivot constructions would be expected in the sequence proposed by Gruber—but pivot construction was not the dominant pattern in her language, and 'subjectless predicates' did not occur.

The Topic + Comment designation is a linguistically descriptive but superficial account of Gia's sentences at Time I in that it does not explain the semantic relationship between noun forms that occurred in juxtaposition. The first explanation—that Gia had learned subject-object order but had not yet learned relational features of verbs—is the preferred account in view of the ordered relationship of Noun + Noun constructions at Time I and the subsequent development of verb forms in relation to nouns observed at Time II, six weeks later.

4.1.2. Utterances Not Accounted For by the Gia I Grammar
There were 12 occurrences of "here Mommy," 9 occurrences when Gia gave something to the investigator and 3 occurrences when she did not give anything to anyone—for example:

(37) (Gia taking the lambs out of a basket)   here Mommy.

(38) (Gia holding pen and paper)   here Mommy.
     (subsequently gave the pen to Lois)

"Here" occurred as a single-word utterance only once, and "here

Mommy" was interpreted as a stereotype form that was noncontrastive; that is, it did not signal Gia's giving something to Mommy, nor any other interpretable meaning.

There were eight occurrences of "ah: baby" and one occurrence of "make ah: baby" as Gia either hugged her doll or rocked her doll carriage.

4.1.3. Comparison of the Gia I and Kathryn I Grammars

The grammar for Gia I is more primitive than the Kathryn I grammar in a number of important ways. Because the position of verbs appeared to be variable in relation to nouns in the Gia I text, it was not possible to specify the underlying relationships between nouns and verbs, and relationships between nouns (as subject or object constituents) could be identified only tentatively. As a result, the Gia I rules are more superficial and less precise than were the rules proposed for the Kathryn I grammar.

A significant omission in the Gia I grammar is that, except for "more" and "'nother"—which have been discussed as syntactic operators—there was no occurrence of forms with adjective status in the adult model. In fact, there were no adjective forms as single-word utterances in the Gia I corpus at all. The list of words that occurred in isolation in the text is presented with their frequencies of occurrence in Appendix D. In a total of 138 forms that occurred singly, there were none that would be classed as adjectives in the adult model. Whereas, at Kathryn I, a productive sentence type was the elaborated noun phrase (for example, "ə funny man"), this same construction did not occur at Gia I.

The sentence rewrite rule:

$$(iii) \quad S \to N_i + N_j, \quad \text{where } N_i \text{ has the feature } [+\text{animate}]$$

was one of the alternative rules for Noun + Noun constructions at Kathryn I, discussed in Chapter 3. The order of the constituents and the inferred semantic relationship between them at Gia I anticipated a potential hierarchical syntactic relationship. But in the proposed grammar, the relationship is a linear one—both constituents of a Noun + Noun sentence would be derived from the same node, S, in the phrase-marker representation—because there was insufficient evidence for postulating the derivation of the second-position noun from a VP node.

There was only slight evidence of the operation of reduction at Gia

I—for example, in the sequence

(36) (Gia pulling Mommy toward her
stroller, wanting to go outside)   go byebye. go byebye.
Mommy.↑
> go Mommy.
go byebye. go.

Otherwise, the nonoccurrence of subject-verb-object strings was attributable to (1) vocabulary insufficiency—Gia knew few verb forms; and (2) syntactic immaturity—Gia had not learned syntactic features of verbs in relation to nouns. In the list of lexical items that occurred in isolation (in Appendix D), there are only 14 verb forms (including "(a)way," which occurred frequently and with verbal force).

4.1.4. Differences Between the Gia I Grammar and Pivot Grammars

Although there were productive pivot constructions with "more" and "Hi," a more frequent pattern was an utterance that juxtaposed two substantive forms; this pattern could not be described as pivotal. The Gia I grammar includes the specification of the pivot constructions that occurred but also specifies the occurrence of Noun + Noun and Noun + Verb strings. The Gia I grammar is not a pivot grammar if the notion of pivot grammar means that Gia's linguistic expression was limited, at Time I, to syntactic juxtaposition of just two classes of forms: a small class of operators and a larger class of substantives. Although her linguistic expression was primitive, Gia had learned some of the possibilities for combining substantive forms in relation to semantic experience. The use of "more" to signal recurrence, and the inherent relationship between noun forms in juxtaposition were the important features of Gia's linguistic behavior at Time I. Only the syntactic operation of "more" and the occurrence of /ə/ and "Hi" could be accounted for by a pivot grammar.

4.2. Gia II

At Time II, Gia was 20 months, 2 weeks old, and mean length of utterance was 1.34 morphemes—compared to 1.12 morphemes six weeks earlier. The language sample was approximately seven and one-half hours and consisted of an estimated total of 1,790 utterances of which exactly 451 consisted of more than one morpheme—compared to approximately 1,015 utterances at Time I, of which 141 were phonologically longer than one morpheme.

The syntactic component of a tentative grammar for Gia II, presented in the section that follows, consists of (1) the phrase structure, (2) lexicon feature rules, and (3) transformations. The lexicon of the Gia II text is presented in Appendix E.

4.2.1. Gia II Grammar

Phrase structure:

1. $S_1 \rightarrow N(Q) \begin{Bmatrix} NP \\ VP \end{Bmatrix}$

2. $S_2 \rightarrow Hi + N$

3. $VP \rightarrow V + NP$

4. $NP \rightarrow (\partial)(N)N$

Lexicon feature rules:

i. $N \rightarrow [+N, \pm animate]$
ii. $[+animate] \rightarrow +[\_\_VB]$
iii. $Q \rightarrow [+quantifier]$
iv. $[+quantifier] \rightarrow more$
v. $V \rightarrow [+V]$
vi. $[+V] \rightarrow \pm[\_\_NP]$
vii. $\partial \rightarrow +[/d/\_\_], -[Q\_\_]$

Transformations:

(1) $T_{Placement}$
    (optional)
    S.D.: $away + X$
    S.C.: $x_1 - x_2 \Rightarrow x_2 - x_1$

(2) $T_{Reduction}$
    (obligatory)
    S.D.: $\# - X - Y - Z$, where X, Y, Z are category
    symbols[1]
    S.C.: $\# - x_1 - x_2 - x_3 \Rightarrow \# - x_i - x_j$,
    where $0 \leqslant i < j \leqslant 3$

(3) $T_{/\partial/\ Placement}$
    (optional)
    S.D.: $X - VP$, where X may be Q or null
    S.C.: $x_1 - x_2 \Rightarrow \partial - x_1 - x_2$

The Gia II grammar is more complex than the Gia I grammar and reflects syntactic maturity in a number of important respects—although the grammars are also similar in a number of important ways.

---

[1] Category symbols are those symbols in underlying strings from which lexical items are derived. Thus, the constituents NP, VP, N, and V are deletable, but such elements as /ə/, "Mommy," and "read" are not.

One of the most productive constructions at Gia II was the juxtaposition of two nouns—with 66 occurrences (compared with 11 at Time I and 59 at Kathryn I). Table 4.4 presents the classification of the

Table 4.4. Classification and Distribution of Noun + Noun Utterances at Gia II

Classification	Example		Frequency
Conjunction	(39) (G looking at a photo of M and G)	Mommy Gia.	6
Genitive	(40) (G holding M's keys)	$\begin{bmatrix} \text{Mommy's.} \\ > \text{Mommy key.} \end{bmatrix}$	12
	(41) (G pointing to doll's hat)	dolly hat.	
Subject-Object	(42) (G pointing to her jacket hanging up to dry after M washed it)	Mommy jacket.	19
	(43) (G saying goodbye to M, who was bringing a package to Roger)	Mommy Roger.↑	
	(44) (G asking L to play one of her records)	Lois baby record.	
Attributive	(45) (G looking at photo of herself)	picture Gia.	20
	(46) (G holding book about animals)	animal book.	
Locative	(47) (G pointing to cow hanging from mobile)	cow mobile.	3
Equivocal: Subject-Object Genitive Conjunction	(48) (G looking at a picture of a Daddy shaving)	Daddy beard.	4
	(49) (G looking at a picture of a girl and fish in bathtub)	girl fish.	

Table 4.4, *continued*

Classification	Example		Frequency
Anomalous	(50) (G picking up girl figure to put on form board)	Daddy man.	2

Noun + Noun constructions at Gia II, with examples of each classification and the frequency with which each type occurred in the text. Classification was based on the criteria discussed in Chapter 3 for the utterances with the surface form Noun + Noun in the texts of Kathryn I.

The two most important features of the sentences exemplified in Table 4.4 are the order of the constituents and the occurrence of 'animate' nouns in first position in all but *attributive* constructions. The same observations had been made for most of the Noun + Noun utterances in the Gia I text—that there was an inherent order of the constituents, and the initial-position noun could be described as 'animate' (or 'movable').

Classification of Noun + Noun utterances had been necessarily tentative at Time I inasmuch as there were only 11 instances. Six of these had been characterized as equivocal *subject-object* strings with the probability that 3 of the 6 ("Gia eyes," "Gia Blueyes," "sheep ear") could be more specifically identified as *genitive* strings. In comparison, only 4 Noun + Noun utterances at Time II were equivocal, whereas 12 were unequivocally *genitive* strings and 19 were *subject-object* strings. At Time I, 3 of the 11 sentences were classed as *locative* constructions; at Time II, 3 of the 66 sentences were *locative* constructions.

Attributive constructions formed the one classification at Time II that was not represented at Time I, and, at Time II, *attributive* Noun + Noun constructions occurred as frequently as *subject-object* strings (with 20 instances). None of the constructions signaled *identity, disjunction,* or *indirect object.*

The most significant difference between the Gia I and the Gia II grammars was the occurrence of subject-nouns and object-nouns in syntactic contexts with verbs—with nouns occurring in sentence-initial position having the function of sentence-subject, and nouns in sentence-final position having the function of sentence-object most often. However, there were exceptions: "read book" and "book read" (both /ri:d/) occurred in virtually identical speech events—attesting to the recent development of verb forms in relation to nouns.

Except for the sentence "Gia more read book," three-term strings did not occur; there were 15 subject-verb strings, 23 subject-object strings (including the 4 equivocal cases in Table 4.4), and 38 verb-object strings. Verb-object strings, which did not occur at Gia I, were the most frequent of these two-term strings at Gia II, and the least frequent were subject-verb strings—the same pattern, with similar frequencies, as was obtained in the Kathryn I text.

Thus, two important changes at Gia II were (1) the introduction of hierarchical structure, with constituents derived from more than one major category node in the underlying representation; and (2) the obligatory operation of reduction on three-term strings in the underlying structure. These two changes at Gia II were also two of the significant features of the Kathryn I grammar.

Table 4.5. Classification and Distribution of Utterances with "more" at Gia I and Gia II

Time	Request for Recurrence of Event		Request for Recurrence of Object		Comment on Recurrence of Object or Event		Comment on Coexistence of Objects
"more"							
I	18(90)		12(92)		7(70)		0
II		32(63)		20(40)		9(24)	4(67)
"more" + N							
I	1(5)		1(8)		2(20)		1
II		8(16)		30(60)		15(41)	2(33)
"more" + V							
I	1(5)		0		1(10)		0
II		11(22)		0		13(35)	0
	(100)	(100)	(100)	(100)	(100)	(100)	(100)

Note: The figures in parentheses represent the percentage of times the particular form ("more," "more" + N, or "more" + V) was used within each classification at Gia I and Gia II. For example, at Gia I the request for recurrence of an object was expressed with isolated "more" 92 percent of the time and with "more" + N only once. However, at Gia II isolated "more" was used for requesting recurrence of an object 40 percent of the time, while the construction "more" + N was used 60 percent of the time. In addition, at Time I there were 14 indeterminate instances of "more"; at Time II there were 21 indeterminate utterances—13 instances of "more," 6 instances of "more" + N, and 2 instances of "more" + V.

As at Gia I, one of the most productive constructions was "more" in syntactic contexts before nouns (64 occurrences), and before verbs (23 occurrences). These utterances have been classified according to the following criteria: (1) Gia asking for a recurrence of an event that occurred previously; (2) Gia asking for an object that she had previously but no longer had; (3) Gia commenting on the recurrence of an object or event after a previous occurrence; (4) Gia commenting on the coexistence of more than one object in the environment—simultaneous occurrence, as opposed to recurrence; and (5) equivocal reference. Table 4.5 presents the distribution of "more" (1) as a single word utterance, (2) in context with nouns, and (3) in context with verbs, according to the foregoing classification, for Gia I and for Gia II.

There were no instances of "more" in contexts where Gia asked for an object or an event that had not occurred previously. It seems apparent that the concept of "more" in relation to *recurrence* or 'another instance of' had been well learned at Gia II. Also, "more" occurred marginally to signal plurality—the coexistence of objects. There was only one instance of "another" ("another man"), with the function of *recurrence*.

There were nine instances of the operation of reduction in constructions with "more." These occurred in contexts where "more" did not operate directly on (did not 'modify') the adjacent constituent with which it occurred—for example:

(51) (Gia giving Lois label and truck, to stick label
       on the truck as Lois had done previously)   more truck.

(52) (Gia looking for second wire man to put on
       train, after putting first wire man on)   more train.

The form "more" has been specified in the Gia I grammar as a syntactic operator, Q (signaling *recurrence*), in syntactic contexts before predicate constituents and after subject noun forms (which were expressed in production only marginally):

$$\text{1.i.} \quad S_1 \rightarrow N + Q \begin{Bmatrix} NP \\ VP \end{Bmatrix}$$

This structural description differs from the specification of Q at Time I—where it had been included as a member of a pivot class with privileges of occurrence in syntactic contexts before noun and verb forms. But in the Gia II grammar, "more" occurred (1) in hierarchical construction (expressed marginally in three-term strings, for example, "more play block"), and (2) in syntactic contexts before predicate forms and after /ə/ (for example, "ə more in," "ə more upidown").

As at Time I, the most frequent sentence type was /ə/ (or occasionally a phonological variant such as /e/ or /i/) in syntactic contexts before noun and verb constituents. Examples included "ə record," "ə lamb," "ə peekboo," "ə Gia Mommy," "ə push ə carriage"—utterances that were similar to the utterances with /ə/ at Kathryn I. Again, as at Kathryn I, the reduction rule did not operate on /ə/, allowing such strings as "ə push ə carriage" to occur.

The other pivot form that occurred productively was "Hi" in juxtaposition with nouns and with the same use as at Gia I. Gia did not use "Hi" as a salutation or greeting; "Hi" occurred as she watched the children on the playground, frequently after someone said "I see___." Gia's living room window faced the playground and was above the building entrance, so she frequently watched the playground traffic and waved to the children she knew.

Except for "'nother," the pivot forms that occurred at Time I were productive at Time II; there were no new pivot forms. Moreover, "more" and /ə/ could be accounted for in relation to the categorial rules of a phrase structure grammar, leaving "Hi" as the one-word pivot class.

4.2.2. Utterances Not Accounted For by the Gia II Grammar
The utterances that occurred at Gia II that could not be generated by the Gia II grammar included the most 'complete' sentences that occurred:

(53) (Lois rolling wheel on slide; Gia
     picking up book which she and
     Lois had read previously)   > Gia more read book.
     Hm?

     (Gia bringing book to Lois)   more book.↑

(54) (Gia picking up a piece of chew-
     ing gum)   I got gum.

The other three-term strings that occurred were "more play block," "Papa Gia barrette," "more Mommy picture" (Gia wanting to see Mommy's photographs), "more picture bee," and "more picture animal."

There were occurrences of single words with "-s" suffix—for example, "Mommy's," which Gia said (1) as she picked up Mommy's keys; (2)

as she pointed to Mommy's photographs, which she had been told repeatedly not to touch because they were "Mommy's"; but also (3) as she pointed to Lois' sweater.

Also unaccounted for were three Noun + Noun constructions with unordered constituents—or order that did not fit the classification summarized in Table 4.4.

(55) (Gia eating lunch in the kitchen
with Lois' book on high chair
tray; Lois walked out; Gia
calling out to Lois)   > book Lois!

(56) (Gia putting the doll's shoe into
a shopping bag)   > shopping bag shoe.

(57) (same context as (43); Mommy
preparing to leave)

Byebye. Mommy's going to give
something to Roger. O.K.?
Mommy'll be back soon.   Roger.

Roger.   > back Roger Mommy.↑

What, Sweetie?   Mommy Roger.↑

Roger, yes. Mommy's going to
give something to Roger.

There were also utterances that were uninterpretable from the context—for example:

(58) (Gia lying down on floor)   Mommy tire.

4.2.3. Comparison of the Gia II and Kathryn I Grammars

The grammar for Gia II is more similar to the Kathryn I grammar than it is different, and the two are directly comparable in a number of important details. Mean lengths of utterance for the two texts were similar (1.32 for Kathryn at Time I and 1.34 for Gia at Time II).

As has been seen, both grammars provided productive rules for verb-object and subject-object strings and, less frequently, for subject-verb strings. A significant feature of both grammars was the constraint on three-term subject-verb-object strings in production—when the underlying structure of sentences, as inferred on the basis of semantic interpretation, specified inclusion of major category components with these inherent grammatical relationships.

Both texts contained pivot constructions, and both contained utterances that extended the phonological structure of a single morpheme with inclusion of /ə/ or a phonetic variant in pre-position (without contrast).

There were three noteworthy differences between the Kathryn I and Gia II texts that precluded the specification of a single grammar for both.

The first important difference was the absence of a negative operator in the Gia II grammar—there was no provision for syntactic expression of negation at Gia II. There were two negative constructions in appropriate contexts:

(59) (Gia pushing the car with driver in it; driver fell out)   no more man.

(60) (Gia trying to connect train cars but unable to)   no right.

Otherwise, the few syntactic utterances with "no" that occurred were not contrastive—for example:

(61) (Gia eating peaches) $\left[\begin{array}{l}\text{no more.}\\ \text{no more peaches.}\end{array}\right]$

(Gia continued to eat peaches; did not produce similar utterance when, indeed, there were no more peaches)

The two other negative constructions occurred in sequence with "more" in context with the same noun:

(62) (Gia turning pages of pad of paper, looking for fresh piece of paper to scribble on) $\left[\begin{array}{l}\text{no more write.}\\ \text{more write.}\end{array}\right]$

(63) (Gia reaching for her empty bottle in her crib) $\left[\begin{array}{l}\text{no more bottle.}\\ \text{more bottle.}\uparrow\end{array}\right]$

(five repetitions of "more bottle," Gia wanted more milk)

In the discussion of the semantic and syntactic development of negation by the three children in Chapter 7, it is reported that "no" occurred contrastively at Gia I and Gia II as a single-word utterance. However, the syntactic expression of negation was marginal at Gia II— even though an argument could be advanced for the appropriateness of the negative element in (61) "no more peaches"—that is, Gia was creating the state of 'no more peaches'; but the argument is weak. An argument might also be made for (62) "no more write" and (63) "no more bottle" to the effect that Gia was expressing nonexistence (of paper to write on or milk in her bottle) and, subsequently, the contrastive form signifying the positive alternative. However, both utterances occurred within the same speech events, and from the available context, interpretation of negative predication in these constructions was necessarily equivocal.

"More" was a productive form in both grammars, but far more productive in Gia II than in Kathryn I. Also, in Gia II "more" occurred productively with verbal predication ("more write," "more stand up"), whereas there was no verbal predication with "more" at Kathryn I, nor is there in the adult model. In the different grammars of the two children, "more" in Gia II and the negative element in Kathryn I are placed in the same prepredicate position—within the structure of the sentence.

Speculating on this difference, it may be possible that Gia's use of "more" to signal *recurrence* operated somehow to preclude the alternative predication, *negation*, in the same sentence position—that cognitive attention to syntactic expression of the concept of "more", *another instance of*, could not occur simultaneously with attention to the syntactic expression of the semantic converse, *no instance of*. The cooccurrence of both forms in the same syntactic and semantic contexts, (62) with "write" and (63) with "bottle," may have reflected this cognitive confusion. The possible relation between the syntactic function of "more" and the absence of negation in Gia's early grammars is discussed further in Chapter 7.

A second important difference between the Gia II and Kathryn I grammars was the absence of adjective forms in the Gia II grammar that were not also noun forms—and, indeed, the small number of adjective forms in the single-word utterances as well (see Appendix E). The noun phrase rule for Kathryn I specified adjectives in attributive position, but the noun phrase rule for Gia II specified attributive nouns—for example, "animal book," "baby record." Thus, the first 'adjectives' (modifying attributives) in Gia's lexicon were forms with noun status in the adult model. Also, the syntactic occurrence of these forms differed from the Kathryn I adjectives in that the attributive noun also occurred in predicative position in other structures—for example, "picture Gia" (a picture of Gia) and "picture bee" (a picture of bees), but "Mommy picture", (Mommy's pictures).

There was one occurrence of a predicate adjective:

(64) (Gia reaching for the micro-
     phone)

    (drawing back)

$$\begin{bmatrix} \text{Lois microphone.} \\ \text{no.} \\ > \text{microphone hot.} \end{bmatrix}$$

At Gia I Gia had referred to the microphone as "iron"—apparently because of the electrical cord.

Two similar utterances, which were not accounted for by the Gia II grammar, were:

(65) (Gia reaching for her silver bank, which
     was not broken)   bank ə broke.

(66) Gia looking at her hands after Lois had
     wiped them clean)   hand ə wipe.

A third difference between the two grammars was the absence of demonstrative pronouns at Gia II. "That" appeared in the text only twice: "that mine" and "that lion."

In summary, the comparison of the grammars prepared for the texts obtained at Gia II and Kathryn I—when both children were approximately the same age and mean length of utterance was virtually the same—revealed that the grammars were quite similar, even though there were differences between them that precluded the specification of a single grammar to account for the texts obtained from both children. Pivot forms—such as have been reported in children's texts collected in other studies—existed in the Kathryn I and Gia II texts, but the grammars that have been proposed are not pivot grammars. Rather, the grammars reflect the fact that Kathryn and Gia had learned the subject-verb-object order of constituents in English sentences, even though there were constraints on the extent to which these relationships could be expressed within the bounds of a single utterance.

Chapter 5 discusses the data obtained from the third child, Eric, and the grammars that have been proposed for his first three texts.

5 Eric's Language at I, II, and III

At the time of the first two observation sessions, Eric produced single-word utterances that generally could be understood. More often, he produced extended strings of sounds with recognizable English sentence intonation patterns—but containing few intelligible words, if any. Although not observed with Kathryn and Gia, this kind of linguistic behavior has been described in other children and often is referred to in the literature as "jargon" (McCarthy, 1954). This characterization may be imprecise if the term implies 'language.' Eric's unintelligible production did not appear to have the status of an idiolect; rather, it appeared to represent an attempt at imitating the superficial, acoustic aspects of heard speech.

Both question and statement contours were common in Eric's expressive vocalization, the expression was often directed to a listener, and a response from the listener was expected; Eric would wait for a response before continuing or repeat what he had said with emphasis. The investigator was able to initiate 'dialogues' by producing an approximation of Eric's unintelligible production in response, and the exchange was repeated as often as 14 times. When the response to what Eric said was varied—for example, by including intelligible words or his name—he was usually able to reproduce these words when they occurred at the beginning or end of the expression, but not when the words occurred within the expression.

The ability of children to reproduce adult intonation patterns at an early age—before using the phonetic patterns of adult speech—was

102

described by Lewis (1951). Weir (1966) reviewed investigations of children's learning intonation patterns in different languages and reported a conclusion by Ohnesorg that "the rising intonation pattern requiring a 'yes' or 'no' answer that is most frequently used with children . . . often remains structurally ambiguous [in the child's expression]until other patterns are learned as well." This observation coincided with Weir's "inability to find systematically contrasting [intonation] patterns with a two-and-a-half-year-old child."

Lieberman (1967, p. 46) observed that children were able to mimic the different fundamental frequencies of individual parents in their babbling and early speech attempts and commented that this mimicry may represent "a social use of speech."

In subsequent sessions, Eric often exhorted or reprimanded the toys, his baby sister, or the investigator with duplication of adult expression, intonation, and affect. It is probable that his earlier, extended unintelligible vocalization was an attempt to mimic the stream of heard adult speech in much the same way.

5.1. Eric I

The first observation of Eric, when he was 19 months, 1 week old, was four hours long. There were 207 intelligible utterances, of which 19 were phonologically longer than one morpheme, and mean length of utterance was 1.10. Table 5.1 presents all the utterances that were longer than one morpheme, and Table 5.2 presents all the intelligible single-word utterances and the frequency with which each occurred in the corpus.

Table 5.1. All Utterances Phonologically Longer than One Morpheme at Eric I

Description of Speech Event	Eric's Utterance
(1) (E putting clown on floor)	ə sit.
(2) (E trying to open closet door)	ə ə door.
(3) (E closing lid of toy chest)	ə ə door.
(4) (E looking out window at car parked at curb, door open, and infant seat visible)	ə baby.
(5) (E stacking rings on cone)	$\left[\begin{array}{l} \text{on. on.} \\ > \text{ə on.} \\ \text{on. on. on.} \end{array}\right]$

Table 5.1, *continued*

Description of Speech Event	Eric's Utterance
(6) (E asking L to spin top)	ə ə turn.
(7) (E asking L to spin top again)	ə ə more ə.
(8) (E showing clown to L)	ə ə see.↑
(9) (Same as (11) in Chapter 1) (E watching tape recorder reels through window in lid)	see↑ window.
(10) (E pointing to picture of a rabbit on his wall)	see↑ rabbit.
(11) (L hiding behind curtain in peek-a-boo game)	I see you.↓
(12) (E picking up parts of a vacuum cleaner)	I got.
(13) (E waving out window; cars and traffic going by)	Hi car.
(14) (E watching man get into car parked at curb)	/hi/ car. Hello.
(15) (E trying to see lollipop stick he had dropped into radiator grille)	/ɑ/ 'pop.
(16) (same as (15))	/hə/ 'pop.
(17) (E looking into grille) What's in there?	/hɑ/ 'pop.
(18) (E closed the lid of his toy chest)	⎡ all gone. ⎤ no more. ⎣ make all gone. ⎦
(19) (E watching trucks on building lot across the street)	/tə/ truck.

A 'grammar' of Eric's language at this point would be presumptuous —the data were meager. However, this sample proved to be valuable in that it may have recorded utterances that were among the earliest true syntactic constructions—"see↑ window" and "see↑ rabbit." Eric's parents had reported that he was not producing sentences or putting two words together as yet—although "he says a lot that we can't understand." The original intention for obtaining a sample of his speech at this time was, first, to determine if, indeed, he was producing utterances that might prove to be intelligible on careful relistening, and second, to obtain a record of his presyntax lexicon.

Table 5.2. Lexicon: Single-Word Utterances and Their Frequencies of Occurrence, Eric I

all gone	Eric	O.K.
		on, 2
baby	foot	one
ball, 3		one more
bear, 2	goose, 2	pacifier
bed, 3		'pop, 3
birdie	hand, 4	
blanket	heavy, 4	rabbit
boy	Hello, 8	ride
bunny	Hi, 3	
byebye	horsie, 6	see↑, 23
	hug	sheep
car, 4		shoe, 2
carrot	kangaroo, 5	shoes
cat, 5		shovel
cherry	Mommy	sit, 6
'chine, 4	mole, 3	sock
cleaner, 2	more, 2	squirrel
clown	mouse	
cold		Teddy
cookie, 5	nice, 6	there
	no, 13	three
Daddy, 3	no more	
dog, 5	noise, 16	whale, 2
door, 7		window, 5

The earliest utterances that were longer than one morpheme were most often single words extended phonologically—right to left—with some phonetic element, which was most often /ə/. These phonetic elements were counted in computing mean length of utterance, although they probably did not have morpheme status. Reduplication of /ə/, as in "ə ə door," was not counted.

The occurrence of /ə/ with single words was also the most frequent utterance type longer than one word in the early texts of Kathryn and Gia. The form did not appear to be contrastive—there was no 'meaning' or linguistic referent that distinguished its occurrence, although a number of possible interpretations could be made: that /ə/ represented the article "a" or a primitive form of the pronoun "I." Utterances often referred to events with Eric as actor-agent, and the stereotype sentences "I got" and "I see you" also occurred.

It appears that at Time I Eric's linguistic expression consisted of single-word utterances primarily; most of the words produced were those that are nouns in the adult model—the names of 'things' or objects in his environment. In this early lexicon, there were three forms that are verbs in the adult model—"see↑," "sit," and "ride"—one of which, "see↑," was the most frequent form to appear in the entire corpus, with 23 occurrences. The two syntactic constructions (9) "see↑ window," and (10) "see↑ rabbit" consisted of the most frequent word in his lexicon (with rising intonation contour, as it occurred in isolation) in syntactic construction with the names of two different objects in the environment.

5.2. Eric II

The second observation was six hours long, and Eric was 20 months, 2 weeks old. In addition to many unintelligible utterances, he produced 490 utterances that were intelligible; 87 of these were more than one morpheme long—mean length of utterance was 1.19.

5.2.1. Productive Phrase Structures

The most frequent utterance with more than one word continued to be /ə/ (or some other phonetic element) in juxtaposition with other forms, which were most often nouns and verbs in the adult model. The form /ə/ occurred six times in contexts with verb forms when Eric was the actor-agent of events—for example:

(20) (Eric about to sit down)   ə sit.

and twice when he was not:

(21) (Eric hearing Mommy come
       in the front door)   ə home.

(22) (Eric pointing to his record
       player, which he had broken
       earlier in the week)   ə broke. broke.

One possible source for /ə/ may have been the pronoun "I"; this interpretation of /ə/ in constructions with verbs became more tenable at Eric III, when the form was often "I" in context before verbs only. A second possible source may have been the prenoun article "a" or "the"—for example:

(23) (Eric turning to open his
       toy chest)   ə toy.

(24) (Eric pointing to his doll)   ə baby.↑

However, the following also occurred:

(25) (Eric had tried to move his
  rocking chair aside but he
  couldn't; Lois moving it so he
  could reach the window
  ledge)   ə heavy.

(26) (Eric stacking blocks)
$$\left[\begin{array}{l} \text{one more. one more.}\\ \text{one more.}\\ > /i/ \text{ up.}\\ \text{one more. one more.}\end{array}\right]$$

As at Eric I, this utterance type appeared to represent his linearly extending a monomorphemic element—perhaps in an effort superficially to duplicate syntactic speech—without either grammatical or semantic motivation.

The two other productive phrase structures in the Eric II text consisted of nouns in contexts after verb or pivot forms. Nouns did not occur productively in constructions with other nouns (as they did with Gia and Kathryn), and there were no adjective forms in constructions (except possibly after /ə/, as in "ə heavy"). It was possible to establish tentative criteria for form class distinction on the basis of occurrence of forms in syntactic contexts with pivots, nouns, and /ə/, as follows:

	Pivot	Verb	Noun
/ə —	−	+	+
/— Noun	+	+	−
/ Pivot —	−	−	+

Pivot forms were mutually exclusive with /ə/ and verb forms; pivots occurred only in contexts with nouns, and verbs occurred only in contexts with nouns, although verbs occurred also after /ə/.

Table 5.3 presents all the utterances with verb forms in syntactic contexts (other than "ə + Verb"). Of the utterances in Table 5.3, (35) "shake hands," (38) "make pee," and (40) "show me" were probably not constructions but, rather, wholly learned stereotype expressions. Utterance (39) "/də/ down" appears to include a consonantal variant of /ə/ as in (37) "/də/ see the 'chine." However, it was also possible that "/də/" might have been "duck" in (39). "Ducky" and "down" each occurred once as single-word utterances. The verb forms did not share contexts with any other forms—except for "house" with "build" and "in," and "it" in sentence-final position.

Table 5.3. Syntactic Utterances with Verbs at Eric II

Description of Speech Event	Eric's Utterance
(27) (E holding toy drum) Play the drum. (still holding drum)	play it. ə play it.
(28) (E picking up his pail)	ə find it.
(29) (E running after a wheel after kicking it across the room)	get it.
(30) (E watching the tape recorder)	
(31) (E looking at a picture of a baby eating cereal) What's he doing?	eating cereal.
(32) (L starting to stack blocks; E joining) Will you help me?	ə help you
(33) (E pointing to cookie he dropped on the floor)	down ə cookie.
(34) (E putting wheels into round window of stacked blocks)	⎡ one more. ⎤ > build house. house. ⎣ > in house. ⎦
(35) (L showing E the figures that fit on the form board) and Mommy. (E pointing to the hand) hand.	 hand. shake hands.
(36) (E picking up the baby to put it on the board)	ə put ə baby.
(37) (E wanting to lift tape recorder cover; whining) You can't play with the machine.	- - - - 'chine. /də/ see the 'chine.
(38) (E holding his overalls; he had wet his diaper; "make pee" was the expression his parents used for "urinate")	 make pee.
(39) (E bending to pick up a toy duck from the floor)	⎡ > /də/ down. ⎤ ⎣ this. ⎦
(40) (L playing with the train; E sitting on window ledge) Did you see my train? (E climbing off the ledge)	 ⎡ out. ⎤ ⎣ > show me. ⎦

Table 5.4. Examples and Frequency of Pivot Constructions at Eric II

Pivot	Example	Frequency
1. here(s) $\begin{cases} \text{the} \\ \text{ə} \\ \text{comes} \end{cases}$	(41) Where are the clowns? (E pointing to clown on the chair) here the clown.	5
	(42) (E trying to turn control knobs on the tape recorder) We can't play with the machine. What? here comes ə 'chine. here's ə ə 'chine.	
2. Hi	(43) (E looking at bear in his crib) Hi Teddy.	4
	(44) (E picking up Mother figure to put on the form board) Hi Mommy.	
3. 'nother	(45) (E looking for the second clown after finding the first one) 'nother clown.	7
	(46) (E picking up block after playing with blocks) 'nother toy.	
	(47) (E going toward the air conditioner, which was off) (subsequently tried to turn it on) 'nother noise. noise!	
	(48) (L and E playing with the slide) My turn? or Eric's turn? Whose turn is it? $\vdots$ (E rolled wheel, retrieved it; coming back handing the wheel to L) $\begin{bmatrix} \text{turn on.} \\ > \text{'nother turn.} \end{bmatrix}$	

Table 5.4, *continued*

Pivot	Example	Frequency
4. no more	(49) (E pointing to the lamp, which was off) no more light.	10
	(50) (L getting the tape recorder and micro-phone together, preparing to leave) no more noise.	
	(51) (E standing in front of closed closet door where the vacuum cleaner, his favorite toy, was stored) no more cleaner.	

In contrast, the pivot forms did share contexts and also occurred far more frequently. Table 5.4 presents examples and frequency of occurrence of the pivot constructions in the text.

Function of Pivot Forms

There were 26 pivot constructions accounted for in Table 5.4, and there were several other utterances with indeterminate interpretation that contained pivot forms. The special case of *negation* is discussed in Chapter 7. The pivot " 'nother" signaled *recurrence* as the form "more" did in the texts of Kathryn and Gia. At Eric I " 'nother" did not occur and "more" occurred only in the forms "no more" and "one more," which ultimately were specified as single words. The function of "Hi" was similar to its use in the Gia and Kathryn texts—it was not used as a salutation and appeared to signal 'taking notice.'

Syntactically, "here" occurred twice in response to a Where-question; elsewhere (three instances), it appeared to signal *locative* reference (as in (41) "here the clown"). However, in eight occurrences of "here" as a single word, it indicated location only once; seven occurrences of isolated "here" accompanied Eric's giving something to someone else—a *deictic* function that did not occur syntactically.

In addition to the utterances described so far, there were forms originally considered 'more than one morpheme' that were ultimately specified as single words—for example, "no more," "one more" (the forms "one" and "more" did not occur elsewhere), the verb form "go get" (as Eric picked up wheels for the slide), and seven occurrences of variants of noun forms that added "-s" (for example, "blocks," "hats," "babies") where the "-s" did not occur contrastively to signal plurality.

5.2.2. Eric II Phrase Structures
The following base rule will generate the utterances that have been described; the Eric II lexicon is presented in Appendix F.

$$S \rightarrow \begin{pmatrix} \text{Pivot} \\ (\text{ə}) \text{ V} \end{pmatrix} ((\text{ə}) \text{ N}),$$ where Pivot is here(s), Hi, 'nother, no more, with syntactic restriction on occurrence with /ə/.

Sentences with "it," which occurred marginally, would not be accounted for by the above rule:

(27) (ə) play it.
(28) ə find it.
(29) get it.

The form "it" was included in the grammar proposed by Braine (1963) as a pivot in sentence-final position with the rule $S \rightarrow X + P$, where P is pivot. The verbs that occurred with "it"—"play," "find," and "get"—did not also occur elsewhere in the texts at Eric I or II, except for one instance of "find" in isolation and "go get" (which is discussed later) at Time II, and "it" never occurred alone. The forms "it," "play," "find," and "get" could be included in the lexicon as bound forms, or, alternatively, "play it," "find it," and "get it" could be included as single words that do not occur in syntactic contexts, except after /ə/.

In addition to syntactic occurrence, pivots and nouns were also one-word utterances, so their specification in strings is optional. Moreover, the pivots and nouns that occurred in constructions were among the most frequent lexical items that occurred alone in the text: the pivots "Hi," "here," "no more" and the nouns "noise," "cookie," " 'chine," and "baby."[1] The single-word lexicon at Time II is presented in Appendix F.2.

In contrast, the verbs that occurred in syntactic contexts with nouns occurred alone less often. Of the verb class represented in Table 5.3, "see" occurred five times as a single-word utterance. The forms "down" and "find" each occurred elsewhere only once, and the other verbs— "shake," "put," "make," "eating," "help," "in," "play"—occurred in the text only in the syntactic contexts presented in Table 5.3.

---

[1] This account contrasts with McNeill's (1966) report that pivot forms did not occur as single words in the data collected by Roger Brown and his associates.

There appeared to be two different syntactic processes underlying the grammar proposed for the Eric II text.

1. Certain constructions occurred as the result of the juxtaposition of two forms that were frequent single-word utterances—the pivots, except " 'nother," and "see," with the noun class generally. Several of the most frequent words at Time II were also among the most frequent words at Time I: "noise," "see," and "cookie." Eric appeared to learn a set of single items and then the semantic and syntactic possibilities for combining them.

2. Other constructions occurred as new forms were acquired or learned with particular semantic intent in syntactic contexts with more familiar forms—the pivot " 'nother" and the verb class except for "see." Thus, the syntactic features of certain forms, such as most of the verbs, were learned before or at least in conjunction with the inherent or semantic features of the forms. For example, in the following,

(34) (Eric putting wheels into round
window of stacked blocks)

$$\begin{bmatrix} \text{one more.} \\ > \text{build house.} \\ \text{house.} \\ > \text{in house.} \end{bmatrix}$$

"build" and "in" occurred in syntactic context before "house," in a referential situation for which both forms were somehow relevant. "Build" and "in" did not occur in isolation in the corpus, but appeared as forms with the syntactic feature of sentence placement before certain other forms. The syntactic feature of sentence position may have been learned along with the 'meaning' of "build" and "in"—if it can be assumed that the two words did not also occur in isolation outside the recorded speech sample. In contrast, "house" appeared as a member of the larger class of words that have privileges of occurrence in sentence-final position, after other forms. This account of early syntax is essentially the conclusion reached by Braine (1963)—that children learn the positions in which words can occur in an utterance. However, learning sentence position was only one aspect of what the children learned about grammar in these early stages.

It might be argued, also, that pivot forms produced endocentric constructions as the earliest noun phrase constructions. The pivots were mutually exclusive with /ə/, which may have been interpretable as the primitive article before single noun forms. The argument for including /ə/ and the pivots in one as yet undifferentiated prenoun category would suggest a rule for a noun phrase sentence type such as the following:

$$S \rightarrow \begin{Bmatrix} \partial \\ \text{Pivot} \end{Bmatrix} N$$

However, as counter evidence, /ə/ did occur marginally in syntactic contexts before verb-object constructions but never before pivot-object constructions. Pivot constructions never occurred as constituents in larger constructions. The only conclusion that can be supported by the available evidence was that the pivots "no more," " 'nother," "Hi," and, also, "see" occurred as syntactic operators to signal specific semantic concepts in relation to noun forms.

5.2.3. Utterances Not Accounted For by the Eric II Grammar
Several utterances were unique in structure. There was one Noun + Noun construction in a speech event which occurred twice:

(52) (Eric pointing to the air
     conditioner, which was not on)   air conditioner noise.

There was one occurrence of subject-verb which was actually a distant imitation:

(53) (Eric was squeezing a rubber duck,
     which made a squealing noise)
     What's that?   cry.
     (Eric squeezing duck)
     Does Eric cry?
     (Lois and Eric producing extended
     unintelligible vocalization in
     'dialogue,' Lois imitating Eric;
     4 exchanges)
     Eric squeezing duck) $\begin{bmatrix} > \text{Eric cry.} \\ \text{kə}\_\_ \text{ kə}\_\_ \text{ cry.} \end{bmatrix}$

     You're gonna cry?
     Let me see.
     (Eric screwed up his face, as
     though crying)

There were two utterances with " 'nother" and nonnoun forms:

(54) (Eric had wet his pants)   'nother wet.

(55) (Eric pulling at the tape
     recorder, which Lois was carrying
     to the door, preparing to leave)   'nother off.

There were two occurrences of attributive constructions:

(56) (Eric picking up the girl
figure to put on the form
board, after putting the
mother on)   little mommy.

(57) (Eric holding his doll)   my baby.

There were also unique utterances that appeared to be wholly learned stereotype phrases: "right here," "how 'bout it," "show me," "turn 'round," "turn on" and

(58) (Eric dropping the doll;
immediately after (57))   ə don't want baby.

There was only one utterance that presented clear semantic evidence for the operation of reduction, as discussed in the Kathryn I and Gia II grammars:

(59) (Eric pointing to the tape
recorder as Mommy walked in,
after being told earlier that
he couldn't play with it)   no 'chine.

"No 'chine" was the only example of predicate negation, which became productive subsequently, and the only use of "no" as the negative operator. In the subsequent Eric III text, as will be seen, "no" and "no more" were in complementary distribution: "no more" occurred with noun forms, and "no" occurred with predicates. As with other un-accounted-for utterances at Eric II and in the Gia and Kathryn texts, unique or marginal structures often anticipated structures that were to become productive in subsequent samples.

5.2.4. Comparison of the Eric II Grammar with the Grammars Proposed for Kathryn and Gia

It should be pointed out that each corpus collected from Eric was considerably smaller than those collected from Kathryn and Gia. In order to compare them, Table 5.5 presents a description of each speech sample in terms of duration, estimated total number of utterances, and the percentage of utterances that were longer than one morpheme.

Clearly, Eric was not as talkative as either of the girls; even at Time III, when the sample totaled eight and one-half hours, the total number of utterances produced was less than half the number produced in less

Table 5.5. Description of the Language Samples

	K:I	G:I	G:II	E:I	E:II	E:III
Age (months, weeks)	21,0	19,1	20,2	19,1	20,2	22,0
Time (hours)	7.5	7.0	7.5	4.0	6.0	8.5
Mean length of utterance (morphemes)	1.32	1.12	1.34	1.10	1.19	1.42
Total number of utterances	1,225	1,015	1,790	207	490	564
Utterances longer than one morpheme	397	141	451	19	87	243
Percentage of utterances longer than one morpheme	.32	.14	.25	.09	.18	.43

time at Kathryn I and Gia II. In this context, it is pertinent that Eric's mother frequently commented to the investigator that Eric "talks more when you're here."

Also, mean length of utterance was not comparable for the grammars being compared; the utterances of Gia and Kathryn were somewhat longer in terms of mean length of utterance than the utterances produced by Eric at Time II.

However, there were more significant differences that had to do with the kinds of sentences the children produced. Kathryn and Gia both produced pivot constructions, but the majority of productive phrase structures that occurred could not have been accounted for by a pivot grammar. It was necessary for the grammars to generate strings that specified inherent semantic relationships between lexical items and were often hierarchical in structure.

In contrast, the Eric II grammar was a pivot grammar. A number of object nouns occurred in directive constructions with a smaller class of forms. The smaller form class was subdivided into a class of syntactic operators (or pivots) and a class of verbs. Pivots occurred frequently, shared contexts with a larger number of different noun forms, and occurred with identifiable general semantic function in conjunction with different substantives; for example, " 'nother" signaled recurrence of the referents of whatever noun forms with which it occurred. Verb forms were less productive in that each member of the class occurred less frequently than pivots, generally did not share contexts, and occurred with narrower, more special semantic intent (in relation to the particular nouns with which they occurred). Whereas there were multiple occurrences of pivots with different nouns, verb forms were generally restricted to specialized occurrence with specific nouns. There was optional occurrence of /ə/ before verb forms but never before pivot forms. Finally, the two categories were mutually exclusive.

Whereas Kathryn and Gia both produced Noun + Noun constructions with different inherent relationships between the constituents, Eric did not. The only grammatical relationship that existed between categories in Eric's sentences was a linear direct object relation—object noun to verb—and that structure was less productive than pivotal structures. There was no provision for hierarchical structure in the Eric II grammar. There was a direct linear relationship between the immediate constituents of each utterance, and there was no evidence for postulating a richer underlying structure. There was no need for a transformational component in the grammar to account for the shapes of the sentences that were actually produced. The surface structure was the only structure.

However, the Eric II grammar was not less systematic than the Gia II and Kathryn I grammars. On the contrary, the form classes in the Eric II grammar were well defined syntactically, and the order of elements and their privileges of occurrence were scrupulously observed.

5.3. Eric III

At Time III, Eric's level of linguistic development could be compared more directly with the levels observed at Kathryn I and Gia II. Mean length of utterance for the three children was more similar, although still below 1.5 morphemes—the upper limit of mean length of utterance for the texts discussed in this study. Interestingly, although Eric produced far fewer utterances than either Kathryn or Gia (as seen in Table 5.5), the proportion of utterances that were longer than one word was highest for the Eric III text (.43), as compared with the Gia II (.25) and Kathryn I (.32) texts.

Eric produced 243 utterances that were phonologically longer than one morpheme. There were multiple occurrences of many of these, and often an utterance was produced repeatedly with minor, apparently unmotivated variation, as in the sequence:

(60) (Eric nesting blocks)

$$\begin{bmatrix} \text{ə fit.} \\ \text{ə made ə fit.} \\ \text{/ɑ/ fit.} \\ \text{/i/ fit.} \end{bmatrix}$$

and in the following sequence:

(61) (Eric holding the tank,
     looking for the tank car)

(62) (Eric put the tank on the tank
     car; pointing to the tank)

(63) Does that fit?

$$\begin{bmatrix} \text{ə fit.}\uparrow \\ \begin{bmatrix} \text{I fit.} \\ \text{/e/ fit.} \end{bmatrix} \\ \text{this ə fit.} \\ \text{this fit.} \end{bmatrix}$$

(64) (Eric assembling the train again)

$$\begin{bmatrix} \text{/e/ fit.} \\ \text{ə fit.} \end{bmatrix}$$

⋮

(completing the train)   there is fit.

(65) (Eric assembling the train again,
     putting a car at the wrong end
     of the engine)

(putting it right)

$$\begin{bmatrix} \text{ə fit.} \\ \text{/e/ fit.} \\ \text{no fit.} \\ \text{/e/ fit.} \end{bmatrix}$$

The most frequent construction type continued to be a single lexical item (67 utterances) or a phrase (36 utterances) with some phonological element in pre-position. Although the phonological element was /ə/ most often, there were variants, as in the examples with "fit" and with nouns: "/i/ lamb," "/e/ bunny," "/i/ man," "/i/ toy," "/e/ baby," and four occurrences of "/e/ naughty," referring to a picture of naughty babies.

There were 64 utterances in which the phonological element occurred before verbs in reference to events in which Eric was actor-agent and none where he was not. In 22 of these 64 utterances the form of the phonological element was /ɑɪ/ or /əɪ/, allowing interpretation as the first person pronoun "I." Moreover, this was the only variant of /ə/

that did not also occur before noun forms. If "I" was productive as the first person subject pronoun at this time, then a significant question was why it did not occur exclusively—why did the variants /i/, /e/, /ɑ/ occur if all had the same referent? One possible answer might have been that the form was still transitional—that "I" was productive but not completely so. But looking ahead to the Eric IV corpus, where one might expect the form to occur most often if, indeed, it was transitional at Time III, the same pattern prevailed—"I" occurred frequently with verbs in events with Eric as actor-agent, but so did the variants.

The contexts of the speech events did not reveal a rationale for determining a possible motivation for the variants of "I." A superficial observation was that there may be a differentiation of "I" in contrast with the inanimate "it"; "it" was a reasonable variant in (64) "/e/ fit" and (65) "ə fit." But "it" occurred 28 times after verbs—for example, "I find it," "/e/ fix it," "hə look for it," "hold it," "throw it." "It" never occurred in other sentence positions. It may be that "it" was a pivot with fixed position, but it was also likely that "it" did not have agent-function status for Eric but existed in his lexicon only as a proform occurring in direct object constructions.

Sentences with a phonological element before a verb and optional "it" in sentence-final position accounted for 48 of the total number of utterances that occurred at Eric III; they would be generated by the following rule:

$$\text{(i)} \quad S \rightarrow \begin{Bmatrix} \text{ə} \\ \text{I} \end{Bmatrix} V \quad \text{(it)}$$

This rule is different from the sentence rewrite rule at Eric II only in the specification of "I" as a variant of /ə/ and the inclusion of "it" as a postposition pivot form.

Clearly, (i) was a productive rule at Eric III, and the sentence type could be described as an interpivotal construction—a verb form juxtaposed between the initial-position phonological element and the proform "it," which was mutually exclusive with nouns. The specification of "I," which in the adult model is a lexical item derived from a major category (NP), created the potentiality that the sentences generated by Rule (i) expressed the underlying grammatical relationship subject-verb-object. Adding the specification of object nouns to (i), as follows:

$$\text{(ii)} \quad S \rightarrow \begin{Bmatrix} \text{ə} \\ \text{I} \end{Bmatrix} V \begin{pmatrix} & \text{it} \\ \text{(ə)} & \text{N} \end{pmatrix}$$

extended this potentiality. But there were other pivot constructions to consider as well.

Four pivot forms had been identified in the earlier Eric II text: "no more," "here," "Hi," and " 'nother." Of these, "Hi" did not occur at Eric III at all; "here" occurred marginally—once in sentence-initial position, once in sentence-final position as the complement of "go," and once after /ə/, "ə here." Thus, only two of the four pivot forms that were productive at Time II also occurred productively at Time III: "no more" and " 'nother."

But, whereas " 'nother" occurred pivotally with other substantives at Eric II to signal recurrence of an object, it did not occur in pivot constructions at Eric III. Rather, " 'nother" and the variant "another" occurred exclusively with the proform "one." There were seven occurrences of the form "(a)nother one," which signaled request for the recurrence of an object, and three occurrences that commented on the recurrence of an object. The following also occurred:

(66) (Eric took the car driver and
        tried to fit it into the truck)
        Will that go in?

$$\vdots$$

        (Eric turned to stack the blocks)
        (Eric stacked all the blocks;
        looked around; going to the toy
        bag, presumably for more blocks)   'nother go in.

There were seven utterances intervening between the model and Eric's utterance (66) " 'nother go in"—but this unique utterance was the only occurrence of " 'nother" with a substantive. Further, the substantive was a verb form; at Eric II, pivots had not occurred with verbs.

The negative element "no more" occurred syntactically at Time III 26 times and was in complementary distribution with the negative element "no," which occurred 5 times. These forms are discussed at length in Chapter 7 where a full description of the syntactic and semantic development of negation is presented for the three children.

There were two new pivot forms in the Eric III text: "there" occurred, with deictic function, four times—"there ə birdie" and "there phone" as Eric pointed to the birdie and the phone, respectively, "there more" as Eric looked into the toy bag for more toys and found the last wheel, (64) "there is fit," and one occurrence of "right there." The following routine also occurred:

> (67) (Eric sitting on Mommy's lap as
> she dressed him; Mommy had just
> put on one of his shoes; Eric
> reaching down for the second
> shoe on the floor)

$$\left[\begin{array}{l} \text{where's the shoe.} \uparrow \\ > \text{there is.} \end{array} \right]$$

It is plausible that "there" at Eric III replaced the similar form "here" at Eric II in similar contexts, but both forms were only marginally productive.

The second pivot form that emerged at Eric III was productive— "more." Table 5.6 summarizes the functional distribution of the form

Table 5.6. Classification and Distribution of Utterances with "more" at Eric III

	Request for Recurrence of Event	Request for Recurrence of Object	Comment on Recurrence of Event	Comment on Recurrence of Object	Comment on Coexistence	Indeter-minate
"more"	4	13	0	7	1	16
"ə more"	2	3	3	1	0	0
"more" + N	0	6	0	5	0	0
"ə more" + N	0	0	0	1	0	0

as a single morpheme utterance and in constructions with nouns and /ə/. The same form occurred in the Kathryn I, Gia I, and Gia II texts with the same function—to signal *recurrence*, either as a comment or a direction. However the form occurred in Eric III in constructions with nouns only, as at Kathryn I, and not, as in Gia II, in constructions with verbs. Further, at Eric III, "more" contrasted with the negative marker "no more." "No more" signaled *nonexistence* of the referent;

"more" signaled *recurrence* of the referent. There were five repetitions of the following routine, produced with great delight:

(68) (Eric had inserted a tinker toy
     axle into a wheel and made a
     friction noise by turning the wheel
     around the axle; putting the axle
     in the wheel)   more noise.
     (turning it)   more noise.
     (stopping it)   no more noise.

It appeared that the two notions were related (1) conceptually—the *nonexistence* of the referent as contrasted with its *recurrence* after nonexistence; and (2) syntactically—with similarity in the shape of the two operators "more" and "no more," as well as syntactic occurrence in identical contexts.

Thus, the rule of grammar that generated pivot constructions at Eric II continued to be operative at Eric III, with two important differences. First, the actual pivot forms that occurred in the two texts differed— certain Eric II pivots no longer occurred and others were replaced by different forms with similar function ("here" was replaced with "there"; " 'nother" was replaced with "more").

The second difference in the pivot rules was that /ə/ was no longer mutually exclusive with pivot forms—/ə/ occurred frequently with "more," with one occurrence in a fuller construction, "ə more apple," and also with "no more." The earlier observation, that one of the first attempts at syntax consisted of phonologically extending a single verb or noun form, applied, at Eric III, to pivot forms as well. An alternative explanation would seek to account for the source of /ə/ in functional terms. One such function has already been offered to explain the occurrence of /ə/ with verbs as a primitive first person pronoun. But no functional explanation for the /ə/ with "more" is apparent from the data. A third rule, to account for pivot constructions, can be specified:

(iii)   S → (Pivot) + (N.)

with the lexical entry for "more," a pivot, specifying optional occurrence after /ə/.

However, there were more significant differences between the Eric II and the Eric III grammars. Although pivot constructions continued to be the most productive sentence type at Eric III, there were also

Table 5.7. All Utterances with Nouns in Direct Object Constructions
with Verbs at Eric III

Description of Speech Event	Eric's Utterance
(69) (Immediately after (68); E twisting wheel and axle again)	> watch noise.
(70) (E trying to get nested blocks out of toy bag) (takes out the car driver) ⋮	toy. ə: toys.
(E pulling at blocks again) (takes out lambs and gives them to L) ⋮	> out toy. here. here. here.
(71) (Pulling at blocks again)	> out ə toy.
(72) (E had just eaten an apple) You ate the apple all up. There's no more apple. (E starts to cry and hits the toys) What's the matter? (crying) You ate the whole apple. (running to kitchen)	more apple. > want more apple. more apple.
(73) (E sitting in his high chair, wearing socks but not shoes) Do you have shoes on? (Pointing to top of the kitchen cabinet) Your shoes aren't up there. Yes, we'll get your shoes. After you go to the bathroom we'll get your shoes. (E pointing to top of the cabinet again) Whatever gave you the idea your shoes were up there?	 I /íəò/ shoes. /íəò/. /ə^{n}ó^i/ shoes. > ə need shoes.
(74) (E going after his unfinished cup of juice) (drinks it)	> ə eat juice.
(75) (E's favorite toy was M's discarded vacuum cleaner; he spent much time connecting the hose; pushing the on-off button; and 'cleaning.' He also stored small blocks, pegs, and toys in the tank) (E and L looking for the truck driver) I don't see him. Oh! I remember. Somebody put him in the cleaner. (E going toward the cleaner)	⎡ hə look for it. here! ⎤ ⎢ - - - - - - - - cleaner. ⎥ ⎣ > ə look ə cleaner. ⎦

Table 5.7, *continued*

Description of Speech Event	Eric's Utterance
(76) (E threw the slide upright across the room; to distract him, L picked up a stuffed kitten) I found a kittie. I found a kitten. Where's Daddy? (L hearing "doggie" as "Daddy") (77) (E going to window to look outside) (seeing a boy on sidewalk)	⎡ > i found ə doggie. > I want ə doggie. boy. ⎦
(78) (L taking wooden pegs out of the cleaner tank; E watching) Oh there's one more. Here it is. I got them all. I'm gonna put them all on the train. (E taking pegs from L) (E going with pegs to the cleaner, passing his hobby horse and tape recorder) (79) (E putting pegs into the cleaner)	⎡ I get down. > I get horsie 'chine. > I get cleaner. ⎦
(80) (E climbed under his bed and lay there 'talking'; L imitated his unintelligible production and he repeated it; 'dialogue' continued for several minutes) It my truck under there? What? Away? Are you going away? ∶ (E coming out from under bed with L's truck	ɔ́ nɔ́ gɔ́ dɔ́ bái gwei > ɑ see you truck.
(81) (E seating wire man on large block)	⎡ blocks. > man sit blocks. ⎦
(82) (E and L playing; M walked past door) (E running after her) Now you want your apple? O.K. I'll give you the apple.	Mommy! > here ə need apple.

constructions without pivot forms. Returning to the rule discussed earlier:

$$\text{(ii)} \quad S \rightarrow \begin{Bmatrix} ə \\ I \end{Bmatrix} V \begin{pmatrix} & it \\ {}_{(ə)} & N \end{pmatrix}$$

there were 14 sentences that included noun forms as verbal complements. These are presented in Table 5.7. The constructions with verbs
and object nouns in Table 5.7 were not developmentally innovative—
except for (81) "man sit blocks," all would be generated by the earlier
Eric II grammar.

However, there were also six occurrences of noun forms before verbs;
these are presented in Table 5.8. The verbs in Table 5.8 were among
Eric II as single-word utterances, and "sit" and "cry" were also among
the most frequent words at Eric II.

Table 5.8. All Noun + Verb Utterances at Eric III

Description of Speech Event	Eric's Utterance
(83) (Wire man, riding on the train, fell off)	off.
⋮	
(E replaced it and it fell again; E picking up man)	⎡ cry. man səi⎤ ⎣ > man cry. ⎦
(84) (Shortly after (83); same context: wire man, riding train, fell off)	⎡ cry. ⎤ ⎣ > man cry. ⎦
(85) (same as (81); E seating wire man on large block)	⎡⎡ blocks. ⎤⎤ ⎢⎣ > man sit blocks. ⎦⎥
(86) (E walking away; leaving man sitting on block)	⎣ > ə man sit. ⎦
(87) (E's foot caught in the tape recorder wire, trying to free it)	> /u/ 'chine off.
(88) (E dropped his apple) What happened?	> apple down.

From the contexts of the speech events, it was clear that the noun
forms in Table 5.8 related to the verb forms as sentence-subject. Of
particular interest was (88) "apple down." At Eric II, Eric had produced
the sentence "down ə cookie" in a slightly different context—the cookie
was on the floor and had not fallen as part of the speech event. But in
(88), "apple" as sentence-subject was more plausible than "apple" as
sentence-object, and the fact of its occurrence in appropriate subject-
verb order was even more impressive in view of the fact that "apple"
occurred in sentence-final position 11 times in the text—for example,
"no more apple" and (82) "here ə need apple."

Three other sentences with "apple" were:

(89) (Eric looking at a picture of a
raccoon holding an apple)   'coon apple.
(two occurrences of the same
speech event)

(90) (Eric holding his apple with
both hands)   cold.
cold?   cold.
cold. yes.   > apple cold.

At Eric II there had been only two syntactic possibilities for constructions with nouns—nouns always occurred in sentence-final position as direct objects or pivot complements. But at Eric II the order of constituents was more variable and was motivated by the potentiality for expressing different inherent grammatical relations between elements of a predication. Nouns occurred before and after verbs, but except for "man sit blocks," nouns never occurred in both positions in a single sentence.

The only other utterance that was similar in form to (90) "apple cold" was

(91) (Eric was blowing through a
broken whistle)
I think it's broken.   / bókət. /
(Eric pointing to the broken
record player)   / bókət. /
broken. The record player's
broken too.
(Eric pointing to lamp which
was off)   light.
Is the light broken?   light. light.
Is it broken? No.   > light hot.

This utterance was ambiguous because the light was not hot at the time, but lights are often hot. "Apple cold" and "light hot" were marginal forms.

Attributive adjectives occurred only twice—"orange juice" and "red car," referring to the truck, which was not red. Eric also said "my medicine" as he picked up his nose drops, and "two man" as he watched while the second wire man was placed next to the first one.

There were three other Noun + Noun utterances in addition to the two occurrences of "'coon apple":

(92) (Eric feeding juice to his doll)   juice baby.

(93) (Eric sitting precariously on the big block)

Do you want to sit on your chair over there?

(Eric looking at the doll and his blanket on the chair)   baby blanket.

(94) (Eric finding the car driver)   Eric big boy.

"Eric big boy" (and also "orange juice" and "red car") were clearly repetitions of familiar phrases. "Baby blanket" was a conjunction, and interpretation of "juice baby" was open, although direct-indirect object was most likely. These last utterances, (90) through (94), were marginal forms and could not be included as phrase structures generated by a grammar for Eric III. But the occurrence of a noun form as sentence-subject in initial position began to be productive and represented the most important developmental difference between the texts at Time II and Time III.

5.3.1. Eric III Phrase Structure

There were at least two possibilities for specifying the phrase structure in a grammar for Eric III. The first specification, (A), presents an account of the three sentence types that could occur at Eric III, with three sentence rewrite rules ordered on the basis of frequency of occurrence (see Appendix G for the Eric III lexicon).

$$(A)\ S_1 \rightarrow \binom{\text{ə}}{\text{I}}\ V\ \binom{\text{it}}{\text{(ə)N}}$$

$S_2 \rightarrow$ (Pivot)(N), where Pivot is /ə/, no more, more, there(is)

$$S_3 \rightarrow \binom{N}{\text{no}}(V)$$

Thus, the most productive rule would rewrite S as a verb form in direct object constructions with "it" or N, after optional /ə/ or "I." Whereas at Time II the preferred sentence type was generated by S_2 ("Pivot + N"), S_1 was the most frequent of the sentences that occurred at Time III.

The two rules, S_1 and S_2, differ from the earlier Eric II phrase structure:

$$\text{Eric II: } S \rightarrow \begin{pmatrix} \text{Pivot} \\ \text{(ə)V} \end{pmatrix} ((\text{ə})N)$$

only in the specification of "I" as an alternant of /ə/ in sentence-subject position and the inclusion of "it" as a direct object alternant. The rule generating S_3 was innovative, and, even though only marginally productive, it represented an important developmental difference in structure between the texts at Eric II and III. Otherwise, the pattern of sentence that was emerging at Time II became more productive at Time III with certain developmental changes in the specification of constituents and the relationship between constituents. The rules for S_1, S_2, and S_3 in account (A) will generate the linear surface structure of most of the utterances that occurred at Time III.

The alternative account (B) consisted of collapsing the S_1 and S_2 rules in (A) as follows:

(B) 1. $S_1 \rightarrow (\text{Pivot}) \begin{pmatrix} \text{NP} \\ \text{VP} \end{pmatrix}$

2. $S_2 \rightarrow (N)(V)$

3. $VP \rightarrow V \begin{pmatrix} \text{it} \\ \text{(ə)N} \end{pmatrix}$

4. $NP \rightarrow (Q)N$

with a feature representation that specifies:

(i) Pivot → no, there(is), /ə/
(ii) /ə/ → "I"/__V
(iii) Q → more
(iv) no + NP → no + Q + N

The inclusion of the pivot forms "more," "no," "there(is)," and /ə/ in the (B) phrase structure attempted to account for the different functions of the forms (such as "more" and "no") in relation to the lexical items with which they occurred. The pivot "more" was represented as a quantifier (Q) that said something specific about the category constituent N: the *recurrence* of the referent.

As will be discussed in Chapter 7, "no more airplane" and "no more noise" signaled that the object named did not exist, but "no go in" meant that one block did not fit into another and "no train" meant that Eric did not want the wire man to ride the train. The negative particle "no" appeared only in predicative constructions, in complementary distribution with "no more," which appeared in constructions with nouns.

Occurrence of the negative particle with NP required the occurrence of Q in NP, and the result was the negation of recurrence, expressing *nonexistence*. Thus, the account of negation at Eric III specified the constituent structure of the pivot construction "no more noise" with the following phrase-marker:

(a)

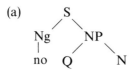

and not:

(b)
```
            S
          /   \
        Ng     NP
        |      |
      no more  N
```

The evidence that "no more" and "more" were conceptually contrastive at Eric III (as demonstrated in the sequence (68) "more noise, no more noise") was impressive and favored the phrase-marker (a), as generated by the (B) phrase structure.

"There(is)" was only marginally productive, but the specification in (B) rules accounted for the varied occurrence of "there" in contexts with noun, verb, and pivot ("there more") forms.

Because it was not possible to account for the variation in the form of preverbal /ə/, and the occurrence of "I" was noncontrastive (in that it occurred only in reference to events with Eric as actor-agent, but other variants of /ə/ also occurred in such events), the most appropriate specification of "I" appeared to be as a variant of /ə/ in preverbal position.

The (B) phrase structure was the preferred account because, in addition to describing sentence patterns, it also specified the relation of pivot forms to other category constituents through a primitive sequence of base rules for the derivation of phrase structure. However, the account (B) also provided for the potentiality of hierarchical relationship between the constituents "I," V, and N (or "it"). A reasonable objection to this account could be made inasmuch as the status of "I" was not yet substantiated in the text as sentence-subject. The only other possibility for hierarchical structure was in the account of negation, where the constituents "no" and Q, and N or, alternatively, constituents of VP, were derived from different nodes in underlying phrase-markers. Otherwise, the relationship between constituents was essentially linear.

A comparison of the Eric II and Eric III grammars revealed that pivot and verb forms were no longer mutually exclusive. The phrase structure proposed for the text at Time III was essentially a pivot grammar, as was the emerging grammar described at Time II. But increased complexity was introduced into the grammar at Time III by (1) elaboration of the sentence-final constituent in contexts after the pivot constituent, and (2) the fact that pivots were no longer mutually exclusive with verb forms. Thus, the original pattern at Time II, which differentiated the prenoun class into pivot and verb classes:

$$\left\{ {P \atop V} \right\} N$$

was replaced, at Time III, with the pattern:

$$P \left\{ {N \atop V(N)} \right\}$$

which represented a differentiation of postpivot constituents.

Finally, there was evidence of reduction in only a few utterances in which the negative element had direct effect on an intervening constituent that was not produced. For example, "no more dumpcar" occurred as Eric dumped a peg from the dump-car; "no train" occurred as Eric took the man off the train. Although only marginal, it is of some interest that evidence of reduction occurred only with expression of negation, one of the few syntactic structures in Eric's grammar that was potentially hierarchical. A marginal reduction transformation might be as follows:

$$T_{\substack{\text{Reduction} \\ \text{(obligatory)}}} \quad \text{S.D.}: \left\{ {\text{no} \atop \text{no more}} \right\} X - Y$$

$$\text{S.C.}: \; x_1 - x_2 - x_3 \Rightarrow x_1 \left\{ {x_2 \atop x_3} \right\}$$

5.3.2. Utterances Not Accounted For by the Eric III Grammar

Several utterances so far discussed were not accounted for in the grammar because of their marginal status. There was no specification for either attributive or predicate adjective forms. There was no specification for the three occurrences of demonstrative pronouns—"this ə fit," "this fit," and "this is fit"—because all occurred in only one context, with "fit."

As at Time II, there was frequent occurrence of inflectional affixes that were noncontrastive, for example, " – s" in "foots" (Eric was on the window ledge and unable to climb down unaided), "ə babies," "naughtys," and "-ing" in "crying." The forms "sitting down" and "sit down" were considered variants of the form "sit."

In addition to the only three-term string that occurred, "man sit blocks," there were two other sentences that anticipated a more complex grammar with catenative verbs and were not accounted for: "ə want off" and "ə made ə fit."

There were also unique occurrences of pivotlike forms—for example, "byebye Mommys" as Mommy walked by with her coat on.

Other unique utterances, as in the previous texts of Kathryn and Gia, appeared to be unanalyzed stereotype sentences that probably represented imitations occurring at a distance from their models. Examples included the routine "where's the shoe.↑ there is" and

(96) (Eric taking the slide from Lois)   I need that.

(96) (Eric unable to fit a block on the
       train)   it won't fit.

(97) (Eric not wanting to wear shoes)   ə want any shoes.

(98) (Eric looking for the wire man)   where's ə man.↑

(99) (Eric finding the car driver)   Eric big boy.

Generally, in the early texts of all three children, the unaccounted-for sentences other than stereotype sentences were often forms that anticipated subsequent, more complex developmental stages that were not yet productive. There were also occasional, unique utterances that might be interpreted as production 'errors' because of their lack of 'fit' with the productive structures described. One such utterance was "cleaner more," as Eric looked into the cleaner for pegs he had stored there, after taking out others. The sentence "I get horsie 'chine" probably reflected the effect of distraction as Eric was on the way to his cleaner, passing the hobby horse and tape recorder.

5.3.3. Comparison of the Eric III Grammar with the Grammars Proposed for Kathryn and Gia

The phrase structure grammars proposed for the second and third texts of Eric were characterized by (1) essentially linear relationship between constituents and (2) provision for a small class of function forms that occurred frequently, with identifiable meaning, in juxtaposition with a larger class of lexical constituents. Such constructions, which have been described as pivotal because of the way in which the forms combine with one another, were the predominant pattern in the texts. Of the possibilities for expressing grammatical function in the relationships between substantive constituents, verb-object strings were most productive and developed first. Subject-verb strings did not appear until Time III and were only marginally productive.

In contrast, the grammars proposed for the texts collected from Kathryn and Gia were characterized by provision for hierarchical relationship between constituents and the expression of verb-object, subject-object, and subject-verb relationships. Although subject-verb-object strings were not produced, these constituent relationships were postulated in the underlying structure of two-term utterances to account for their inferred semantic interpretations. To account for underlying structure that was more complex than surface structure, a reduction transformation was postulated that deleted constituents as a result of increased complexity—for example, with the inclusion of sentence-subjects or negation in a sentence.

Thus, a transformational component was productive in the Gia and Kathryn grammars and accounted for the differences between structures generated in base strings and the surface form of the sentences that occurred. A transformational component was a marginal component of the Eric III grammar and operated in conjunction with the syntactic expression of negation. Otherwise, the relationships between constituents in Eric's sentences could be described in terms of surface structure. Although both subject and object nouns did not occur within the same sentence, sentence-subjects were only marginally productive, so their nonoccurrence with verb-object strings could not be attributed to the process of reduction.

There were pivot constructions in the Kathryn and Gia texts, but the three children used different forms as syntactic operators (or pivots) or used the same or similar forms in different ways. The productive demonstrative pronoun at Kathryn I was only a marginal form at Eric III and Gia II. Negation was fully productive at Kathryn I and Eric II and III, but the syntactic operation of negation was more elaborated at Eric III, with different negative markers in complementary distribution with NP and VP constituents. Negation was not a productive syntactic process at Gia II.

The form "more" was a syntactic operator that signaled recurrence in all three grammars, but its specification was different in each. Only Gia used the form in predicative constructions, so the node Q from which "more" was derived was a category constituent in the sentence rewrite rule in the Gia II grammar. In contrast, in Kathryn's lexicon, "more" shared syntactic features with attributive adjectives and was included as a member of the productive form class of adjectives in the NP rewrite rule. In Eric's grammar, "more" was the only attributive form to occur with nouns and was derived from the Q node in the NP rewrite rule. Noun phrases were more elaborate at Kathryn I with specification of attributive adjectives and at Gia II with specification of attributive noun forms.

It was possible to distinguish inherent features of nouns as [±animate] in the Gia and Kathryn texts on the basis of the syntactic occurrence of animate and inanimate nouns. Generally, people and 'animate' objects were the agents of events and occurred as sentence-subjects; inanimate objects were 'acted upon' and occurred as direct objects in sentence-final position. However, when Eric began to produce subject-verb strings at Time III, the nouns that occurred in initial position were the same forms that also occurred as object nouns —"apple," "'chine"—so the same distinction could not be made for the nouns in Eric's lexicon.

Eric did not produce any proper nouns or names of people, except in isolation, and he referred to himself by his first name only rarely. The subject pronoun "I"—in reference to Eric as agent of events—developed as a variant of preverbal /ə/ and not as a proform in relation to the subject noun "Eric." In contrast, both Gia and Kathryn used their proper names to refer to themselves as agents of events in the early texts and proforms developed subsequently. "I," "me," and "my" all occurred as sentence-subjects in the later texts of Kathryn and Gia, although "I" was the preferred form.

Prepositions were specified only in the Kathryn I feature rules. Forms with the status of prepositions in the adult model functioned as verb forms at Gia II and Eric III, with invariable syntactic occurrence before object nouns and after subject nouns. But at Kathryn I, although only marginally productive, they occurred before and after object nouns, and this variability was accounted for transformationally.

Finally, the comparison of the three children's grammars must conclude with the observation that there were important differences among them but that there were also similarities. Most important, their linguistic behavior was systematic and rule-governed. Although the children faltered, took misteps, and overreached, it was clear that all three had learned (1) that the subject-verb-object order of English sentences is necessary for the meanings of sentences; (2) that a large number of words can occur, with inherent and syntactic restrictions, as formatives with these sentence functions; and (3) that a small number of words can occur in restricted positions as syntactic operators to signal certain semantic concepts. These appear to be the basic facts of English sentences; although Kathryn, Eric, and Gia knew something about all of them, their competence was limited to a minimal, but basic knowledge of each. It also appeared that Eric knew most about (3), Kathryn and Gia knew more about (1) and (2), and Kathryn knew most about (2).

It was not the case that Eric's grammar represented a more immature linguistic system. At Eric III, Eric's grammar could be described as pivotal inasmuch as the predominant syntactic pattern was the juxtaposition of function forms with substantive forms. But at the same time, mean length of utterance was somewhat longer than mean length of utterance in the Gia and Kathryn texts, and the proportion of utterances that were longer than one word was also greater.

The investigation of the children's emerging grammars was concluded when the children had reached superficially similar levels of linguistic maturity in terms of mean length of utterance. However, although mean length of utterance for Gia and Eric was similar to Kathryn's (and less than 1.5 for all three), their linguistic competence did not merge with Kathryn's at that point. Rather, the earlier linguistic behavior of Gia and Eric (Gia I and Eric I and II) was more like their own later behavior. Thus, Gia at Time II was more like Gia at Time I, and Eric at Time III was more like Eric at Times I and II than they were either to each other or to Kathryn at Time I.

From what has been observed of the course of development of Gia and Eric and subsequently surmised about Kathryn's previous development, one reason for the differences among the children is that they appeared to use different strategies in approaching the model language. Perceptual-cognitive function interacted in some way with linguistic and nonlinguistic experience to determine what these strategies were, and it would have been unlikely that these three factors, or their mutual effects, would be the same for any three children. A discussion of what these strategies might have been is presented in Chapter 8.

An important feature of the grammars proposed earlier for Kathryn and Gia was the operation of reduction—the specification of a transformation that accounted for the differences between the surface structure of obtained sentences and what was postulated to be a richer underlying structure. In Chapter 6, the reduction transformation is discussed in relation to constraints on the length and complexity of the children's earliest sentences.

6 The Reduction Transformation and Constraints on Sentence Length

The formal notation in the grammars proposed for the texts of Kathryn and Gia specified that categories from which subject and predicate constituents were derived were obligatory rather than optional in the underlying phrase structure. It was pointed out that specifying categories as optional—meaning that one or more could occur in final derived strings—would ascribe the ability to exercise all options in a string to the child's linguistic competence when, in fact, such sentences (subject-verb-object) did not occur. In order to account for the differences between the underlying structure of sentences—which accounted for their semantic interpretation—and the reduced surface structure of these sentences as they were actually produced, a reduction transformation was postulated that mapped the richer base form into the reduced surface form.

But there needs to be justification in the data for the existence of categories in the phrase structure in order to be able to specify their deletion in terminal strings. For example, there was no category in the grammar of Eric II with the grammatical function *subject of the sentence*—Eric did not produce nouns in sentence-subject relation to verbs—so the nonoccurrence of sentence-subjects in Eric's earliest sentences could not be attributed to reduction. Whether or not Eric understood the grammatical function of sentence-subjects in the speech he heard, there was no evidence that he could produce sentences with grammatical subjects. Similarly, at Time I, Gia did not produce noun forms in subject or object relation to verbs, so the nonoccurrence of verbs in Noun + Noun constructions could not be attributed to reduction.

The problem of justifying the representation of category components in the phrase structure grammars, so that their nonoccurrence in terminal strings could be accounted for by the syntactic process of deletion, is considered in the following discussion of the evidence in the data that provided support for the specification of reduction rules to account for the reduced form of children's sentences.

6.1. The Nature of Sentence Accretion

Looking at the grammars presented in Chapters 3, 4, and 5 and at the linguistic data for which they were constructed, it appears that, in a general sense, growth in sentence constructing proceeded with a linear concatenation of constituents from right to left. Object-nouns predominated in the children's lexicons and were combined in syntactic constructions with verb forms, modifying forms, subject-noun forms, or pivot forms. At the same time, as a general rule, such object-nouns did not also function as sentence-subjects. Subsequently, subjects or demonstrative pronouns occurred before elaborated predicates.

Going beyond the data presented here and looking at the subsequent texts collected for the three children, it was apparent that the noun phrase construction that appeared in predicate positions was far more complex at every stage than noun phrases that appeared in subject positions. For example, when the children were 3 years old, they could produce such sentences as:

(1) I want the little green man who rides the truck, or
(2) That's the little green man who rides the truck,

but such a sentence as:

(3) The little green man who rides the truck goes on top,

did not occur.

Brown, Cazden, and Bellugi (1969) reported that in writing complete grammars for the children they studied there were differential rules for accounting for noun phrase constructions at the earliest stage studied by them—that the object noun phrase and the predicate nominal noun phrase were more complex than the subject noun phrase. However, contrary to the findings reported here and referred to in the 'little green man' example, they observed that "one of the things that happened between I and III [roman numerals refer to the levels at which grammars were constructed for their three subjects] was that the four 'NP' [predicate nominal, direct object, subject of a predicate nominal, and subject of a verb] came to resemble one another closely enough so that a single 'NP' symbol ... rewritten by a single set of rules, could be entered in all four positions."

There is additional support for the notion of the linear increase in sentence length from right to left in the findings reported by other investigators of children's language. In the "sentence-generating" and "nominal phrase-generating" rules presented by Ervin (1966), a number of optional word-classes have privileges of occurrence, in a specified order, before a required class and the required class occurs in sentence-final position. The rule that Brown and Bellugi (1964, p. 148) proposed for the early development of the noun phrase represented a series of ordered but optional elements preceding an obligatory form in sentence-final position:

"NP → (Dem) + (Art) + (M) + N,"

where Dem is "demonstrative," Art is "article," M is "modifier," and N is "noun."

There is evidence of similarity in the direction of sentence accretion in the acquisition of one aspect of Japanese syntax—where the word order of object and verb is the reverse of English order. In a study of the early development of linguistic forms of requests that combined both longitudinal and cross-sectional data, Murata (1961) reported that "verb-forms denoting requests" were "differentiated from the inter-jectional words" in the second half of the second year. Toward the end of this period "syntactical integrations [of words in an utterance] increased rapidly. Their typical forms were word-chain utterances of requests which were constituted of 'Object + Verb' (Japanese word-order of sentences, which constitutes one of the most striking differences from that of Europeans)."[1] Thus, it appears that the Japanese children produced verbs and then object-verb strings as request forms— extending the original single-word utterance from right to left.

In explanation of the fact that their subjects tended to imitate the most recent words in a model sentence, Brown and Fraser (1963, p. 193) suggested that "perhaps the human mind operates on an un-learned 'recency' principle, and ... sentences ... are nicely adapted to this principle in that the least predictable, most informative words usually fall into the final position."

[1] Quotations were taken from an abstract, in English, supplied by the author.

However, the generalization about the direction of sentence accretion is true in only a limited sense. The addition of elements to utterances in forming longer or more complex utterances was not cumulative and, as will be shown, not strictly linear. That is, the children's ability to construct sentences did not proceed sequentially as the following hypothetical paradigm might suggest:

(4) bridge.
    big bridge.
    a big bridge.
    build a big bridge.
    will build a big bridge.
    Eric will build a big bridge.

The following examples of consecutive utterances, produced within the boundaries of single speech events, illustrated that increase in structure or complexity was not a matter of simply increasing length of utterance by adding structure to structure or adding elements within a structure:

(5) G:II (Gia taking train cars
        from the bag of toys)

$$\begin{bmatrix} \text{more block.} \\ \text{more.} \\ \text{Gia block.} \end{bmatrix}$$

(6) K:II (Kathryn looking at
        a picture of a mother
        cooking)

$$\begin{bmatrix} \text{cereal. hmmmmm.} \\ \text{raisin there.} \\ \text{buy more grocery store.} \\ \text{raisins.} \\ \text{buy more grocery store.} \\ \text{grocery store.} \\ \text{raisin ə grocery store.} \end{bmatrix}$$

As the children learned certain basic phrase structures that increased the complexity of sentences, there were constraints on the extent to which these structures could be realized in the actual production of a single sentence. This kind of limitation in the surface structure of sentences due to increased complexity or length was most obvious when the child produced such consecutive utterances as "more block. more. Gia block." But it was also apparent that there were missing elements in the single, nonsequential sentences produced by all three children, with occurrence of adjacent constituents that could be accounted for only by postulating unrealized intervening constituents.

6.2. 'Telegraphic' Speech

Even the most casual observer is aware that children's sentences are incomplete and fragmented, that elements are omitted that can generally be predicted. These early, incomplete sentences were characterized as "telegraphic" by Brown and Fraser (1963). In their description of the child's imitation of sentences he has just heard, they reported that the child omits some words or morphemes from the longer model sentences. The result is an abbreviated utterance that can be compared to the kinds of sentences produced by an adult who is under pressure to be brief—for example, when sending a telegram or taking lecture notes.

This phenomenon of "imitation and reduction" was discussed by Brown and Bellugi (1964) in describing the processes involved in children's acquisition of syntax. They observed that in the interaction between mother and child the child listens to sentences spoken by his mother; his attempts to reproduce what she has said consist of "highly systematic reductions" of the models. Also, the sentences produced by the child spontaneously, without an immediately previous adult model, have the same 'telegraphic' properties.

In describing which forms are retained and which forms are omitted in 'telegraphic' sentences, Brown and Bellugi and Brown and Fraser noted that the sentences consisted generally of nouns, verbs, and, less often, adjectives—the substantive, lexical items or "contentives" of the language. Grammatical formatives or 'functors'—for example, the articles "the," "an"; verb inflection, "-ing," "-ed," "-s"; possessive noun inflection, "-s"—were the forms generally omitted.

In comparing sentences produced in imitation with sentences produced in spontaneous speech, Ervin (1966) found that both kinds of sentences "were equally predictable" from the same rules for four of the five children studied; that is, that imitated and spontaneous sentences were similar in complexity and characterized by omission of predictable forms. The forms omitted tended to be the unstressed segments—for example, articles, prepositions, auxiliaries, and pronouns, the same kinds of words omitted in the 'telegraphic' sentences described by Brown and his associates.

In these studies, the nature of the language that the child was learning was considered to be the dominant influence on the form of his sentences. In addition to the description of sentences in terms of form class membership of constituents, Ervin reported three further characteristics of imitated sentences. The words retained and repeated by the child occurred in the same order and consisted of the words that were most recent and most heavily stressed in the model sentences.

Brown and Fraser (1963) also observed the preservation of original word order and the influence of sentence position and relative stress on the determination of the forms retained in the children's imitation of sentences, and by extension, included in spontaneous sentences as well. They also pointed out that these words (the content words of the language) carry the greatest information value—as the "reference-making" forms in the language. Brown and Bellugi (1964) suggested that the words produced by the child in imitated and spontaneous utterances tend to be those words with which he is most familiar—having 'practiced' them as single-word utterances before the development of syntax.

Thus, it appears that the characterization of children's imitated and spontaneous sentences as 'telegraphic' depends on the distinction between (1) the substantive, lexical items that receive heaviest stress in production, have semantic correlates and so carry the most information, and are least predictable, and (2) grammatical formatives that are weakly stressed, carry little information value, are most predictable, and tend to occur in sentence-interior positions.

There is an interesting paradox in the literature that describes children's language, on the one hand, as *telegraphic*—consisting only of substantive words with omission of function words—and, on the other hand, in terms of *pivot grammars*—syntactic constructions that consist of a class of function words in juxtaposition with the more diverse and open class of substantive words. Both characterizations have been used by Brown and his associates and by Miller and Ervin. It appears that the distinction between content and function words that underlies the pivot–x-word designation of children's earliest grammars contradicts the general characterization of children's sentences as 'telegraphic.'

There has been no published discussion of the relationship between pivot grammars and 'telegraphic' speech, and the two phenomena appear to coexist in the data reported by Brown and by Miller and Ervin. However, Braine (1963) reported that x-word + x-word constructions (a string of substantive, content words) appeared subsequent to pivot constructions in his data.

6.3. Evidence for the Operation of Reduction

The phrase structure grammars presented earlier accounted for the underlying structure of the obtained sentences; this structure was rarely realized completely in the surface structure of the sentences that occurred. In order to obtain the reduced surface form from the base form, a transformation was postulated that deleted those elements in the base that did not occur in production:

K:I $T_{\text{Reduction}}$
(obligatory)

(a) S.D.: $X - Ng - Y$,

where X and Y are category symbols (which dominate lexical items)

S.C.: $x_1 - x_2 - x_3 \Rightarrow x_2 - x_3$

(b) S.D.: $\# - X - Y - Z$,

where X, Y, Z are category symbols

S.C.: $\# - x_1 - x_2 - x_3 \Rightarrow \# - x_i - x_j$,

where $0 \leqslant i < j \leqslant 3$

It is important to emphasize that the reduction transformation did not account for the 'telegraphic' nature of children's sentences as this notion has been described in the literature just reviewed. Rather than operating to delete the grammatical formatives or function words that did not occur in such sentences—*for which there were not representations in the base* as yet—the reduction rules operated to account for the non-occurrence of the *substantive* forms for which evidence existed to specify their representation in underlying strings. It was not possible to speak of deletion of function words as a syntactic process in accounting for their nonoccurrence in 'telegraphic' sentences, because, in the early stages when the reduction transformation operated obligatorily, there was limited evidence for the existence of grammatical formatives in the children's grammars.

The kind of reduction accounted for by the reduction rules occurred in the 'buying more raisins at the grocery store' example. Kathryn was apparently constrained to delete the verb "buy" with expression of the object noun in the last sentence in the sequence, "raisin ə grocery store"—for which the presence of the verb was obligatory in the underlying representation to account for the semantic interpretation (the grammatical relationship between "raisin" and "grocery store") of the sentence. The occurrence of such sequential utterances with simultaneous expansion and deletion provided strong evidence for the operation of reduction and the child's inability to handle increased complexity or extended length.

It was more difficult to justify the operation of reduction in the occurrence of an isolated sentence. Evidence for inclusion of elements in the underlying representations of sentences was obtained from two courses: (1) the semantic interpretation of the utterance as described in Chapter 1, and (2) the observed distribution of structures in the entire text. To illustrate the operation of reduction in the distribution of structures, all utterances that included the form "make" have been extracted from the corpus of utterances obtained from Kathryn at Time II and presented in Table 6.1.

Choosing the verb "make" to illustrate the operation of reduction actually distorts the example in favor of nonreduction or the relative completeness of sentences, because the verb was not only very frequent in occurrence but was well learned in contexts with direct object nouns. That is, the verb "make" did not occur as a single-word utterance at Time I or Time II and appeared to have been learned as a form with the syntactic feature [+__Noun], although this claim must be qualified somewhat by noting that no data were collected previous to Time I, when "make" may have occurred as a single-word utterance. Also, "make" was one of the most frequent verbs to occur at Time I, so its existence in Kathryn's lexicon was well established at Time II. The utterances with "make" should have been less vulnerable to deletion, and Kathryn should have had less difficulty using this word in syntactic constructions than other verbs that occurred infrequently—for example, "buy," "bring," "eat."

The mean length of utterance of the total number of 48 utterances was 3.77 morphemes. In comparison, the mean length of utterance of the entire text at Time II was 1.92 morphemes. It is evident that these sentences were among the longest sentences produced by Kathryn at Time II—another factor that distorts the example in favor of non-reduction.

The utterances in which "make" did not appear:

(14) Kathryn under bridge.
(28) Kathryn bear tie.
(54) no plop.

were included in Table 6.1 because of their occurrence in the same

Table 6.1. Sentences with "make" Produced by Kathryn at Time II

Description of Speech Event	Kathryn's Utterance
(7) (K taking out train cars)	⎡ > making building house. ⎤
(8)	⎣ > make ə choochoo train. ⎦
(9) (K picking up blocks) Shall we build a house? What shall we do?	> make ə house.↑
(10) (K pushed tower of blocks after she had stacked them) (stacked blocks again)	> make ə house again.
(11) (L going to train cars on floor) I'm going to make a train (K joining her)	⎡ > make ə tree. ⎤
(12)	⎢ > make ə flower. ⎢
(13)	⎣ > make ə tree. ⎦
(14) (L pushing train under bridge; K going to train and bridge; subsequently pushed it under)	> Kathryn under bridge.
(15) (Bridge collapsed; K asking for another one)	> Lois ə make ə bridge.
(16) (K trying to seat second wire man, after seating first one)	> made ə sit down again.
	⎡ man sit down. ⎤
(17) (K trying to seat man again)	⎣ > made this sit down. ⎦
(18) (K spilled her blocks on the floor) What shall we do with the blocks?	⎡ > Kathryn ə making house. ⎤
(19)	⎣ > making train. ⎦
(20) (K took the train apart) Let's make the train again. Let's make the train go under the bridge. (L hadn't made bridge)	⎡ train under bridge. ⎤ ⎣ > make ə bridge.↑ ⎦
(21) (L pushed the train under the bridge; L picked up the truck) Let's make the truck__ (K interrupting) No make a truck? (K pushing train under)	> no make ə truck. ə bridge. under bridge.

Table 6.1, *continued*

Description of Speech Event	Kathryn's Utterance
(22) Who's going to go under the bridge? I know who's going under the bridge. (K holding a lamb) What is this? Let's make him go under the bridge. (K taking lamb to bridge)	this under bridge. lamb. > Kathryn ə make ə under bridge.
(23) (K pushed first lamb under bridge; picking up another lamb)	⌈ go lamb. ⌉ ⌊ > make ə more under bridge. ⌋
(24) (Bridge collapsed as K was about to push lamb through) (25)	⌈ > make ə more under more. ⌉ ⌊ > make another bridge. ⌋
(26) (Bridge collapsed) What happened to it? (K didn't make bridge)	> Kathryn ə make another bridge.
(27) (K picked up bear with a loose ribbon on its neck) (28) (K fumbling with the ribbon)	⌈ > Kathryn make ə ties. ⌉ > Kathryn bear tie. Kathryn /fɪk/ ə tie. ⌊ Kathryn /fɪk/ ə ties. ⌋
(29) (K 'tied' the ribbon; whispered) (K left bear) Did you fix the bear's tie?	there > make ə bear tie.
(30) (K replacing small block that had fallen out of hole in big block, after she had put it in before)	> Kathryn ə make again.
(31) (L making a bridge with book)	> Lois make ə bridge.
(32) (K snapping plastic beads together)	> Kathryn make this.
(33) (K taking out box of wooden snap blocks) (34) (K trying to snap blocks together) (35) (36)	⌈ > make ə cars. ⌉ ⌈ > make ə foot. ⌉ > this ə make ə foot. ⌊ > make arms. ⌋
(37) (M preparing dinner; opening a box of frozen food)	> make ə vegetable.

Table 6.1, *continued*

Description of Speech Event	Kathryn's Utterance
(38) (In response to (37)) Make the vegetables? Make pineapple?	⎡ no. ⎣ > make pineapple. ⎤ yes.
(39) Go get the man with the truck. (K going after man and truck)	> go make ə man truck.
(40) (K picking up a bag of blocks)	> ə want make ə blocks.
(41) (In response to (40)) We can build a bridge with the blocks. (42) (43)	⎡ > make ə block. ⎤ > make ə house. blocks. ⎣ > make ə house. ⎦
(44) (K stacking blocks)	> make another bridge.
(45) (K pushing car under bridge)	> make ə car under bridge.
(46) (K knocked bridge over)	> make another one.
(47) (In response to (46)) Make another one? Will you help me? Will you help me? (L making a bridge)	> making one.
(48) (K picked up a wheel while L was making a bridge with the blocks) That's the green one.	> make another. go slides.
(49) (K starting out of room) Where are you going? (K picking up her car)	car. /æn/ go gets it. > make it sit.
(50) (L stacking blocks; K sits on floor to stack blocks also)	> make another one.
(51) (K stacking blocks) (52)	⎡ > Kathryn make ə house. ⎤ that's mine. ⎣ > Kathryn make ə seat. ⎦
(53) (K going into the bathroom; "plop" was K's word for "defecate"; subse- (54) quently urinated)	⎡ > ə make plop. ⎤ ⎣ > no plop. ⎦

behavioral contexts as existed with the occurrence of utterances

(22) Kathryn ə make ə under bridge.
(27) Kathryn make ə ties.
(53) ə make plop.

Looking at the entire group of sentences, it could be seen that when the subject of the sentence was expressed, either the verb, the object, the adverbial phrase, or more than one of these was not expressed. If all the possible constituent positions were filled, the ultimate result might be the production of such a sentence as

(55) Kathryn ə want ə make ə more choochoo train

$$\text{under bridge} \begin{Bmatrix} \text{again} \\ \text{more} \end{Bmatrix}$$

with at least nine morphemes. No sentence like this in extent of completion was produced in the Kathryn II text. Characteristically, elaboration of what preceded or followed the verbal position was accompanied by a deletion of some or all other constituents. There was deletion of categories as well as deletion within major categories when other categories occurred or were expanded.

It was possible for Kathryn to increase the complexity of sentences without necessarily increasing sentence length, and sentence accretion occurred with hierarchical and not strictly linear effect. That is, the structure of sentences could be represented on more than one hierarchical level with constituents derived from more than one phrase-marker node, as in the following tree-diagram:

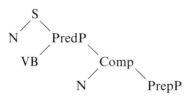

for the possible derivation of such sentences as

(14) Kathryn under bridge.
(22) Kathryn ə make ə under bridge.
(23) make ə more under bridge.
(45) make ə car under bridge.

Although the nodes of the tree-diagram were not 'filled' in the utterances that Kathryn produced, the existence of the nodes in underlying representations of the sentences would be needed to account for their semantic interpretation, for example, of "Kathryn under bridge"—that is, to account for the relationship between "Kathryn" and "bridge." Kathryn was not under the bridge. Specifying the grammatical relationship between the constituents in "Kathryn under bridge" would imply the existence of nodes V (directly dominated by the node PredP, predicate phrase) and N (dominated by the node Comp, complement, which in turn is dominated by PredP).

Thus, the notion of *reduction* is presented here as a grammatical process that attempts to explain the surface structure of children's sentences—rather than a notion that describes how children's sentences differ from the adult model.

In his examination of the data collected by Brown and his associates, McNeill (1966) observed that there were limitations on the inclusion of structure within the boundary of a single sentence. However, he concluded that "the child's first grammatical productions are the NP's and PredP's of adult grammar. Most often he produces them independently, though occasionally they are brought together to result in the skeleton of a well-formed sentence." McNeill suggested an alternative set of rules for children's early constructions that would replace, but also include, the 'pivot + x-word' and 'x-word + x-word' rules. The two rules with which McNeill "assume[d] that the child generated all his sentences" at Time I in the Brown data are reproduced here in the form of their phrase-markers, as presented by McNeill (p. 44), where P is "Pivot":

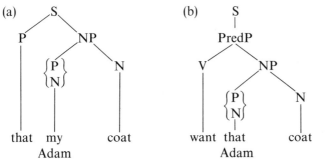

McNeill concluded that "all the child lacks [at this time] is the simultaneous application of both rules in the generation of a single sentence." According to McNeill, these rules represent the NP and PredP of adult grammar, and McNeill concluded that the frequency of their combination in a single sentence increases as the child matures, probably as a result of "the child's growing memory span." This account implies that the increase in sentence complexity was simply an additive process; two syntactic structures that occurred first as two different 'sentence types' were ultimately combined within the same sentence.

Before continuing the discussion of the operation of reduction, a word should be said about the NP generated by McNeill's Rule (a) (actually Rule (7) in the McNeill text). In the grammars proposed for Kathryn and Gia, the NP construction occurred as a predicate nominal or direct object. The forms that occurred in subject position in constructions with predicate phrases were less complex, and, rather than being a noun phrase, these forms consisted of single nouns—most often the names of people or animals—or pronouns. Brown, Cazden, and Bellugi (1969) reported, similarly, that "subject NP at [Time] I never consisted of more than one morpheme—a simple pronoun or noun," and subjects of verbs "were almost always names of persons or animals."

It would appear that there was not an equivalence of subject and predicate NP's (as concluded also by Brown, Cazden, and Bellugi) at this stage, and the NP of McNeill Rule (a) may be the same NP as in McNeill Rule (b), and not the subject NP, as he suggested. Rules (a) and (b) may indeed represent two different sentence types, that is, predicate nominative and verb plus complement.

It is felt that McNeill's account of the acquisition of syntax, as a process of increasing structural complexity by adding structure to structure, cannot explain the variable relationships between constituents in the distribution of such sentences as those with "make" in the text of Kathryn II. The analysis of the grammatical functions of the constituents in these sentences was not simply disjunctive—they did not just represent either the subject noun phrase or the predicate phrase of adult sentences.

An account of the development of grammar as an additive process becomes less tenable with consideration of the effect of the syntactic operation of negation on the internal structure of sentences.

6.3.1. Reduction and Negation

The example of reduction with negation will be discussed at length for two reasons: (1) the semantic correlates of negation were relatively clear in the texts, so that the nonrealization of constituents in the surface structure of sentences could be demonstrated; and (2) negation was a syntactic operation that entered the grammars at a time when the development of the system was under way, so that its effects on the system could be examined.

All the syntactic constructions with a negative particle ("no") from the Kathryn I text are presented in table 6.2.[2] Looking at these negative

Table 6.2. All Negative Sentences Produced by Kathryn at Time I

Description of Speech Event	Kathryn's Utterance
(56) (K unable to find a pocket in M's skirt)	⌐ > no pocket. ⌐
(57)	∟ > no pocket in there. ⌡
(58) (K waiting for M to make 'pretend' socks for her feet)	no sock.
(59) (K unable to nest blocks or fit lambs into blocks; 7 instances of utterance in similar situations)	> no fit.
(60) (K standing in unzipped boots)	> no zip.
(61) (K unable to turn plastic screw in washer)	> no turn.
(62) (K unable to close box)	> no close.
(63) (K picked up clean sock)	⌐ this sock ⌐ ∟ dirty. ⌡
Oh that's not a dirty one. That just has a big hole in it.	hole.
It has a big hole in it.	> no dirty.
(64) (K pushing away a piece of worn soap in the bathtub, wanting to be washed with new pink soap)	> no dirty soap.
(66) (K pulling away from L, who had offered to comb her hair)	> no Mommy.
(67) (K protested taking a bath, wanted to go outside)	> no outside.

[2] For the purpose of this discussion, the negative sentences at Kathryn I in Table 6.2 will be used as primary examples, although the discussion and conclusions that have been drawn apply as well to the negative sentences in the data presented and discussed in Chapter 7 (Kathryn II and III, Eric I to VI, and Gia I to VI).

Table 6.2, *continued*

Description of Speech Event	Kathryn's Utterance
(68) (K put lamb into block upside down; head was not in round window like the other lambs) He can't see out of the window. Can he see out of the window?	> no window.
(69) (K pushed lambs off the chair) Now why did you do that? They wanta sit on the chair. (K trying to climb on the chair) (M putting lambs on chair) (K pushing lambs off chair) They wanta sit on the chair. (K pushing lambs off)	ə wanta sit down chair. no! no. no. > ə no chair.
(70) (Indeterminate utterance; M washing K's face after lunch) Clean your nose.	milk > no milk.

utterances and the contexts in which each occurred, there appear to be two broad classes of sentences (excluding (70) "no milk," which could not be interpreted). These can be distinguished according to the relation of the surface constituents of the utterance to the negative predication: (1) sentences in which the negative particle preceded an element that was clearly being negated:

(56) no pocket.
(57) no pocket in there.
(58) no sock.
(59) no fit.
(60) no zip.
(61) no turn.
(62) no close.
(63) no dirty.
(64) no dirty soap.
(65) no sock.

and (2) sentences in which the "no" occurred and the remainder of the sentence was clearly not being negated directly:

(66) no Mommy.
(67) no outside.
(68) no window.
(69) ə no chair.

With "no pocket," there was no pocket; with "no sock," there was no sock; with "no zip," the boots were not zipped; with "no dirty soap," Kathryn did not want the dirty soap. However, with "no outside," Kathryn wanted to go outside; with "no window," there was a window; and with "ə no chair," Kathryn wanted to sit on the chair.

There were two alternative explanations for the occurrence of "no" in utterances where the segment after "no" was clearly not negated. In (66) "no Mommy" and (67) "no outside," the "no" was anaphoric and applied to a prior utterance (Lois, not Mommy, offering to comb Kathryn's hair, and Mommy telling Kathryn it was bath time, respectively). Anaphoric "no" in these sentences occurred in juxtaposition with an affirmative utterance that expressed a positive alternative to something said by someone else. Although there were only two such examples at Kathryn I, this type of utterance increased in frequency in subsequent samples. For example, the following are two of the eight occurrences of the sentence type *no plus affirmative sentence* at Kathryn II:

(71) K:II (Kathryn, looking for a
book about dragons, picked
up a book about bears)
$$\left[\begin{array}{l} \text{this.} \\ > \text{no that's ə bear book.} \end{array} \right]$$

(and dropped it)

(72) K:II (Kathryn, unable to
connect the train, giving the
cars to Lois)   no Lois do it.

Prosodic features of juncture or stress did not assist in interpreting these sentences. There was not a pause after "no," and "no" did not receive differential stress. Acoustically, these sentences did not differ from negative sentences—for example:

(73) K:II (Kathryn looking at Lois'
bare head)   Lois no hat.

where "no" occurred after the sentence subject and before a negated constituent. Superficially, such sentences as "no that's ə bear book" and "no Lois do it" were ambiguous, and, as discussed presently, only the nonlinguistic cues of context and behavior were available for interpreting the sentences in order to resolve the ambiguity.

The second explanation of "no" in juxtaposition with a segment not being negated applied to (68) "no window," (69) "ə no chair," and the example that follows, in which the surface structure is, at first glance, paradoxical:

(74) E:II (Eric pointing to the tape
recorder as Mommy entered the
room, after being told he could
not play with it)   no 'chine.

Looking at these utterances—(68) "no window," (69) "ə no chair," and (74) "no 'chine"—without knowing the accompanying behavior and context in which they occurred, the adult could be misled by his own grammar into interpreting them to mean that there was no window, no chair, and no machine. But the children had demonstrated the ability to use the negative operator to indicate nonexistence—for example, "no pocket" when there was no pocket and "no more noise" (at Eric II) when the noise had stopped. It appeared that the same superficial form was used to express a more complex negative-syntactic relation.

For each of these sentences—"no window," "ə no chair," and "no 'chine"—a semantic interpretation would depend on an underlying structure that specified a semantic relation between the negative element and a constituent intervening between "no" and the sentence complement. It appeared that in these sentences the negative element had immediate effect on an aspect of the sentence that did not get produced in its surface structure. A similar analysis could be made with (64) "no dirty soap" and (65) "no sock," where the semantic correlates of negation were different; for example, the dirty soap was being negated, but indirectly in that Kathryn was negating 'using' or 'wanting' the dirty soap.

Such utterances as (68) "no window," (69) "ə no chair," and (74) "no 'chine" appeared to represent the reduced form of an implicit, more complex underlying structure. This postulation of *reduction* in linguistic expression of negation was supported by the following observations. First, the children had learned something about the semantics and syntax of negation; that is, they used the negative particle as a syntactic operator, with semantic effect on immediate constituents, as Kathryn did in (56) "no pocket," (58) "no sock," and (60) "no zip." If the child knows that "no" plus a substantive element signals negation of that element, as in "no pocket," then it is reasonable to assume that the child's use of that same superficial syntactic structure with different intent, as in "no window," 'means' something else. "No pocket" signaled direct negation of "pocket," but "no window" did not signal negation of "window" in quite the same way. Second, the semantic interpretation of these negative sentences, given the speech events of which they were a part, depended on the postulation of unrealized constituents in more complex syntactic structures than were actually produced. Otherwise, the utterances could not be interpreted as 'negative' in the same sense that other utterances with "no" were interpretable at the same time. In each instance, there was negation of a predicative structure but there was expression of only the object complement. "Window," "chair," and " 'chine" functioned grammatically as predicate objects in relation to unrealized constituents that were obligatory in the inherent structure of the sentences.

But it appeared necessary for the children to have produced a syntactic construction (conjoining two or more constituents with an inherent relationship between them) in order to postulate the operation of reduction. In the texts of the three children there was frequent occurrence of "no" as a single-word utterance and there were also instances in which the child produced a single word with apparent negative intent, although a negative element was not expressed—for example:

(75) K:I (Kathryn taking off the lavaliere
microphone, not wanting to wear it)   necklace.

An argument for the operation of reduction in these two instances— that is, the occurrence of "no" alone or single-word utterances such as "necklace"—would be necessarily weak. The response "no" is an acceptable elliptical response to yes-no questions or imperatives, and grammatical ellipsis is necessarily distinguished from *reduction*. In the other instance, "necklace," the nonlinguistic evidence of negative semantic intent was strong, but so was the possibility for ambiguity. Kathryn could have intended the fuller sentence "off necklace" (an utterance that actually occurred in a different but identical speech event at Kathryn I) as easily as the negative sentence "no necklace," and the context and behavior could support both interpretations.

There were instances of sentence reduction with deletion of the negative element—for example:

(76) K:II (Lois had said "coffee
store?"; Kathryn was reminded
of having the "coffee 'chine"
fixed and then said, shaking her
head negatively)   ⎡ > me like coffee.   ⎤
(no longer shaking her head)   Daddy like coffee.
(shaking her head)   ⎣ Lois ə no coffee.   ⎦

(77) E:III (Eric unable to find a
    particular block and giving up)   ə find it.

However, the possible deletion of the negative element was less interesting—and somewhat more difficult to evaluate—than the reduction that occurred in the remainder of a sentence when the negative element was expressed. Sequential utterances in a single speech event—where the child subsequently expanded or changed an utterance and reduced it at the same time—provided clear-cut evidence of the effect of the syntactic operation of negation on sentence complexity, as in "Lois ə no coffee" in (76). In the utterances "no window," "ə no chair," "no 'chine," the semantic correlates of negation provided evidence of the nonrealization of constituents, that is, reduction in surface structures of negative sentences (as manifest in the relation of the negative element to the rest of the sentence). However, a more important question with respect to the effect of negation on syntactic complexity was how all the negative sentences compared in syntactic structure with the affirmative sentences that also occurred in the same texts. Was there any evidence that negative utterances were syntactically different?

The structural form of the first negative sentences was a negative particle before nominal or predicate forms. There were certain missing elements in these negative utterances that were irrelevant; for example, the fact that there were no verb and noun inflections was immaterial because verb and noun inflections were not realized in the early grammars at all. However, there were other structural omissions in the negative utterances that were significant in that they did characterize the negative sentences in a way that set them apart from the other, affirmative sentences that occurred.

First, there was no expression of sentence-subject in any of the sentences, except "no Mommy" (in which, it turned out, "Mommy" was not the subject of a negative predication). However, at the same time, the nominal subject was expressed in more than 60 of the total of 397 utterances analyzed in the text of Kathryn I, excluding the occurrence of preverbal /ə/. Second, there were no occurrences of both a predicate complement and a verb in a single sentence with "no," although Kathryn expressed such 'complete' verb phrases in more than 40 of the 397 utterances and verb-object phrases were among the most productive constructions in the texts of all three children. These omissions of subject, verb, or object complement were not attributable to lack of vocabulary; Kathryn 'had' the words in her lexicon—for example, "want," "see," "boot," "box," "lamb," "Mommy," "Kathryn."

Looking at the rest of the surface structure of these sentences, it was apparent that without the "no" they were comparable to the most primitive utterances that Kathryn produced. However, the more complex underlying structures for these sentences, which would account for their semantic interpretation—for example, "no window": roughly, "X no Y window" (where X and Y represent inferred underlying category symbols with the grammatical functions of sentence-subject and predicate)—could be accounted for by the same grammar that would generate the affirmative sentences that also occurred.

A number of affirmative sentences in the data could be considered semantically reciprocal to, or the affirmative correlates of certain of the negative sentences that also occurred, for example, at Kathryn I: "no turn" and "this turn"; "no dirty" and "this dirty." But it was significant that the negation of "this turn" and "this dirty" did not result in *"this no turn" or *"this no dirty," nor *"no this turn" or *"no this dirty."

At Kathryn II there were two examples of an immediate denial of an affirmative statement in which the affirmative sentence was reduced with the operation of negation:

(78) K:II (Kathryn sticking out her
　　　tongue)
　　　Whose tongue do I see?
　　　Who?

$$\left[\begin{array}{l} \text{that ə Wendy.} \\ \text{no Wendy.} \\ \text{Kathryn. no Wendy.} \end{array} \right]$$

(79) K:II (Kathryn going into the
　　　bathroom)

$$\left[\begin{array}{l} \text{ə make plop.} \\ \text{no plop.} \end{array} \right]$$

　　　("plop" was Kathryn's word
　　　for "defecate"; Kathryn
　　　subsequently urinated)

The following example from the text at Gia V illustrated the comparative simplicity of a negative utterance in an extended sequence with more complex utterances, several of which appeared to be plausible positive correlates of the negative. At this time Gia produced sentence subjects (usually pronoun forms) frequently, but none appeared in the negative sentences that also occurred at Gia V.

(80) G:V
Do you wanta read "Mop
Top"? (Gia's newest book)   yes
(Lois picking up the book;
Gia reaching for it)   > no Mop Top.
Hm?
(Gia reaching for it)   ⎡ Móp Tòp. ⎤
What?   ⎣ /mǽdàp/ ⎦
(Lois going to the sofa with it;
Gia following, holding out
her arms for the book)   ⎡ read ə m⎯/æ · æʷ/.   ⎤
                                 ⎢ I wanta read new /mádə/. ⎥
(whining)   ⎣ I wanta read ə my book. ⎦
                                 . . . . .
(Lois gave Gia the book;
after 'reading' it, Gia
giving it to Lois)   you read wə⎯Móp Tòp.

One possible explanation for the differences between the surface structures of affirmative and negative sentences might be that they are learned separately; that is, as different sentence patterns, they are accounted for by 'different grammars' or different sets of rules. Such an explanation could not be argued very productively; learning separate 'grammars' for different sentence types would be inefficient and would increase the child's cognitive tasks. One of the most attractive aspects of the theory of transformational grammar in application to children's language is the specification of the 'relatedness' of sentences so that one set of rules is learned that underlies all the sentences of the language. It is more likely that children learn the semantic component of negation as an option in generating sentences so that two kinds of semantic realities—affirmative and negative—can be distinguished. However, exercising the option to include the element of negation in a sentence operates to increase the syntactic complexity of the sentence. It appeared that in negating a sentence it was necessary to reduce it at the same time—that the syntactic operation occasioned the reduction.

There was further support for the notion that the operation of negation *within* a sentence increased its complexity, and thereby necessitated reduction in the surface structure, in the fact that structure of the affirmative sentences with anaphoric "no" (the sentence type "*no*" plus *affirmative sentence*) was more structurally 'complete' in all the texts, when compared with the negative sentences that occurred at the same time. Thus, the inclusion of "no" (without juncture) did not affect sentence length when "no" was anaphoric and without effect on the internal syntax of the sentence.

The account of the operation of negation just presented differs from Bellugi's description of the first of five stages in the development of the syntax of negation (Bellugi, 1967; Klima and Bellugi, 1966). In the first stage described by Bellugi, Period A, the mean lengths of utterance of the three subjects she studied were 1.96, 1.80, and 1.74. Comparing these figures with the information in Table 2.1, it can be seen that text collection began with Kathryn, Eric, and Gia somewhat earlier in terms of mean length of utterance, which was less than 1.5 for all three children.[3]

Period A was described by Bellugi as "negation outside the sentence nucleus," where a negative element is attached to a "rudimentary sentence." The grammar of the "rudimentary sentence" or its relation to the children's nonnegative sentences were not specified. Negative sentences were described as having "little internal structure, consisting only of noun phrases or unmarked nouns and verbs."

The negative sentences that Bellugi reported—for example, "no heavy," "no the sun shining," "no sit there," "no more string," "no Mommy read," "no no put glove"—are similar in surface structure to the sentences of Kathryn, Eric, and Gia over the course of several observations. The more complex sentences, such as "no the sun shining" or "no no put glove," are comparable to the surface form of utterances in the texts of Kathryn II, Eric V, and Gia V.

In the phrase structure for the text of Kathryn I, the negative element was an optional semantic choice within the internal structure of the sentence:

$$K:I \quad S \rightarrow Nom \ (Ng) \begin{Bmatrix} NP \\ VP \end{Bmatrix}$$

In contrast, Bellugi described the operation of negation in terms of an element "outside" the sentence "nucleus":

$$\text{``}\left[\begin{Bmatrix} no \\ not \end{Bmatrix} \text{--Nucleus} \right] S \quad \text{or} \quad [\text{Nucleus--}no] \ S\text{''}$$

---

[3] It should also be noted that Bellugi's Period A was based on a 10-hour speech sample from each of the children, obtained over a 10-week period for two of the children and over a 20-week period for the third child. The individual observations of Kathryn, Eric, and Gia were spaced over a period of a few days, and obtained every six weeks. Thus, the period discussed as the first stage (Period A) by Bellugi overlaps the first several observations of Kathryn, Eric, and Gia.

A grammar is constructed to answer the question of what it is the child knows about the language—the system that underlies the observed behavior. In this sense, Bellugi has characterized this first syntactic operation of negation as a "primitive abstraction which later drops out, having been replaced by a much more complex system of negation" and "not the primitive version of some later structure which adds constituents to form longer sentences." The principal evidence Bellugi provided for placing the negative element "outside" the sentence nucleus was the observation that the "children seldom place the negative morpheme in an internal position in the sentence structure" (for example, "no Mommy read," "no the sun shining"), and here Bellugi was describing *surface* structure only. No evidence of the function of negation or of the relation of the negative element to the rest of the sentence, in terms of content, was presented: ". . . we have stripped the speech of paralinguistic features . . . of information arising from discourse relations by omitting interchanges, and of information from the setting or situation." However, when this kind of information was taken into account in analyzing the texts of Kathryn, Eric, and Gia, semantic interpretation of negative sentences was possible in most cases. Isolating the semantics of these sentences made it possible to analyze the internal structure of the syntax—revealing that inclusion of the negative element operated to replace or delete other forms.

In the earliest sentences, the negative element did occupy the initial position in the surface structure of sentences (except for the few occurrences after /ə/), as also observed by Bellugi. However, this occurred as a consequence of the deletion of other constituents, that is, sentence-subjects, in the earliest negative sentences. In the subsequent texts (Kathryn II, Gia V, and Eric V) there were sentences that contained both sentence-subject and the negative particle, and these later texts could still be described as having occurred in Bellugi's Period A; that is, there were no noun and verb inflections and the form of the negative element was invariant.

Table 6.3 presents all the sentences that contained both sentence-subject and a negative element in the texts of Kathryn II, Gia V, and Eric V (such sentences did not occur in the earlier texts). These sentences happened to include the most complex negative sentences the children produced—precisely because of the inclusion of sentence-subjects.

Differentiation of the negative element had not begun at Kathryn II; the only form was "no." Gia, at Time V, produced a few sentences with the form "can't," and Eric, at Time V, had begun to use the forms "didn't" and "doesn't"—but the primitive forms "no" and "no more"

Table 6.3. Utterances with Negative Element and Sentence-Subject, Without Identifying Information

(81)	K : II	Lois no hat.
(82)	K : II	Kathryn no shoe.
(83)	K : II	Mommy no picture there.
(84)	K : II	man no go in there.
(85)	K : II	Kathryn no /fɪk/ this.
(86)	K : II	Kathryn no fix this.
(87)	K : II	Kathryn no like celery.
(88)	K : II	Lois ə no coffee.
(89)	K : II	this ə no goes.
(90)	E : V	you no bring ə choochoo train.↑
(91)	E : V	I no reach it.
(92)	E : V	I no like to.
(93)	K : II	no Lois do it.
(94)	K : II	no Kathryn want play with self.
(95)	K : II	no Kathryn playing self.
(96)	K : II	no my have ə this.
(97)	K : II	no I my have ə this.
(98)	K : II	no that's ə bear book.
(99)	E : V	no car going there.
(100)	E : V	no this Daddy.
(101)	E : V	no this ə Mommy.
(102)	E : V	no this Mommy Daddy.
(103)	G : V	no man ride *this* tank car.
(104)	G : V	no now I do ə /dɪt/.
(105)	G : V	no doll sleep.
(106)	K : II	no Daddy hungry.

were far more frequent in both children's texts. Thus, Kathryn's and Gia's sentences in Table 6.3 could be described as having occurred in

Period A—before the use of different forms of the negative element, which characterized the second stage, Period B, in Bellugi's account. Eric's sentences might be characterized as transitional—occurring somewhere between Periods A and B. Eric's sentences with "didn't" and "doesn't" were not included in Table 6.3.

When presented in this way (as in Table 6.3), in an unordered list without identifying information, the position of "no" in relation to the rest of the sentence appears to be variable. It occurred both before and after the sentence-subject.

However, when the contexts of the speech events of which the utterances were a part were studied, these sentences were seen to fall into two distinctive groups (see Table 6.4). In the first group, (N), the "no" occurred before a predicate that was clearly being negated—for example, "Lois no hat" (Lois was not wearing a hat), "Kathryn no shoe" (Kathryn was not wearing shoes), "Mommy no picture there" (Mommy was reading a novel), "Kathryn no fix this" (Kathryn could not fix the

Table 6.4. Identification of Utterances in Table 6.3

(N) Negative Sentences

(81)	K:II	Lois no hat. (L not wearing a hat)
(82)	K:II	Kathryn no shoe. (K pointing to her bare feet)
(83)	K:II	Mommy no picture there. (M reading a novel)
(84)	K:II	man no go in there. (K holding her toy clown; watching L pack up toys to leave)
(85)	K:II	Kathryn no /fɪk/ this. (K unable to snap blocks)
(86)	K:II	Kathryn no fix this. (K unable to snap blocks)
(87)	K:II	Kathryn no like celery. (K watching M eat celery after not taking celery when M offered it to her)
(88)	K:II	Lois ə no coffee. (in sequence (76): "me like coffee, Daddy like coffee, Lois ə no coffee.")
(89)	K:II	this ə no goes. (K trying to fit puzzle piece into the wrong space)
(90)	E:V	you no bring ə choochoo train.↑ (E disappointed because L had not brought the train)
(91)	E:V	I no reach it. (E pointing to the window blind, which he wanted L to open for him)
(92)	E:V	I no like to. (M had asked E if he wanted to go on a roller coaster again)

Table 6.4, *continued*

(A) Affirmative Sentences

(93) K:II no Lois do it. (K, unable to connect the train cars, giving them to L to connect)

(94) K:II no Kathryn want play with self. (K didn't want to play with the slide; L asked, "Shall I do it myself?"; K climbing into her playpen to play with her toys)

(95) K:II no Kathryn playing self. (In sequence with (94))

(96) K:II no my have ə this. (In response to "Kathryn'll have two and I'll have two"; K refusing to give wheel to L)

(97) K:II no I my have ə this. (In response to "Lois'll have this"; L reaching for K's snap block; K holding on to it)

(98) K:II no that's ə bear book. (K, looking for her book about dragons, picked up a book about bears, then dropped it)

(99) E:V *no* car going there. (E insisting that he sees a car in a picture in the animal book)

(100) E:V no this Daddy. (E had called the boy figure "Daddy"; L asked "Is this Daddy?"; E pointing to the Daddy figure)

(101) E:V no this ə Mommy. (E had named all the figures; L pointed to the baby, asked "Is this Mommy?"; E pointing to Mommy figure)

(102) E:V no this Mommy Daddy. (E pointing to Mommy and Daddy on the form board, in response to "Is this Mommy?")

(103) G:V no man ride *this* tank car. (G pointing to a different car for the man to ride on)

(104) G:V no now I do ə /dɪt/. (G had completed a puzzle; L asked "Now can I do it?"; G refusing to let L do the puzzle; did it again herself)

(105) G:V no doll sleep. (G had pretended to sleep; getting up and taking her doll to put to sleep)

(106) K:II no Daddy hungry. (This utterance is presented with the context of the speech event in which it occurred in the following discussion)

train). In the second group, (A), the "no" was clearly anaphoric and did not apply to the remainder of the sentence, which was an affirmative statement: "no Kathryn playing self" (Kathryn did not want to play with the slide and went into the playpen to play alone), "no Lois do it" (Kathryn was giving the train to Lois to fix), "no man ride *this* tank car"

(Gia was pointing to a different car for the man to ride), "no doll sleep" (Gia wanted to put the doll to sleep).

There was only one exception in the data to this clear distinction between the (N) negative sentences, where the negative particle followed the sentence-subject, and (A) affirmative sentences, where the negative particle preceded the sentence-subject—the utterance "no Daddy hungry," which occurred as follows:

(106)   K:II (Kathryn looking at a
         picture of a family at a dinner
         table; in the picture the
         mother and children are
         seated at the table and the
         father is walking toward the
         table carrying a platter of
         food)

$$
\begin{bmatrix}
\text{hungry. hmmmmm.} \\
\text{girl hungry.} \\
\text{Daddy hungry.} \ldots \\
> \text{no Daddy hungry.} \\
\text{Daddy up.} \\
\text{Mommy hungry.} \\
\text{boy hungry.}
\end{bmatrix}
$$

If the distinction between the two kinds of sentences with sentence-subject and a negative element in the texts of Kathryn, Gia, and Eric did not exist in the Bellugi data, it represents an important difference in the development of negation in the two groups of children. In a personal communication to William Labov at Columbia University (1967), Bellugi described the nonlinguistic context that accompanied the utterance "no I see truck" in a published "section from Adam's first record" (Brown and Bellugi, 1964, p. 135) that would support characterization of the sentence as negative; that is, Adam could not see the truck.

The account of the operation of negation proposed here—that introduction of additional structure in a sentence, such as including the element of negation in its base form, has a limiting effect on production, causing reduction of the sentence with deletion of constituents—contradicts the Bellugi account. If the negative element is outside the sentence in its underlying structure, then, it is presumed, it would not affect the internal structure of the sentence. Such was the case in sentences with preceding anaphoric "no," where the negative element was without effect on the remainder of the sentence.

Further, such a rule as that proposed by Bellugi appears to imply that there are no constraints on sentence complexity or sentence length with the operation of negation—if the choice of negation simply adds an element to an otherwise affirmative utterance. But in the texts of Kathryn, Eric, and Gia, the negative utterances were otherwise among the least syntactically complex when compared with affirmative utterances. There was strong evidence that the inclusion of the negative particle reduced surface form.

Finally, the specification of the negative particle outside the sentence is inconsistent with sentence negation in the adult model of English, where negation is an inherent semantic fact of English sentences. In the fully realized system of negation in the adult grammar of English, the "structural position of the negative element in the sentence" is related to the "scope of negation (i.e., the structures over which the negative element has its effect)" (Klima, 1964, p. 316). And, indeed, the constituents that were most often deleted in these early negative sentences were sentence-subjects, which were not within the immediate scope of negation.

Bellugi (1967) suggested that, in Period A, negation outside the sentence represented a syntactic structure that has no relation to the adult model of the language—"a primitive abstraction which later drops out." In contrast, the development of Kathryn, Eric, and Gia suggested that the earliest system of negation was more similar to the adult model than it was different—but it was a much simpler, fragmented, and far more generalized system.

The evidence for this conclusion included the following observations:

1. The relation of the negative element to the content of the rest of the surface structure of sentences was direct or else, in some utterances, appeared to be semantically paradoxical (for example, "no 'chine," "no window") unless an unrealized element was postulated between the adjacent constituents "no" and " 'chine," "no" and "window," on which the negative element would have direct effect in the internal structure of the sentence.

2. The negative element never occurred before the subject of a negative sentence. In the earliest examples, there was no occurrence of sentence-subject in negative sentences, although sentence-subjects were fully productive in affirmative sentences in the texts of Kathryn and Gia. Indeed, even at Time V, when Gia produced the sentences in Table 6.4 with anaphoric "no" and an affirmative sentence that included sentence-subjects, she did not produce any negative sentences with sentence-subject at the same time. When, at a subsequent stage, subjects

were expressed in negative sentences, the negative element always followed the subject—preceding the negated predicate.

3. The negative element occurred after /ə/, when a possible source for /ə/ might have been "I" or "it," or when in the absence of semantic correlates, /ə/ was designated in the phrase structure only as a pre-verbal element.

The latter two observations correspond to the attraction of the negative element to the essential verb of a sentence in the adult model. When "the whole combination of a subject and a predicate is negativized—the negative element [is] joined more or less closely to the finite verb" (Jespersen, 1961, p. 438). An objection to this interpretation could be raised when the finite verb did not occur. But it was just this non-occurrence of the verb—for example, "want" or "use" in "no dirty soap," "play" in "no 'chine"—that was an effect of the constraints that operated to reduce the surface structure of the children's early sentences. The sentences could not otherwise be interpretable as negative sentences, given the facts of behavior and context in the speech events in which they occurred.

4. The negative element never occurred before (outside of) a syntactic structure that could be construed as the affirmative correlate of a negative structure. For example, the most frequent early verbal construction in the texts of all three children consisted of /ə/ (or, occasionally, some other noncontrastive phonological element) before a verb form—for example, "ə fit" and "ə turn"—but the negative correlates of these sentences in the same texts were "no fit" and "no turn," not *"no ə fit." Similarly, in other examples already cited, "this dirty" occurred, but "this dirty" plus the negative operator resulted in "no dirty" in the same text, not *"no this dirty."

Negative sentences could not be construed as simply a positive sentence with a negative sign attached, outside the sentence. Rather, the negative element was intrinsic to the structure of the sentence and as such operated to increase its complexity, as in adult grammar. This account has attempted to show that the earliest system of negation in the children's grammar differed from the account of the adult system only in the fact of its essential immaturity.

6.4. Constraints on the Form of Children's Speech

It appeared that pivot and 'telegraphic' sentences were often the reduced forms of more complex underlying structures. The results of an experimental study by Shipley, Smith, and Gleitman (1969) provide support for the contention that children's speech may not be isomorphic with what is known about linguistic structure. They reported that "children whose speech is telegraphic readily obey well-formed commands, and less readily obey telegraphic commands," thus indicating that the children know more about grammatical structure than their speech would indicate.

When the total distribution of sentences in a text was examined, it was observed that sentences were incomplete (in terms of basic subject-verb-object representation), but the pattern was variable. There were subject-verb, subject-object, and verb-object strings, but subject-verb-object strings did not occur. Leopold (1949, Vol. III, p. 28) observed the same restriction on the production of sentences in his daughter's development. At the time (20 to 23 months) that "sentence span was limited to two words," he observed that "where the standard [the adult model utterance] required at least three words because the predicate was not a simple verb, the child was forced to omit one of them." It might be argued that inclusion of "no" in such strings simply increased sentence length beyond the 'permitted' two morphemes—that constraint on complexity *is* a constraint on length. But it appeared that reduction was the result of something more than a production limitation on sentence *length*. The evidence presented here suggests that some sort of cognitive limitation in handling structural complexity (such as accompanies sentence negation) *underlies* the constraint on length of children's utterances—that the constraint on sentence length reflects an inherent limitation in linguistic operations. It was clear that the earliest negative sentences did not simply add a negative marker or operator to an otherwise affirmative sentence. Rather, the linguistic operation of negation had a limiting effect on structural complexity and length of utterances.

Thus, the operation of the reduction transformation has been ascribed to a constraint on sentence complexity; with an increase in the underlying complexity of a sentence, something had to give in its production. If this was so, what determined which constituents were deleted and which were retained? The factors that operated to influence the production or deletion of particular forms in a sentence appeared to be related to the nature of the language the child was learning (linguistic constraints) and the basic fact of the immaturity of the cognitive system (cognitive constraints).

6.4.1. Linguistic Constraints

Vocabulary. The nonoccurrence of elements in production often resulted from the fact that the child operated with a primitive lexical system—primitive in the sense that the lexicon was insufficient in the number of words, but also in the sense that the inherent and syntactic features of particular items were rudimentary. 'Learning' a word did not imply that the word, with the features that govern its combination with other words in the adult model, appeared full-blown in the child's lexicon. For example, at Kathryn I, "hurt" and "ə hurt" occurred in the text. The following also occurred, in different speech events:

(107) K : I (Jocelyn, Kathryn's friend,
       had bruised her cheek on the
       playground and cried a few days
       previously; Kathryn reporting
       this to Mommy at lunch)   Jocelyn cheek.
       Jocelyn hurt her cheek.

(108) K : I (Kathryn's doll 'cried')
       What happened to the baby doll?
       Is she crying?   /ɑ/ baby cheek.

Although Kathryn had used "hurt" and "ə hurt" in appropriate contexts (talking about chapped hands), it appeared that she might not have learned the complex symbol features of "hurt" as a verb that can appear in environments before and after nouns. "Hurt" was at least a possible lexical item that might have occurred in the utterances "Jocelyn cheek" and "/ɑ/ baby cheek." But the effect of reduction was the deletion of the intervening (dummy) constituent in the base form of the sentences that accounted for the grammatical relationship between "Jocelyn" and "cheek" and between "/ɑ/ baby" and "cheek"—not the deletion of the lexical item "hurt." The reduction rules did not operate on particular lexical items but, rather, on the categories in the under-lying structure from which lexical items are derived. However, the motivation for reduction could have occurred in the fact that a lexical item that could be substituted for the terminal, category symbols (N or V) in a derived string did not exist in the lexicon or existed without the necessary contextual or syntactic features.

Syntax. Two sources of deletion are not pertinent to this discussion and need to be distinguished. Grammatical ellipsis could have resulted in the production of acceptable sentence fragments that represented full sentences in particular environments—for example, the response "making a house" to the question, "What are you doing?" Eventually, in the later texts, there was also grammatical deletion of elements in sentence embedding—for example, deletion of the subject in the constituent sentence of "I see the man who rides the truck." These grammatical deletion transformations, which are necessary for a linguistic account of such utterances, were not related to immaturity.

If it is true—as it was for Eric and Gia and probably for Kathryn also, although the evidence for Kathryn was incomplete—that children learn predicate-objects (the names of the 'things' that can be acted upon, counted, modified, owned) first, then the learning of these forms in complement constructions with verbs and as constituents of predicates that say something about sentence-subjects constitutes the substance of the child's earliest syntactic learning.

Brown, Cazden, and Bellugi (1969) reported that, on the basis of their data, "the child's knowledge of these [grammatical] relations which, in English, are chiefly expressed by order undergoes no development. He seems to express the relations he means to express from the very start." This conclusion was based on the fact that children make few errors in word order; subjects of sentences occur before objects. This order is one of the universals of language reported by Greenberg (1963); with rare exception, subjects precede objects in all languages.

Gia did make 'mistakes' in word order. For example, at Time II, Gia produced "book read" and "read book" in virtually identical speech events. At Gia I, object nouns occurred before verbs—for example, "balloon throw" as Gia dropped the balloon as if throwing it—although subjects always preceded objects in Noun + Noun constructions. It appeared that 'errors' in word order at Gia I and II were related to the tentative position of verbs as they emerged in the grammar.

The grammatical relations subject-verb-object did not exist in the sentences that Gia and Eric produced in the earliest texts. Gia learned the subject-object relation first; Eric learned the verb-object relation first. Both children subsequently learned the subject-verb relation—the structure that was least productive in the texts of all three children.

The nonoccurrence of sentence-subject in relation to verbs or object nouns in Eric I and Eric II and the nonoccurrence of verbs in relation to nouns in Gia I were not attributed to the operation of reduction rules. Category forms with these functions did not exist in the total distribution of the sentences that occurred. However, in the subsequent grammars—Eric III and Gia II, when Eric began to produce subject-verb strings and Gia began to produce subject-verb and verb-object strings—the previously nonproductive forms appeared to be the forms that were most likely to be reduced in three-term strings.

In the operation of negation, it was observed that sentence-subjects were deleted, and verbs were deleted in negated predicates when the predicate complement occurred. Generally, it appeared that, in the case of negation, the reduction rules deleted elements from left to right. It may have been that deleted elements were somehow those elements that were most vulnerable—sentence-subjects being less productive than, for example, predicate-objects.

The operation of reduction appeared to be systematic. In answer to the question of the factors that determined which constituents were deleted and which were retained with the operation of reduction, the following linguistic factors appeared to be influential: (1) the relative recency of the appearance of the category components that dominated the deleted or retained constituents in the phrase structure; (2) the child's cognizance of lexical items and the relative 'completeness' of the semantic and syntactic feature representation of particular items in his lexicon; and (3) in the case of negation, the deletion of constituents that were most often not within the immediate scope of negation, such as sentence-subjects.

At the level represented by Kathryn I, all three children appeared to have learned something about the grammatical relations object-of-verb, predicate-of-sentence, and subject-of-predicate. However, there were lexical and syntactic constraints that interacted with cognitive constraints to limit the production of sentences, so that all three grammatical relations could not occur in the surface structure of a single sentence.

6.4.2. Cognitive Constraints

It was more difficult to specify the nature of the cognitive constraints that influenced production. As pointed out by Brown and Fraser (1963, p. 193), some sort of limitation in memory span is almost certainly a factor in influencing length of imitated responses. The role of memory in influencing the length or complexity of spontaneous utterances is less easily defined. Brown and Fraser referred to "a similar limit of programming span for the situation in which the child is constructing sentences"; mean lengths of imitated and spontaneous utterances in their data were highly similar.

What does a child need to remember when constructing sentences? The names for 'things' and 'actions' are important, but he learns that he can get by without them and begins to use proforms such as "this," "this one," "do," "it," "here" quite early.

The children's ability to remember complex linguistic material was often impressive—as evidenced by the production of stereotype model sentences that had no analogue in the child's grammar; for example, "who has that book?, Kathryn has that book" at Kathryn I. An even more striking example was Eric's ability to 'recite' accurately from memory long passages of text in his favorite story books, turning the pages at the appropriate juncture, when he was two and one-half years old. But he was unable to answer specific questions about the text, and certain phrase structures he recited—sentence adverbials, for example— did not appear in his spontaneous utterances. Perhaps there is a relative distinction, in this context, between more or less 'immediate' memory. But something more than a memory factor appeared to be operating to account for the reduction of spontaneous sentences. Certainly the children presented no evidence of difficulty in remembering what they had intended to say. On the contrary, their utterances were produced as 'wholes'—as if the children assumed reciprocal editing on the part of the listener.

The reduction transformation accounted for the inferred relationship between underlying structure and obtained utterances; evidence of its operation provided insight into the child's ability to handle surface structure. The rule operated on category symbols that were necessary in an underlying representation to account for the inherent relation between two constituents of an utterance, such as between "Mommy" and "pigtail," and between "no" and "chair" (where "chair" was not being negated directly). The number of syntactic operations or the complexity of grammatical relationship within a sentence appears to increase the cognitive weight of the sentence for the child, and his reduced utterance reflects the inability to carry the full sentence load in performance.

When the children played with the train, they had to gather the disconnected cars—engine, dumper, tank car, and tank, as well as all the flat cars—and carry them to a clear space on the floor. This always involved several trips, and each armload of cars deposited on the floor by itself never added up to a 'train.' The analogy is a simple one but fairly direct. The limitations in linguistic performance reflected an inability to carry the full structural load of the underlying representation. Limitations in linguistic operations appear to interact with limitations in cognitive function to influence linguistic expression in an as yet unspecified way.

7 Syntactic and Semantic Development of Early Sentence Negation

The children's use of negative sentences provided a particularly fruitful opportunity to study the correlation of linguistic expression with semantic intent. Negation was usually signaled in the children's utterances by a linguistic marker (such as "no," "no more," "not"), and there was corresponding nonlinguistic evidence of negation in the immediate context of the speech events that contained the utterance. It was possible to observe the relationship between the syntax and semantics of negation to obtain important insight into the question of the relative development of language and cognition.

The syntax of negation in adult English has been described at length in the traditional grammar of Jespersen (1917; 1961, pp. 426–467), and in generative transformational terms by Klima (1964). Of greater significance to this study is the extensive description of the syntactic development of negation in children's language by Bellugi (1967). She described the sequence of developmental changes in the syntactic form of three children's negative sentences from the age of approximately two years, over a period of from one to about two and one-half years— until the structure of the children's sentences approached the adult model. Bellugi provided a formal linguistic description of the acquisition of negation but did not inquire into the inherent semantics and syntax of negation that underlie the formal account.

The rule that Bellugi proposed for the earliest negative sentences in the first phase of development, Period A, placed the negative element outside the sentence. As pointed out in the previous chapter, this rule appears to imply that there are no constraints on sentence complexity or sentence length with the operation of negation—if the choice of negation simply adds an element to an otherwise affirmative utterance. But in the texts of Kathryn, Eric, and Gia, the negative utterances were among the least syntactically complex, and there was strong evidence that the inclusion of the negative element constrained length and complexity of surface form. Also, specification of the negative particle outside the sentence is inconsistent with sentence negation in the adult model of English. Negation is an inherent semantic fact of English sentences and is marked by the attachment of the negative particle to the verbal auxiliary *within* the sentence.

The term *cognitive clutter* was used by Slobin (1966) to describe the child's early development of negation in the light of the Bellugi account. Slobin (p. 91) went on to say that the child "develops negation systems of unwieldy complexity—systems that are presumably too complicated to deal with and must be abandoned or seriously modified." But is this indeed the case? It appeared that the question of the semantic and cognitive aspects of negation was worth pursuing in an effort to describe the underlying syntax of early sentence negation.

The previous discussion of the texts and the grammars proposed for Kathryn, Eric, and Gia dealt with the earliest stage—approximately the same level that was described as Period A in the Bellugi presentation. Bellugi described a second stage, Period B, as one in which the negative element occurs after the sentence-subject and has different forms, including "no," "not," "don't," and "can't." The data to be presented here—from the observations of Kathryn I to III, Eric II to VI, and Gia IV to VI—coincided with the Periods A and B that Bellugi described for the three children she studied.

7.1. Semantic Categories of Negation

In identifying negative sentences, utterances were considered negative if (1) they contained a negative element, such as "no," "no more," "not," or "don't," that signaled negative intent, or (2) they were produced with clearly negative intent (as evidenced, for example, by the child shaking his head, pushing an object away, or refusing to follow a direction) although a negative element was not expressed.

Semantic interpretation of negative sentences was inferred from observation of the status of the referent in the context in which the utterance occurred, or the child's relation to the referent in terms of behavior. For example, 12 of the 15 utterances with "no more" (including 4 instances of "no more" in isolation) at Eric II shared the same semantic feature: the *nonexistence* of the referent in the context of the speech event. When Eric said "no more noise," the noise had stopped; when he said "no more cleaner," the cleaner was gone; when he said "no more juice," he had finished his juice. Thus, the linguistic and contextual features shared by these 12 utterances were the expression of a negative element ("no more") and the *nonexistence* of the referent. The semantic interpretation of 2 of the 15 utterances could not be determined, and 1 utterance had a different interpretation.

At the same time, Eric II, there were 76 occurrences of "no" in the text as a single word, and it was possible to interpret the use of "no" in 41 instances. In only 3 instances did "no" signal *nonexistence* of a referent unequivocally. However, in 33 instances where "no" occurred, the referent did exist in the context. The interpretation of these utterances as negative was based on Eric's behavior as he indicated *rejection*—by pushing away or turning away from an object or otherwise opposing the occurrence of an event. Five occurrences of "no" were interpreted differently.

Clearly, Eric used the negative syntactic operator "no more" to signal *nonexistence* and the single word "no" to signal *rejection*. Most of Eric's first negative sentences, at Time II, referred to the *nonexistence* of objects and included the negative marker "no more." However, at the same time, he expressed *rejection* of something that existed in the context, and he did so by using the isolated negative element "no."

But whereas the expression of *nonexistence* and *rejection* was distinguished formally at Eric II, the same categories were not distinguished formally at Kathryn I:

(1) K:I (Kathryn not finding a pocket in
Mommy's skirt, which had no pocket)   no pocket.

(2) K:I (Kathryn pushing away a sliver of
worn soap in the bathtub, wanting to be
washed with new pink soap)   no dirty soap.

The same form signalled *nonexistence*, "no pocket," and *rejection*, "no dirty soap." Furthermore, at Kathryn II, a third semantic category, *denial*, was distinguished on the basis of function, and the form of expression of *denial* was not structurally different from "no pocket" and "no dirty soap":

(3) K:II (Kathryn, Mommy, and Lois look-
      ing for the truck)

Where's the truck?

(Mommy picking up the car, giving it to
Kathryn)

Here it is. There's the truck.   no truck.

Thus, there appeared to be three semantic categories of negation that characterized the children's earliest negative sentences in terms of function: *nonexistence*—the referent was not manifest in the context, where there was an expectation of its existence, and was correspondingly negated in the linguistic expression (examples included (1) "no pocket" and sentences with "no more" at Eric II); *rejection*—the referent actually existed or was imminent within the contextual space of the speech event and was rejected or opposed by the child, as in "no dirty soap"; *denial*—the negative utterance asserted that an actual (or supposed) predication was not the case. The negated referent was not actually manifest in the context as it was in *rejection*, but it was manifest symbolically in a previous utterance; "no truck" denied the expressed identity of the car as a truck.

In a paper that discussed the acquisition of negation by one child learning Japanese as a first language, McNeill and McNeill (1967) raised the issue of the semantic interpretation of negation in Japanese. They reported that the facts of negation in Japanese are accounted for by four different forms of the negative element organized on the basis of three dimensions or contrasts. These forms are not syntactically differ-ent—each occurs in sentence-final position, after the predicate phrase. However, the shape of the negative element varies according to seman-tic function. The three semantic dimensions described were "Existence-Truth, Internal-External, and Entailment-Non-Entailment." From the descriptions provided, these three dimensions appear to correspond generally to the semantic categories of negation proposed for Kathryn, Eric, and Gia: *nonexistence, rejection* and *denial.* Although the data presented by McNeill and McNeill were incomplete, they reported that the three negation contrasts in Japanese were acquired by their subject in the order given above.

Negation in the adult model of English can also be organized in terms of the three semantic categories identified in the children's speech; certainly the adult grammar allows expression of the contrastive notions—existence-nonexistence, acceptance-rejection, and affirmation-denial. But whereas in Japanese the semantic categories are neatly signaled by morphological markers, the linguistic expression in English is less efficient. Indeed, the thorough account of the syntax of English negation by Klima (1964) presented only the syntactic mechanics for negation generally and ignored the semantic issues: "the analysis ... offers ... no interpretation of notions like *negative* that appear as designations of grammatical symbols" (p. 247).

There were semantic differences in the early negative sentences of Kathryn, Eric, and Gia, as exemplified by the inherent differences among "no pocket," "no dirty soap," and "no truck." It appeared reasonable to approach the inquiry into the children's acquisition of negation by determining whether the three semantic categories of negation—*nonexistence, rejection,* and *denial*—were differentiated in the course of development in terms of (1) sequence of development and (2) structural differences in linguistic expression.

In the children's texts already described (Kathryn I, Gia I and II, and Eric I, II, and III), the syntactic operation of negation was accounted for in the proposed grammars if negative sentences were used productively. The account of the development of the syntax of negation in the later texts is essentially a taxonomic description; utterances have been classified as to semantic category, and the syntactic structure is described. Rules of grammar for the subsystem of negation were not proposed because grammars were not constructed for these later texts.

7.2. Phase 1 in the Development of Negation

The first phase in the development of the syntax of negation was characterized by the earliest meaningful and productive use of a negative element in syntactic contexts. This occurred in the texts of Eric II, Kathryn I, and Gia IV.

7.2.1. Eric I to III

In the first text collected, Time I, mean length of utterance was 1.10, and Eric produced "no" as a single-word utterance 13 times. In four instances, the utterance occurred in apparent response to a yes-no question—for example, "Does it fit?"—but the use of "no" was inappropriate in one instance and indeterminate in the other three. There were four spontaneous occurrences of "no"—not in response to a yes-no question—that were indeterminate; it was not clear from the context or behavior whether or not negation was intended. There were five spontaneous occurrences of "no" that were appropriate, and all occurred at different times but in the same context: Eric was unable to fit the vacuum cleaner pipe and hose together.

The following paradigmatic sequence also occurred:

(4) E:I (Eric closed the lid of his toy chest) ⎡ all gone. ⎤
                                               | no more. |
                                               ⎣ make all gone. ⎦

This occurrence of "no more" was the only instance of "no more" in the text. "All gone" occurred elsewhere four time—once after Eric dropped his lollipop stick into the radiator grille and the investigator commented "It's gone." This occurrence took place just before the "all gone, no more, make all gone" sequence, with ten intervening adult utterances and three intervening utterances by Eric. The three other instances of "all gone" were indeterminate.

There was limited evidence, therefore, for postulating the rudimentary beginning of the linguistic expression of negation at Eric I—the sequence in (4) was semantically appropriate, and there were five occurrences of "no" as a single word in an appropriate context signaling negation. But the data were too meager at Time I to determine with conviction if Eric knew the 'meaning' of "no." There were many more yes-no questions to which he did not respond with "no," and the word "yes" never occurred. All that could be said at Time I was that the form "no" occurred as a single word and that its interpretation was indeterminate more often than not.

There were 76 occurrences of the single word "no" in the subsequent Eric II text. These instances of "no" have been categorized—where there was sufficient evidence to permit unequivocal classification—as expressions of *nonexistence, rejection,* or *denial* and are presented in Table 7.1, along with the functional distribution of "no" at Time III. As at Time I, the word "yes" or its equivalent did not occur at Eric II or III. Comparing the distribution of "no" in the Eric II and III texts, it could be seen that, aside from the indeterminate utterances, "no" was used most frequently to express *rejection.* At the same time, "no more" occurred in isolation and signaled *nonexistence* four times at Eric II and eight times at Eric III; "no more" was not used to express *rejection.* Thus, it appeared that variation in the form of nonsyntactic expressions of negation ("no" and "no more" occurring in isolation)

Table 7.1. Functional Distribution of "no," Eric II and III

	Nonexistence	Rejection	Denial	Indeterminate
Eric II	2 (1)	30 (3)	(5)	20 (15)
Eric III	2	11 (11)	0	14 (4)

Note: Numbers in parentheses refer to utterances that occurred after a prior question or comment from the receiver. It should be emphasized that utterances were interpreted (and classified as to semantic category) only when the contextual and behavioral evidence was clear. Nearly half the occurrences of "no" could not be interpreted; these occurred often while Eric played alone—for example, when stacking the blocks or connecting the train. At such times there was not an evident correspondence between utterance and referent, and what Eric said ("no") did not appear to relate to what he was doing. There were also instances that could not be interpreted because of insufficient information at the time of transcription.

corresponded to variation in function—"no" signaled *rejection*, and "no more" signaled *nonexistence* at Eric II and at Eric III.

The text at Time III was two and one-half hours longer than at Time II, but as can be observed, the number of instances of "no" as a single word decreased from 76 occurrences at Time II to 42 at Time III. Corresponding to the marked decline in the use of "no" as a single word, there was an increase in the number of interpretable syntactic expressions of negation—from 11 sentences at Time II to 35 sentences at Time III—while at the same time mean length of utterance increased from 1.19 to 1.42 morphemes. It appeared that the use of "no" as a single word decreased at Time III with the use of "no" in syntactic expression of negation.

Syntactic Negation at Eric II. The negative sentences that occurred at Eric II have been categorized and are presented in Table 7.2. At this time, Eric used syntactic negation to express *nonexistence* most often—in 9 of the 11 speech events. In order to express *rejection* he used "no" as a single word—in 33 of the 41 interpretable instances of "no." Syntactic expression of *rejection* was marginal and there was no syntactic expression of *denial*.

The grammar proposed for Eric II in Chapter V provided for a class of pivot forms, which included "no more," and the phrase structure rule which accounted for the negative sentences was:

S → (Pivot)   (N).

There are two utterances with unique structure in Table 7.2, "ə don't want baby," and "no 'chine," which were sentences not generated by

Table 7.2. Categorization of Negative Utterances, Eric II

Nonexistence		Rejection	Indeterminate
no more noise	(4)	ə don't want baby	no more noise
no more light	(2)	no more noise	
no more juice			
no more cleaner			
no 'chine			
no more	(4)	no (33)	no (35)
no	(3)		no more

Note: Numbers in parentheses refer to the number of times the utterance occurred in the text, discounting immediate repetitions.

the Eric II grammar. The forms "don't" and "want" did not occur elsewhere in the text at Time II and "don't" did not occur subsequently at Time III. Eric said "ə don't want baby" as he dropped a doll which he had been holding.

The utterance "no more noise" occurred five times in appropriate contexts and in one context in which interpretation was indeterminate:

(5) E:II (Eric and Lois had put
the wire man on Eric's peg
bench; Eric started to whim-
per)   Mommy. Mommy. Mommy.

O.K. Show Mommy.

(Eric began to cry; Lois stood
up)

Let's go find Mommy in the
kitchen.   no.

No?

(Eric refusing to leave) $\begin{bmatrix} \text{no more.} \\ > \text{no more noise.} \end{bmatrix}$

It was not possible to understand what Eric wanted, but he appeared to be using his negation repertoire—"no," "no more," and "no more noise"—to express negation of something. This anomalous occurrence of "no more noise" may have been the most readily available syntactic construction for expressing a negative notion that Eric was unable to express otherwise. That is, "no more noise"—the most frequent syntactic construction—may have been generalized as a negative 'whole' comparable to "no" and "no more."

Whereas "ə don't want baby" was not related structurally to any other utterances at either Eric II or Eric III, the utterance "no 'chine," anticipated a developmental change that did occur subsequently, at Time III.

Syntactic Negation at Eric III. Table 7.3 presents the categorized distribution of the negative sentences that occurred at Eric III. There was a substantial increase in the number of negative sentences; syn-

Table 7.3. Categorization of Negative Utterances, Eric III

Nonexistence		Rejection	Denial
no more noise	(13)	no train	no more birdie
no more light	(2)	no more dumpcar	no more blocks
no more car	(2)	ə want any shoes	
no more seal			
no more airplane		no (22)	
no more round			
no more apple			
no more dumpcar			
ə no more			
no go in			
no goes			
no ready go			
no fit			
no it won't fit			
ə find it			
/jə/ find it			
no more	(8)		
no	(2)		

Note: Numbers in parentheses refer to the number of times the utterance occurred in the text, discounting immediate repetitions.

tactic negation expressed *nonexistence* most productively—in 30 of the 35 negative sentences that occurred. Thus, although the number of sentences increased substantially, the functional distribution was essentially the same as at Eric II—Eric was able to express *nonexistence* syntactically, but *rejection* was signaled most often by isolated "no."

However, two developments occurred that distinguished the data at Eric III from the earlier data at Eric II. First, Eric began to express both *rejection* and *denial* syntactically, although occurrence of sentences with these functions was marginal. In addition, there was a differentiation in the form of the negative element in syntactic contexts. Whereas "no 'chine" at Eric II was the only instance of "no" as a negative operator, this form became productive at Eric III. Further, the two forms of the negative element—"no more" and "no"—were in complementary distribution. "No more" occurred in syntactic contexts with noun forms where the noun referent was negated directly—for example, "no more airplane," "no more noise," "no more apple." Moreover, "no more" was used in contexts where negation signaled *nonexistence* of objects that had occurred previously—the negation of recurrence.

In contrast, the form "no" occurred as a negative operator in syntactic contexts before predicate structures. Thus, the negative element had the form "no" in contexts before verbs—for example, "no go in," "no goes," "no ready go" (referring to sliding the wheels)—and also before nouns that had the grammatical function predicate-object. For example, the sentence "no train" was produced as Eric took the wire man off the train as it was being pushed. Earlier, at Time II, the sentence "no 'chine" occurred after Eric had been told that he couldn't play with the tape recorder. When his mother subsequently entered the room, Eric pointed to the tape recorder saying "no 'chine." The referents of the forms "'chine" and "train" were not negated directly, but they were negated with respect to their function as predicate-objects. Thus, the negative particle "no" appeared only in predicative constructions, in complementary distribution with "no more," which appeared in immediate constituent structure with nouns.

The negative sentences were accounted for in the Eric III grammar as follows:

E : III phrase structure:

1. $S_1 \rightarrow \text{Pivot} \begin{Bmatrix} \text{NP} \\ \text{VP} \end{Bmatrix}$, where Pivot includes "no"

4. $\text{NP} \rightarrow (Q)N$, where Q is the quantifier "more"

Feature rule:

iv. $\text{no} + \text{NP} \rightarrow \text{no} + Q + N$

The utterances "no train," "no 'chine," and also "no more dump-car" (Eric emptying a peg from the dumpcar) were among the few utterances that occurred that involved reduction with deletion of the intervening negated constituent that did not occur in performance.

Again, as in Eric II, "no more noise" occurred more frequently than any other negative sentence. On one occasion "no more noise" occurred when the bridge collapsed; one occurrence of the sentence was anomalous—as beads were being retrieved for the slide. There was one unique 'stereotype' structure: "ə want any shoes." In addition, there were two sentences—"ə find it" and "/jə/ find it"—that appeared to occur with negative intent although the negative element was not expressed; Eric produced both sentences when he was unable to find a block he had been looking for.

In summary, negation was a meaningful cognitive-semantic concept for Eric at Time II and at Time III. The mechanism for the linguistic expression of negation had emerged as a productive syntactic operation, although its function was limited, for the most part, to expression of *nonexistence*, with "no more" used as syntactic operator. Whereas earlier Eric had used two different forms of the negative element in isolation, contrastively, to signal two different semantic functions ("no more" signaled *nonexistence* and "no" signaled *rejection*), when he first began to express *rejection* and *denial* syntactically he used the same, first-learned syntactic operator, "no more," so that semantic differences were not differentiated structurally.

Thus, although Eric had learned something about the different semantic categories of negation, the development of syntactic expression was limited, at first, to syntactic constructions that expressed only one—*nonexistence*—at the same time that the other categories were expressed by isolated "no." Syntactic expression of *rejection* and *denial* began to emerge toward the end of the first phase, but the introduction of the syntactic expression of *rejection* and *denial* was not accompanied by developmental advance in the form of their linguistic expression. Rather, the differentiation of structure that represented the developmental difference between linguistic expression of negation at Time II and Time III was the syntactic occurrence of "no" and "no more" in complementary distribution in the syntactic expression of the category *nonexistence*—the first semantic category expressed syntactically.

7.2.2. Gia I to IV
The grammars that were presented in Chapter 4 for the first two texts collected from Gia did not provide for the derivation of negative sentences. It was pointed out that negation did not appear to have been

learned yet as a concept that could be expressed syntactically in the first two texts, Gia I and II.

The absence of the syntactic process of negation in the Gia grammars may be attributed, as discussed in Chapter 4, to the fact that the syntactic operator "more," signaling recurrence, was fully productive in both noun and predicate constructions. It is possible that this operated somehow to preclude the development of a similarly functioning syntactic operator to signal a contrastive notion (negation) at the same time.

However, there was provision for the syntactic expression of both negation and recurrence in the Kathryn and Eric grammars. But Eric's strategy for learning language was oriented toward the acquisition of simultaneous syntactic operators. That is, Eric's approach to the acquisition of syntax involved learning different markers with different semantic functions that did not differ from one another syntactically— "more" and "no more" occurred in the same syntactic contexts.

In contrast, Gia did not differentiate a class of pivotal syntactic operators in her approach to learning language. Gia learned grammar in terms of the concatenation of categories with grammatical sentence functions, and she differentiated classes of forms on the basis of their categorial function. It was plausible that she was able to learn only one syntactic operator, "more," because such function forms differed grammatically from category forms. Learning an additional class of function forms (which might include "more" and "no" or "no more") would have increased the complexity of her grammatical system, and such an increase in complexity might well have exceeded her cognitive limits at this stage.

However, it was pointed out that Gia and Kathryn were more similar to each other in the acquisition of syntax than they were to Eric. How, then, could the mechanism for expression of both negation and recurrence be explained in Kathryn's grammar? "More," in Kathryn's lexicon, was a member of an adjective form class; a similar class of adjectives did not exist in Gia's lexicon. The form "more" did not operate syntactically in the Kathryn I grammar, as did the negative element "no" or the operator "more" in the Gia grammars. That is, "more" was an attributive constituent in constructions with nouns only at Kathryn I and did not occur in predicate constructions, as did "no" in the Kathryn I grammar and "more" in the Gia grammars.

An explanation for the absence of syntactic expression of negation in the early texts obtained from Gia was problematical. It may be the case that there is an element of 'choice' in what is learned—that children choose to learn certain structures and concepts (perhaps on the basis of such notions as 'need' or 'frequency of exposure')—and that the number of structures that can be learned or *practiced* at any one time is necessarily limited. Thus, having 'chosen' to learn "more" as a syntactic operator, it might have been the case that Gia was unable to attend to syntactic expression of negation at the same time.

There was no evidence that could be used to decide the relative 'need' for sentence negation in the experience of the three children. There was no apparent reason why Eric and Kathryn would need to express negation more than Gia would. Also, the data did not reveal the extent of exposure to negative sentences in the speech the children heard.

At Time III, Gia produced fewer syntactic constructions with a negative element than at Time II and only one utterance expressed negation unequivocally:

(6) G : III (Lois had freed Gia after she had
    gotten stuck climbing onto a chair)   [no more stuck.
                                             no more.   ]

Although Gia produced other sentences that contained a negative element, and the negative element "no more" occurred in isolation at Time III, these utterances were not contrastive—they did not necessarily signal negation. For example, Gia said "no more" as she was stacking blocks, and there was no evidence for an interpretation of negation. She produced the utterance "/nɑt/" while eating lunch and shaking her head negatively; her mother interpreted this at the time as "not hot." The following occurred several minutes later:

(7) G : III (Gia eating lunch at 1:00
    P.M.; Mommy and Lois in kitchen
    with her)   morning. morning.

    Good morning.   > no morning.

Gia might have referred to the fact that the time was early afternoon and not morning, but it was also possible that the appropriateness of the reference was fortuitous or otherwise associated with Gia's eating lunch rather than breakfast. "No morning" was not considered interpretable. These four utterances were the only constructions with a negative element that occurred at Time III. It appeared that Gia had not yet learned syntactic expression of negation at the time of the first three observations.

Gia used "no" as a single word to express negation in the first three texts; the functional distribution of occurrence of "no" is presented in Table 7.4. Generally, Gia used isolated "no" to signal *rejection* most

Table 7.4. Functional Distribution of "no," Gia I to III

	Nonexistence	Rejection	Denial	Indeterminate
Gia I	2 (1)	9 (1)	0	3
Gia II	2 (1)	8 (2)	(9)	2
Gia III	(1)	2 (5)	0	4 (3)

Note: Numbers in parentheses refer to utterances that occurred after a prior question or comment from the receiver.

often. However, at Time II there was frequent use of "no" to signal *denial* in response to questions. This high incidence of "no" signaling denial was due to an effort to 'test' the reliability of Gia's responses to yes-no questions by asking specific questions about the identity of familiar objects. For example, a clown was held up and Gia was asked "Is this a cookie?" Gia's response "no" was classed as a *denial*. The reason for attempting to test the reliability of yes-no responses had to do with the fact that "yes" was a far more frequent utterance than "no" in the second and third texts: 13 occurrences of "yes" at Time I, 145 at Time II, and 137 at Time III.

Gia tended to respond "yes" to almost all yes-no questions. She also responded "yes" to repetitions of her utterances that were presented with rising intonation contour—a question form that attempted to verify what she had said—for example:

(8) G : II (Gia had picked up the train and
     it came apart)   ----train. more.

     (giving the train to Lois)   more.

     What?   more train.

     More train?   > yes.

In similar situations, Eric would produce a subsequent utterance or, less often, repeat his previous utterance—for example:

(9) E : II (Eric watching a cloud of dust on
     the building lot across the street)   hot. hot.

     Hot?   > hot. hot.

Occasionally, Gia said "yes" as a direction—for example, giving the investigator the train to fix, saying "yes." The "yes" responses to questions were sometimes inappropriate; that is, in 14 of the 145 "yes" responses that occurred at Gia II, the context of speech events appeared to call for expression of negation instead. For the most part, "yes" responses had an almost 'automatic' aspect; presentation of an utterance with a rising intonation contour triggered a "yes" response. However, it was usually the case that there was not a meaningful choice available, that "yes" was the only appropriate response, as, for example, when Gia's utterance was repeated to her for verification. But in those situations where Gia was given a choice—for example, "Do you want to read this book?"—Gia responded "yes," whether or not she subsequently complied. In the same situation, Eric simply complied—without expressing agreement—or said "no."

Syntactic Negation at Gia IV. Gia produced six negative utterances at Time IV; these are presented in Table 7.5.

Table 7.5. Categorization of Negative Utterances, Gia IV

Nonexistence	Rejection	Denial	Indeterminate
no more pictures no open it (2) no open the wallet	no more no (15)	 no (4)	not here no (4)

Note: Numbers in parentheses refer to the number of times the utterance occurred, discounting immediate repetitions.

It was not clear at the time what was meant by "not here," but the five other utterances were interpretable and signaled negation. The data at Time IV were no less meager than data obtained in the earlier sessions, but interpretation of these few sentences was unequivocally expression of negation for all but one utterance ("not here").

The functional distribution of "no" in isolation included 15 instances of *rejection*, 4 instances of *denial*, 4 utterances that were indeterminate, and no instances of "no" expressing nonexistence.

In summary, negation was not expressed syntactically in the first three texts collected from Gia. She did use "no" as a single-word utterance, expressing rejection most often, but the occurrence of "no" as a single-word utterance was far less frequent than the occurrence of "yes" at Time II and Time III. In the fourth text, it was possible to draw the tentative conclusion that Gia was able to use syntactic expression of negation, but the structure was only marginally productive. Although not tested, there was evidence that Gia understood negative sentences—she generally attended to negative directions; but evidence of a similar competence in linguistic expression was slight.

Even though the numbers of utterances were small, four of the five negative sentences (including "no more" as a 'sentence') in Table 7.5 signaled *nonexistence*, so that the order of emergence of linguistic expression of the three semantic categories of negation appeared, tentatively, to match the order observed in Eric's early development of negation.

7.2.3. Kathryn I
The negative sentences that Kathryn produced at Time I were presented in Table 6.2, Chapter 6. These utterances have been categorized semantically and are presented once again in Table 7.6 for the purpose of the present discussion.

Table 7.6. Categorization of Negative Utterances, Kathryn I

Nonexistence	Rejection	Denial
no pocket	no dirty soap	no dirty
no pocket in there	ə no chair	
no sock	no sock	
no fit (7)		
no zip		
no turn		
no close		
no window		
ə no		
no (11)	no (24)	no (3)

Note: Numbers in parentheses refer to the number of times the utterance occurred in the text, discounting immediate repetitions.

Kathryn used syntactic negation to express *nonexistence* most productively. She had also begun to express *rejection* and *denial* syntactically; these sentences were few in number and did not differ in structure from those negative sentences that signaled *nonexistence*.

There were also two utterances at Time I that were not classed as negative sentences: "no Mommy" and "no outside." These sentences were extracted from the text and included in the original analysis of sentences for semantic categorization because they appeared, superficially, to be negative sentences—they included a negative marker and they lacked final contour or open juncture after "no." As discussed in Chapter 6, once the contexts in which these utterances occurred was evaluated, it turned out that the negative marker "no" was an anaphoric, external element that applied to a foregone utterance or situation. This anaphoric "no" did not have effect on the rest of the utterance with which it was juxtaposed. Neither "Mommy" nor "outside" were being negated—Kathryn wanted Mommy to comb her hair, Kathryn wanted to go outside.

Kathryn also used "no" as a single-word utterance; the distribution of "no" in terms of function was 11 instances of *nonexistence* (4 in response to questions), 24 instances of *rejection* (15 in response to questions or comments); 3 instances of *denial* (2 in response to comments), and 17 indeterminate instances of "no" (6 in response to questions). As was true with Eric and Gia, "no," when interpretable, signaled *rejection* most often.

Whereas Gia used the reciprocal form "yes" far more frequently than "no" and Eric did not use a reciprocal form at all, Kathryn used two contrasting forms—"no" and affirmative "O.K." There were 55 instances of "no" and 43 instances of "O.K." (including 1 expression of "yes"). When questioned about Kathryn's use of "O.K." rather than "yes," her mother reported that this was a "new stage"—earlier, Kathryn had used only "yes."

7.2.4. Comparison of the Three Children and Summary of Phase 1

The fact that Gia rarely expressed negation was the important difference among the children. She produced fewer constructions with a negative element at Time III than she had at Time II, and all constructions with a negative element in texts I, II, and III were indeterminate in interpretation more often than they could be interpreted as negative. Negation was still a marginal structure at Gia IV, but the constructions that did occur could be interpreted as negative and tended to be appropriate. Although Gia evidently understood negative sentences in the speech she heard, negative constructions were not productive in her own speech. In contrast, Eric and Kathryn each had developed a productive system of syntactic negation that was primitive in structural complexity and did not differentiate semantic function. The children's general linguistic maturity, as measured superficially by mean length of utterance, was essentially similar, although Gia's utterances were somewhat longer than either Eric's or Kathryn's. An account of development in the three semantic categories by the three children in Phase 1 is presented in Figure 7.1.

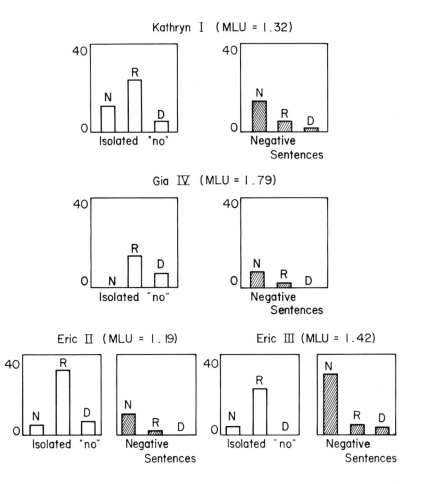

Figure 7.1. Phase 1 in the development of negation: frequency of isolated "no" and negative sentences in the semantic categories nonexistence (N), rejection (R), and denial (D).

The structural form of these first negative sentences was a negative operator in pre-position before nominal or predicate forms. Sentence-subjects were not expressed, even though the children produced affirmative sentences that included sentence-subjects. Negated predicates were reduced—there was deletion of verb or object forms when one or the other occurred in production—even though verb-object phrases were the most productive constructions in the texts of all three children. The syntactic operation of negation served to increase sentence complexity, which resulted in a reduction of the surface structure of sentences—as discussed at length in Chapter 6. The existence of the deleted formatives in the underlying structure of the reduced sentences was postulated on the basis of (1) behavioral and contextual evidence, which revealed that the negative element actually had effect on unexpressed intervening constituents in such sentences as "no window," "no chair" in Kathryn's texts, and "no 'chine," "no more dumpcar," and "no train" in Eric's texts; and (2) the productivity of sentence-subjects in the Kathryn I text.

The grammars that were presented earlier for Kathryn and Eric accounted for the operation of negation, although the syntactic mechanism was different for each. In Kathryn's phrase structure, the negative element appeared as a syntactic operator before the major category constituents—predicate NP and VP—and it was possible to infer an unrealized underlying structure with the grammatical function sentence-subject.

In Eric's phrase structure, there was limited evidence for postulating the occurrence of a subject node before the negative element; subject forms were less productive at Eric III than at Kathryn I and did not occur at Eric II. Interpretation of negative sentences did not depend on the representation of an underlying constituent with the grammatical function sentence-subject.

At Eric II, "no more," was included as a pivot with privileges of occurrence before noun forms only. At Eric III, the negative element "no" was included as an element in the pivot class with effect on sentence NP and VP. Its operation on NP required the specification of Q (the quantifier "more") in the derivation of NP; negation of noun forms at Eric III was specified as negation of recurrence. Nonexistent objects were those that had existed previously. An analogous distinction exists in the adult model between "no bananas," bananas simply do not exist, and the partitive "no more bananas," bananas had existed previous to their nonexistence. Eric had not made this distinction as yet; the nonexistence of objects had only the one dimension for him—nonexistence after his previous experience of it.

All three children used "no" as a single word to signal *rejection* most often. Eric did not use a reciprocal form "yes," Gia used "yes" far more frequently than "no," and Kathryn used both affirmative "O.K." and negative "no."

The earliest negative sentences expressed *nonexistence* most often. Kathryn and Eric had begun to express *rejection* and *denial* syntactically, but sentences signaling *nonexistence* were far more frequent. Both children, although they had begun to differentiate negative sentences semantically, used the same syntactic structure for sentences with different semantic intent. Even though Eric had differentiated two negative forms in isolation, "no more" and "no," in earlier expressions of *nonexistence* and *rejection*, he did not differentiate these same semantic categories in the earliest syntactic constructions. The negative sentences that Gia produced expressed *nonexistence*.

At the close of Phase 1 in the semantic and syntactic development of negation, there was evidence that the children knew something about three different semantic categories of negation—they were able to express *nonexistence, rejection,* and, less often, *denial*. The children were able to produce syntactic constructions that signaled *nonexistence*, but for the most part, expression of *rejection* and *denial* was limited to the single-word utterance "no." As syntactic expression of rejection and denial began to emerge, the syntactic structure of the linguistic expression was the same for the three categories.

Thus, in the early development of negation it was possible to differentiate three alternative interpretations of negative utterances. But the acquisition of linguistic expression was limited at first to only one productive syntactic structure in the speech of each child, and there was no structural differentiation of the three semantic categories.

7.3. Structural Differentiation of Semantic Categories of Negation: Phase 2

The children had begun to use sentences that expressed semantic notions of *rejection* and *denial* in Phase 1, and the syntactic structure was not rich enough to distinguish these sentences from sentences that signaled *nonexistence* and occurred far more frequently.

The first phase was realized in those texts of Kathryn (Time I) and Eric (Time III) in which mean length of utterance was less than 1.5 morphemes and in the text of Gia (Time IV) in which mean length of utterance was 1.79 morphemes. At the conclusion of Phase 2, mean length of utterance was less than 3.0 morphemes for all three children: 2.83 at Kathryn III, 2.84 at Eric VI, and 2.75 at Gia VI.

The distinction between Phase 1 and Phase 2 was most apparent in a comparison of the negative sentences produced by Kathryn at Time I with those at Times II and III.

7.3.1. Syntactic Negation at Kathryn II

There was an increase in the number of interpretable negative sentences from 19 at Kathryn I to 62 at Kathryn II; these have been categorized in terms of function and presented in Table 7.7. Several developmental changes distinguished the sentences at Time II from those that had occurred at Time I.

First, syntactic expression of all three semantic categories was productive at Kathryn II. Although sentences expressing *nonexistence* were most frequent, there was a substantial increase in the number expressing *rejection* and *denial*.

Structurally, 34 of these 62 sentences (the bracketed sentences in each category—for example, "no skirt," "no fit," "no truck") were similar to the negative sentences at Time I and would have been generated by the grammar that was proposed for the earlier Kathryn I text:

K : I phrase structure:

$$1. \ S \rightarrow Nom + Ng \begin{Bmatrix} NP \\ VP \end{Bmatrix}$$

with obligatory operation of the reduction rules as specified in the transformational component:

$$(2)(a) \ X - Ng - Y \Rightarrow Ng - Y$$
$$(b) \ \# - X - Y - Z \Rightarrow \# - x_i - x_j$$

The inclusion of a negative element ("no") in the underlying structure of a sentence at Time I necessitated reduction in its surface structure. Sentence-subjects were deleted obligatorily, and complexity after the negative element—such as inclusion of verb and complement—was also reduced. Having chosen to express negation, there was an obligatory structural constraint on production of the sentence at Time I.

The remaining sentences in Table 7.7 could not have been generated by the Kathryn I grammar because of two important changes: (1) production of the negated predicate was more structurally complete with inclusion of both the verb and predicate complement—for example, "no lock ə door," "no find ə tank"; and (2) sentence-subjects were expressed—for example, "Kathryn no shoe," "Kathryn no like celery."

Table 7.7. Categorization of Negative Sentences, Kathryn II

Nonexistence	Rejection	Denial
⌈ no skirt ⌉	⌈ no bear book ⌉	⌈ no Wendy (2) ⌉
no cup	no meat	no candle
no wagon	no slide away	no tire
no books	⌊ no go outside ⌋	no truck
no driver in the car		no ready
no hat	no put in there	no plop
⌊ all gone magazine ⌋	no make ə truck	no Jocelyn ⌋
Lois no hat	no ə house lambs	
Kathryn no shoe (2)	no want	this ə no Lois
Mommy no picture there	no want this	
	ə no want ə go now	no Daddy hungry
⌈ no fit (8) ⌉		
no fit here		
no stand up		
no under		
no go in		
no go first		
⌊ no go in there (2) ⌋		
no lock ə door		
no find ə tank		
no have ə this		
no like celery, Mommy		
this ə no goes		
man no go in there		
Kathryn no /fɪk/ this		
Kathryn no fix this		
Kathryn no like celery		
Kathryn not quite through		
Lois ə no coffee		
me like coffee		
Kathryn have ə socks on		
can't see (2)		
ə can't see		

Note: The underlined words are those that occurred in an immediately preceding utterance produced by someone other than the child. Utterances within brackets are those that could be accounted for by the grammar at Kathryn I. Numbers in parentheses refer to number of occurrences in the text, discounting immediate repetitions.

However, these changes in the allowed structural complexity of produced sentences applied only to sentences that signaled *nonexistence*; not only did these sentences occur with greatest frequency in the corpus, but they were also the most structurally complete. There was no production of sentence-subject in expression of *rejection,* although the understood subject was Kathryn and "Kathryn" (or "me") occurred as sentence-subject in six sentences that expressed *nonexistence.* The most grammatically primitive sentences were those that signaled *denial*—these were most similar in form to the early negative sentences at Kathryn I and were generally only two morphemes.

The reduction transformation that had operated obligatorily at Kathryn I assumed optional status at Kathryn II. Three-term subject-verb-object strings occurred in performance in affirmative sentences; it was significant that they occurred only in that category of negative sentences that had been most productive in the preceding corpus—sentences that signaled *nonexistence*—but not in the categories *rejection* and *denial,* which had not been productive previously. In the discussion in Chapter 6 of the constraints that motivated reduction, it was pointed out that those structures that were more recently learned (in terms of their productivity in performance) were also those that were most vulnerable to deletion. The evidence just presented gives further support to that conclusion.

However, the constraint on structural complexity in performance was still operative, as demonstrated in a comparison of the three sentences "Kathryn no shoe" (two occurrences) and "Kathryn have ə socks on," which occurred in similar speech events—Kathryn was barefoot. Similarly, the verb form "want" was productive and occurred frequently in affirmative sentences—it had also occurred at Kathryn I —but it was expressed in only three sentences that signaled *rejection,* although its occurrence in the underlying structure was easily postulated from the contextual and behavioral data. For example, Kathryn did not *want* the bear book, Kathryn did not *want* to make a truck. Although a grammar has not been constructed as yet for the later text at Kathryn II, the negative sentences at Time II appeared to be among the least structurally complex sentences that occurred.

Another productive sentence type at Kathryn II that had only marginal occurrence at Kathryn I was the expression of anaphoric "no" with an affirmative sentence—for example, "No Kathryn want play with self" and "No Lois do it." These sentences were discussed at length in Chapter 6—but it is pertinent here to point out again that sentences with the structural description *"no" plus affirmative sentence* were generally more structurally complete than the great majority of the negative sentences that occurred at the same time. The negative element did not apply semantically to the sentence and so did not affect (that is, reduce) its structure.

The form of the negative element was invariant at Kathryn II. As at Kathryn I, the form was "no," with marginal occurrence of "can't" in two sentences expressing *nonexistence.*

In summary, there was a marked increase in the number of negative sentences at Kathryn II. The functional distribution of these sentences followed the distributional trend observed at Kathryn I: the greatest number of sentences that occurred signaled *nonexistence.* But whereas *rejection* and *denial* were marginal at Time I, syntactic expression of these categories was productive at Time II. *Nonexistence*—the only category that was productive at Kathryn I and the category that occurred most frequently at Kathryn II—was also the category that was most structurally complex in performance. Sentences expressing *denial*—the category that was least productive, with only one instance at Time I—were also the least complex negative sentences at Time II.

The syntactic placement of the negative element depended upon the effect of negation within the sentence. The negative element occurred immediately previous to the structure over which it had immediate effect—in prepredicate position, following the sentence-subject. In those sentences where the negative element preceded the sentence-subject, the behavioral and contextual interpretation revealed that the negative reference was anaphoric. Such sentences were actually affirmative and not within the scope of the negative effect, even though the negative element was produced without junctural contour. The one exception was the last sentence in Table 7.7 expressing *denial*: "no Daddy hungry."

Kathryn's negative sentences at Time II, as at Time I, could be described as having occurred in Period A in Bellugi's (1967) account of negation: mean length of utterance was still below 2.0 morphemes; the shape of the negative element was limited to one form—"no"; and there was no inflection of nouns and verbs. However, contrary to Bellugi's observation that the negative element was not positioned within the sentence, expression of sentence-subject in Kathryn's negative sentences always preceded expression of the negative element. Where the negative element preceded the subject of a sentence, the sentence was affirmative. Thus, evaluation of the semantics of these sentences revealed that different uses of "no" were marked by placement of the negative element before or after sentence-subjects.

7.3.2. Syntactic Negation at Kathryn III

Syntactic Expression of Nonexistence. There were fewer sentences expressing *nonexistence* at Kathryn III—25 sentences, as compared with

42 at Kathryn II; these have been extracted from the total number of negative sentences that occurred at Kathryn III and presented in Table 7.8.

There were still a few sentences that were similar in structure to the earliest negative sentences at Kathryn I: "no boy" and "no children." The remaining sentences were similar to the sentences that expressed *nonexistence* at Kathryn II in the inclusion of sentence-subjects and predicate complement constructions with verbs. But the sentences in Table 7.8 also differed from those that expressed *nonexistence* at Kathryn II in two important respects. The proforms "I," "this (one)," or "that" replaced the noun forms that had occurred with the same grammatical function, sentence-subject, at Kathryn II. Further, the form of the negative element was variable. In addition to "no"—the only form at Kathryn I and II—there were alternative forms: "not," "do" (with negative intent), "don't," "doesn't," and "can't."

In contrast to the syntactic placement of the negative element in all the sentences discussed so far, there were two sentences in which "no" occurred in sentence-final position. These appeared to be proforms analogous to "none" in the adult model:

(10) K:III (Kathryn had discovered
     a label on the underside of one of
     the blocks; she picked up a
     different block to see if it had a
     similar label, which it did not)   > this one ə no.

(11) (Picked up a third block as in
     (10); block did not have a label)   > this one have no.
     (Picking up fourth block and
     seeing label on it)   this one have!

There was no immediately apparent motivation for the variation in the form of the negative element in expression of nonexistence. All were present tense forms. Kathryn was the specified actor-agent in sentences with "can't," "don't," and "not." The verb "fit" (the most frequent verb in previous negative sentences at Time I and Time II) occurred with "not," "don't," "do," and "doesn't" (but not with "no," which had always negated "fit" previously).

The sentences expressing *nonexistence* in Table 7.8 are similar to the sentences in the second stage in the acquisition of negation, Period B, described by Bellugi (1967), where the negative element occurred with alternative forms. But as observed also by Bellugi, the different forms

Table 7.8. Negative Sentences that Signaled Nonexistence, Kathryn III

no boy	ə doesn't fit
no children	this not fits!
no more choochoo train	this one don't fit
no part that	this one do fits (2)
ə no hand there	this one don't fits (2)
	this one don't
no bring lambs	that's not ə turn
no stand up	Kathryn not go over here
not going away (2)	ə can't find ə saucer
	I can't open it
this one ə no	I don't go sleep
this one have no	Mommy no play 'corder

Note: Numbers in parentheses refer to number of occurrences in the text, discounting immediate repetitions.

of the negative element "don't," "doesn't," "can't" were not transforms of the auxiliary formatives "do" or "can." Development of the verbal auxiliary in affirmative sentences was limited at Kathryn II to two verb inflections: progressive "-ing," which was productive without "be," and present tense "-s" ("here comeses! here comes!"), which was marginal. The forms "that," "it," "here," "there," "where," and "what" occurred also with final "-s"; the two forms of each were in apparent free variation, as at Kathryn II. But the past tense "-ed" did not occur, and there was no occurrence of forms of "be" or modals before verbs, except occasional occurrence of "this is" and "I'll." The form "do" functioned only as a main verb and was not inflected for person or tense.

However, in two respects, the children described by Bellugi in Period B appeared to be linguistically more mature than Kathryn was at Time III. First, Kathryn had not learned the person and number paradigms for personal pronouns as had the subjects Bellugi studied in Period B. The only productive personal pronoun forms she used in affirmative sentences were the first person alternants "I," "me," "my," and "mine." Second, although progressive "-ing" was productive at Kathryn III in affirmative sentences, it was marginal in negative sentences. This second distinction was important because Bellugi reported that the newly introduced alternative forms of the negative element, "don't" and "can't," were restricted in her data to occurrence before nonprogressive main verbs, whereas "no" and "not" were used before verbs with "-ing." With rare exceptions, however, progressive verbs were affirmative at Kathryn III.

The remaining negative sentences that were obtained at Kathryn III in the categories *rejection* and *denial* are presented in Table 7.9. While both categories continued to be productive at Time III, the number of sentences that signaled *denial*—previously the least productive category—far exceeded the number that expressed *rejection*. Syntactic expression of *denial* occurred as frequently as expression of *nonexistence*.

Table 7.9. Negative Sentences that Signaled Rejection and Denial, Kathryn III

Rejection	Denial
no going home	no Eric
no put it back	not making muffins
	ə not break it
don't get my room	I not tired
don't want go in other room	I not have some fruit
	this man not brother
I ə not go in bathroom	not magic
I don't want play with Lois	that not " " 'body home' "*
I don't want get those ə my room	that not cat
I don't want to comb hairs	that not ə pot
I don't want those shoes	that's not tea
I don't need pants off	that's not scramble
ə don't like that	this not ə pancake
	this not ə doughnut
	that's not ə apple
	that's not apple
	that's not ə man
	this ə not brother
	that not ə sister
	this not ə boy
	that's not ə sister
	that's not ə lady
	that not baabaa black sheep
	that not ə ugly
	that not ə rabbits house
	that not blue one
	that's not ə pink one
	that not brother
	that not

* Kathryn was referring here to the title of the book "Anybody at Home?" which she always referred to as " 'Body Home↓."

Note: The underlined words are those that occurred in an immediately preceding utterance produced by someone other than the child.

In each category there were a few sentences that were similar to the earlier syntactic structures at Time I and Time II: "no put it back" and "no Eric." However, the great majority of the sentences that signaled *rejection* and *denial* were substantially different in syntactic structure from the sentences that occurred with the same functions at Kathryn II. In each of the categories, more complex structures replaced the simpler structures observed earlier, and the sentences within each category were remarkably similar in form. The sentences arranged in Table 7.9 confirmed Bellugi's (1967) observation of "across-the-board appearances of some aspects of grammatical systems in the language, often accompanied by a great rise in frequency of structural types."

Syntactic Expression of Rejection. Just as there were progressive changes in the development of expression of *nonexistence* at Time II, there were significant developmental changes in the form of expression of *rejection* at Time III.

First, sentence-subjects were produced in sentences that expressed *rejection*. Whereas at Time II the understood subject (on the basis of contextual and behavioral information) was Kathryn, sentence-subjects never occurred in the production of sentences that signaled *rejection*— even though the first person subject was expressed in those sentences that signaled *nonexistence* at the same time. At Time III, the understood subject was Kathryn in all but two of the sentences that signaled *rejection* and was expressed (as in expressions of *nonexistence*) with the pronominal form "I."

A second development in the expression of *rejection* was the expression of the catenative verb, "want" or "need," on which the negative element had a direct effect. Such a catenative form had been postulated as a deleted intervening constituent at Kathryn II; "want" had been productive in affirmative sentences and occurred marginally in expression of *rejection* at that time.

However, in the two least complex sentences that expressed *rejection* —"no going home" and "no put it back"—there was no expressed sentence-subject, there was no catenative verb, and the form of the negative element was the primitive "no" (rather than "don't," as in all other sentences in the category). It was also the case that these two sentences involved negation of an event in which someone other than Kathryn was actor-agent. That is, it was the investigator who was going home and putting something back. Thus, Kathryn learned syntactic expression of *rejection* first as expressing negation of her own desire or wish to have or to do something. This was true of all of the previous sentences that signaled rejection, as well as of most such sentences at Time III. As a result, development of the linguistic expression of rejection proceeded toward expression of the first person sentence-subject and the operation of negation on a catenative verb form before a predicative construction at Time III. After gaining a certain competence with this structure, Kathryn began to express *rejection* of an event that involved someone else as actor-agent; in doing so, she reverted to the earlier, more generalized syntactic structure—as in "no going home" and "no put it back." It would be expected that the form of this sentence type in the subsequent texts would approach the adult form of the negative imperative "don't go home" and "don't put it back," where the sentence-subject is the unexpressed "you." But at Kathryn III, use of the negative element "don't" was restricted, in expression of *rejection*, to those sentences in which Kathryn was the subject of the catenative verb (on which the negative element had effect) and the main verb as well.

This interpretation of Kathryn's development of rejection coincides with the description of the semantic contrast "internal-external" proposed by McNeill and McNeill (1967): the negative element in Japanese, "*iya*... conveys the idea of 'I don't want,' and its use, therefore, depends on *internal desire*, or the lack of it." McNeill and McNeill concluded that this was the second category of negation acquired by their Japanese subject after "existence-truth." This was also the second category of negation that Kathryn acquired—after *nonexistence*. The frequency of occurrence of syntactic expression of *rejection* increased from Time I to Time II. Although frequency remained constant at Time III, the produced structure of these sentences had increased in complexity at Kathryn II, and complexity increased again at Kathryn III.

Syntactic Expression of Denial. The linguistic expression of the semantic category *denial* developed last—after *nonexistence* and *rejection*. There had been only one instance of denial at Kathryn I, and although there was an increase in frequency, with ten sentences at Time II, the structure of the ten sentences was the same as the one sentence that signaled *denial* at Time I.

At Kathryn III, *denial* was the most productive category of negative sentences that occurred. It should be pointed out that the substantial increase in the number of these sentences was not contrived. That is, there was no attempt to 'test' Kathryn's ability to express *denial* (as described subsequently in the attempt to 'test' Gia's responses to yes-no questions at Gia V).

In addition to the substantial increase in the frequency of sentences that signaled *denial*, there were significant changes in structural complexity as well. The syntactic structure that Kathryn had used to express *denial* at Times I and II was the same as the first example at Time III in Table 7.9: "no Eric." However, this was the only instance of the primitive structure in the 29 sentences that signaled *denial* at Time III. In all the other sentences, there was only one form of the negative element: "not." In 3 of these sentences, there was inclusion of nominal subjects: "I not tired," "I not have some fruit," and "this man not brother." In 3 other sentences, there was no expression of sentence-subject. But in all the remaining 22 sentences, the sentence-subject was a form of the demonstrative pronoun: "this," "that," or "thats."

In the preceding text at Kathryn II, the occurrence of demonstrative pronouns in sentence-initial position with a predicate nominative was one of the most productive constructions. Examples of the 308 occurrences of this sentence type presented in Table 3.1 of Chapter 3 included "this ə slide," "that ə baby," "this my tiger book." Only one of these 308 sentences expressed negation at Kathryn II; all were affirmative sentences except for "this ə no Lois," which occurred in response to the question "Is this Kathryn's, or is this Lois's?" At the time when this sentence type was one of the most productive structures in her grammar, Kathryn never used it to express negation as she did productively six weeks later, at Time III, to signal *denial*—for example, "that not ə sister," "this not ə doughnut."

This restriction on the use of demonstrative pronouns and negation at Kathryn II was not simply a constraint on sentence length; such sentences as "this ə my Kathryn toys ə floor," "this ə Mommy's fuzzy sweater" occurred at Time II. The fact that "no" was not included as one of the 'permitted' number of words in an utterance could not be attributed simply to some sort of memory limitation. Although Kathryn expressed the semantic concept of *denial* in such utterances as "no candle," "no Wendy" and also used the syntactic structure that subsequently signaled *denial*, there was no evident relation between function and ultimate surface structure in Kathryn's production at Time II. Subsequently, however, at Time III, the linguistic structure and the cognitive semantic concept were somehow joined in production. Thus, the semantics of *denial* (meaning) and the ultimate structure that signaled *denial* (form) existed at Time II but did not exist in concert until Time III.

Progressive Differentiation of the Negative Element. Of the variants of the negative element in the speech Kathryn presumably heard, she chose one form, "no," as the negative element for the earliest syntactic expression of negation: to signal *nonexistence*. At Time I and Time II, when negative sentences began to express *rejection* and *denial*, Kathryn used the same negative element, "no," in the linguistic expression of all three semantic categories. Subsequently, when she began to differentiate the form of the negative element and when the variants "not," "don't," "can't," and "doesn't" appeared in negative sentences, "don't" was used almost exclusively to signal *rejection* and "not" was used exclusively in sentences that signaled *denial*. All the variants appeared in the group of sentences that expressed *nonexistence*.

It is not the case that expression of *rejection* is limited, in the adult model, to constructions with "don't," or that expression of *denial* is limited to constructions with "not." It may be true that rejection of a desire to do or to have something is most often expressed by the structure "I don't want," but there are alternatives—for example, "I won't." Virtually all Kathryn's sentences that signaled *denial* referred to statements of identity (for example, "that's not scramble" in response to "doesn't that look like scrambled egg?" referring to the yellow wheel on a plate). The same structure would occur in contradiction of a statement of identity in the adult model, but, again, there are alternatives—for example, "It isn't a scrambled egg," or the adult might respond to the question with "it doesn't" (look like a scrambled egg).

The form of the negative element in the adult model depends upon the structure of the verbal auxiliary, and the form of the auxiliary directly reflects the notions of tense, aspect, and agreement with subject number and person. Kathryn's linguistic expressions of *rejection* and *denial* were limited, in most cases, to only one dimension (or none) of each of these notions. For example, present tense prevailed in all the sentences, Kathryn was the agent of rejection, and a form of the demonstrative pronoun was the subject in expressions of *denial*.

The status of the verbal element in expressions of *denial* and *rejection* was quite simple. The verb on which the negative element had effect in expression of *rejection* was limited to a stative catenative verb—"want." In most of the expressions of *denial*, there was no verb (exceptions were "not making muffins," "ə not break it," "I not have some fruit"). A form of "be," on which the negative element would have effect in the adult structure, was not included in any of the sentences expressing *denial*. The copular "be" was not yet productive in affirmative sentences, and there was no contrastive notion to account for the alternation of "that" and "that's" in the text.

The relatively homogeneous structures used for statements of *rejection* or *denial* limited the form of the negative element as well. Kathryn learned a particular form ("don't" or "not") as the negative element in a particular structure (for expression of *rejection* or *denial*). In contrast, expression of *nonexistence* involved a number of variables. In addition to nominal negation in reference to objects that did not exist, there was predicate negation expressing nonoccurrence of events. In predicate negation, there was reference to both first and third person agents and negation of predicates with both action and stative verbs. Kathryn attempted to express corresponding variation in the form of the negative element in expression of *nonexistence* with the modal forms "don't" and "can't."

It was also possible that the homogeneous structures and forms of the negative element that Kathryn learned for expressing *rejection* and *denial* were the most frequent structures with these functions in the negative sentences she heard. However, there is no available count of most frequent structures in the adult model or, more specifically, in the speech Kathryn heard.

The effect may also have been developmental. Because linguistic expression of *nonexistence* was differentiated and learned first and *rejection* and *denial* were learned subsequently, the negative sentences at Time III may have reflected the fact that Kathryn also recognized the potentiality for variation in structure and attempted to express it in *nonexistence* before recognizing possibilities for variation in the forms of *rejection* and *denial*.

The important fact was that the differences in the form of the negative element observed at Time III, after occurrence of a single form "no" at Time I and Time II, was not simply a matter of free variation. On the contrary, progressive differentiation in the form of the negative element was a functionally motivated variation that was directly related to the linguistic expression of the three semantic categories—*nonexistence*, *rejection*, and *denial*.

In summary, Kathryn learned the syntactic expression of the semantic categories of negation in the order (1) *nonexistence*, (2) *rejection*, (3) *denial*. Although she had already begun to express *rejection* and *denial* in negative sentences at the time of the first observation, the fact that *nonexistence* was expressed most frequently at Time I and subsequently developed in syntactic complexity before the other two categories at Time II, provided evidence for the conclusion that *nonexistence* was the first category expressed syntactically.

At Time II the occurrence of sentences signaling *rejection* was as frequent as sentences that expressed *denial*, but there was an accompanying increase in structural complexity in *rejection* while the structure of *denial* at Time II was most primitive—the same structure used initially to express *nonexistence*. Subsequently, at Time III, although the number of sentences expressing *rejection* remained constant, there was further increase in structural complexity. However, the most significant change at Time III was a 200 percent increase in the number of sentences that expressed *denial*—accompanied by a substantial change in structural complexity.

The conclusions that have been drawn from the data collected from Kathryn were confirmed by the data collected over a longer period of time from Eric and Gia. But just as the children differed in their rates of acquisition of syntactic negation, there were substantive, although relatively minor, differences among them as well.

7.3.3. Syntactic Negation, Eric IV to VI

The fourth, fifth, and sixth observations of Eric approximated the same developmental period that has just been described as Phase 2 in Kathryn's development of negation.

Eric IV. All the negative sentences that occurred at Time IV have been categorized and are presented in Table 7.10. Sentences that signaled

Table 7.10. Categorization of Negative Sentences, Eric IV

Nonexistence	Rejection	Denial
ə no more	no more tank	no, not blue
ə no more cleaner	no more train	
no more light (2)	no more book	
no more lights	no more noise	
no more cleaner (2)	ə no read ə book	
no more pieces (2)		
no more choochoo train		
no more 'chine		
no more people		
no more man		
no fit /tu/		
no↑·i fit		
no wheels		
no ə think so		
train wheels /tu/ none		

Note: Numbers in parentheses refer to number of occurrences in the text, discounting immediate repetitions. The underlined words are those that occurred in an immediately preceding utterance produced by someone other than the child.

nonexistence continued to occur most frequently in the text, and *denial* was still a marginal class, with only one instance (a decrease from three occurrences at Eric III). There was an increase in the number of sentences that signaled *rejection*; this was the significant development at Time IV—the emergence of *rejection* as a syntactically productive category. However, sentences that expressed *rejection* were not differentiated formally from the other negative sentences that signaled *nonexistence*.

Eric continued to use two forms of the negative element "no" and "no more" in complementary distribution as at Time III : "no" operated in predicative constructions, and "no more" appeared in immediate constituent structure with nouns.

There were no changes in the produced structural complexity of negative sentences, although mean length of utterance increased from 1.42 at Time III to 1.69 at Time IV. Even though sentence-subjects and verbs with predicate complements were fully productive in affirmative sentences, they were not yet expressed in negative sentences.

There were also several unique negative structures, as in all the previous texts from Eric: "no ə think so" (an attempt at a familiar phrase), "train wheels /tu/ none"[1] (an attempt at the negative pronominal form in response to the question "Does the train have wheels?"), and "no, not blue," the only occurrence of "not" (to signal *denial*).

Eric V. There was a substantial increase in the number of negative sentences from 24 at Time IV to 56 at Time V; the sentences that were produced at Time V have been categorized and are presented in Table 7.11.

There was no difference between Time IV and Time V in the relative frequency of occurrence of negative sentences in the three semantic categories. Sentences signaling *nonexistence* occurred most often, and *rejection* was expressed less often, but productively, while *denial* was still not productive. But whereas there was no change in the status of the three categories in terms of relative productivity, there were important changes in the complexity of sentences expressing *nonexistence* and *rejection*.

---

[1] The form "/tu/" occurred frequently in the fourth and fifth texts, with apparent confusion between the homophonous forms "too" and "two," as demonstrated in the example given in Chapter 2: E: V "man ə good boy. /tu/. /tu/ shoe. man ə good boy /tu/. /tu/ shoes/." The utterance "train wheels /tu/ none" at Time IV was part of an extensive speech event in which Eric was comparing the train (which had no wheels) with the car (which did have wheels) and trying to express the difference between them.

Table 7.11. Categorization of Negative Sentences, Eric V

Nonexistence	Rejection	Denial
no more ball	no more cluckcluck	no fire engine
no more tank	no bib	no more fire engine
no more 'chine (3)	no piece ə clay nose	ə no piggies
no more birdie		
no more water	no flush	
no more water, Mommy	no have it	
no more lamb	no throw it (2)	
no more bridge	don't throw it	
no more fire	no in there	
no more pigeon		
no more man	no lollipop	
no more book		
ə no more light (2)	no, I didn't go back roller coaster	
no more fire engine	I no like to	
no more tank	no, I didn't	
no fire engine (3)		
oh no fire engine!		
no fire car		
ə no ice cream		
you no bring choochoo train		
I no reach it		
ə no fall down		
and ə no sit down		
not here		
not crying		
doesn't fit		
oh doesn't fit!		
ə doesn't fit (2)		
I didn't do it		
I didn't crying		
ə didn't have it		
I can't		
I didn't		
no, I didn't		

Note: Numbers in parentheses refer to number of occurrences in the text, discounting immediate repetitions. The underlined words are those that occurred in an immediately preceding utterance produced by someone other than the child.

For the first time, sentences that expressed *nonexistence* included expression of sentence-subject—most often the pronoun "I." However, except for the occurrence of "it" after verbs, there was only one instance of predicate complement construction with verbs: "you no bring choo-choo train." Even though these sentences were longer than the negative sentences at Time IV, with inclusion of sentence-subject, they were still among the least complex sentences that occurred in the entire text. One of the first sentence structures Eric used, at Time II, was verb-object, but he still did not use this structure productively in negative sentences at Time V.

There was a differentiation in the form of the negative element in syntactic position before verbal predicates. The two forms "didn't" and "doesn't" replaced the form "no" in seven sentences with predicate negation. The corresponding affirmative forms "did" and "does" never occurred in the text—"doesn't" and "didn't" appeared to be uniquely negative formatives in the same sense as "no" and "no more." Although it may have been accidental, the forms occurred with appropriate temporal reference in all but one instance of "didn't." Progressive verb inflection was productive in affirmative sentences at this time, but the past tense was not.

Among the sentences that signaled *nonexistence*, there were many that were structurally the same as those that occurred in each of the earlier observations—for example, "no more ball," "no more tank," "no more bridge." However, there was a difference in the distribution of "no" as an alternative form of the negative element. "No" continued to occur in syntactic environments before predicate constructions, as in "I no reach it" and "ə no fall down," but "no" occurred before noun forms that did not have the function sentence-object. That is, in the sentences "no fire car," "no fire engine," and "ə no ice cream," the "no" affected the noun form directly and signaled its nonexistence.

This distinction between "no" and "no more" at Time V may have been analogous to the use of the two forms in the adult model: "no bananas" and the partitive "no more bananas." That is, Eric appeared to distinguish between the nonexistence of something he had experienced previously—for example, "no more fire engine" (Eric was pushing a truck under the bridge and the bridge collapsed on it) and "no fire engine" (Eric looking out the window, not seeing any fire engine on the street). However, it was also the case that "no more," which was the earliest, primitive form of the negative element in Eric's texts, no longer occurred in the subsequent text at Time VI. The use of the form "no" at Time V—to express simple *nonexistence* of objects that were not also predicate objects—may have represented a transitional stage, before Eric relinquished "no more" as a negative marker.

Syntactic expression of *rejection* used the form "no" most often, and there was only one occurrence of the primitive "no more." There were three sentences that included the subject "I" (two of these with "didn't" as the negative element), and these sentences differed from all but one of the rest of the sentences that signaled *rejection*. The last four sentences listed in the category *rejection* in Table 7.11—"no lollipop," "no, I didn't go back roller coaster," "I no like to," and "no, I didn't"— signaled Eric's not wanting to do or to have something—the same kind of *rejection* used productively by Kathryn. The sentences "no, I didn't go back roller coaster" and "I no like to" occurred in the following sequence:

(12) E:V (Eric had been on a roller
coaster the previous weekend;
Mommy was prompting Eric
to tell Lois about it)
Would you like to go again
on the roller coaster?

> no, I didn't go back
roller coaster.
no!

(Eric shaking his head) like to. like to. like to.
You don't want to go again? > I no like to.

However, the remaining nine sentences were negative directions with the second person subject as agent understood. For example, "no more cluckcluck" (Eric wanted Mommy to stop imitating a chicken), "no flush" (Eric didn't want Mommy to flush the toilet until he was out of the way). Only one of these sentences used the adult form of the negative imperative "don't."

There were more indeterminate sentences than occurred previously, and it was possible to infer semantic intent in some of these utterances, but only tentatively—for example:

(13) E:V (Eric standing next to the
baby's bassinet looking at the
bottle of shampoo) no good.

(14) (Eric had picked up the shampoo
and held it, then remonstrating
to Lois, who was watching him) >no had it.
/e/ had it, Bloom.

(Eric put the shampoo back)

It appeared, in (13), that Eric was referring to not being allowed to play with the baby's shampoo, and in (14) he appeared to be acting out this reproof with the investigator.

Table 7.12. Categorization of Negative Sentences, Eric VI

Nonexistence	Rejection	Denial
no more lollipop	I think no more	that not lollipop
no Daddy		that's ə not bridge
oh no Daddy!		no, not ə <u>yellow</u>
no apple (3)	no playing (2)	no, that's ə not
no choochoo train (4)	don't cry (2)	<u>choochoo</u>
oh no choochoo train (2)	don't touch it	<u>train</u> (2)
no choochoo train tonight	don't eat it	
	don't fall down	
	don't fall down, little man	
have no <u>shoes</u>	don't drag it next time	
	don't take ə choochoo train home	
nothing	no, don't touch it (2)	
nothing there		
didn't see choochoo train		
it doešn't go		
it doesn't fit in here		
I can't		
I can't climb up		
/i/ can't fit on		
I can't fit in (2)		
I can't eat it		
ə can't go in		
I can't find the bridge		
they can't go on the door		
choochoo train <u>can't go anyplace</u>		
you can have it. no.		
you can have it		
ə couldn't see ə duck		
Eric couldn't see ə duck		
and I couldn't see piggies		
I couldn't see them		
I couldn't find ə choochoo train		

Note: Numbers in parentheses refer to number of occurrences in the text, discounting immediate repetitions. The underlined words are those that occurred in an immediately preceding utterance produced by someone other than the child.

The three sentences that signaled *denial* used the same structure as negative sentences that had occurred in earlier texts: "no fire engine," "no more fire engine," "ə no piggies." The syntactic expression of *denial* was still nonproductive, and the utterances that did occur were among the least complex negative sentences at Time V.

Eric VI. There were 55 negative sentences in the text at Time VI; these have been categorized according to function and are presented in Table 7.12. Sentences signaling *nonexistence* continued to occur most frequently, and these sentences were more structurally complex than at Time V. The developmental changes that had begun to emerge at Time V were fully productive at Time VI.

Only 4 of the 20 predicate negations occurred without production of sentence-subject and in 3 of these sentences there was a phonological element (/i/ or /ə/) which might be interpretable as a rudimentary pronoun form. In addition to the first person "I," the sentence-subject constituents included "you," "it," "they," and the nominal forms "Eric" and "choochoo train." The person and number paradigms for pronouns were productive in affirmative sentences at Eric VI, whereas they had not begun to emerge at Kathryn III.

The predicate phrase structure with inclusion of verb and complement was productive for the first time in negative sentences at Eric VI—for example, "I couldn't find ə choochoo train" and "they can't go on the door."

There were significant changes in the form of the negative element used in expressions of *nonexistence*. The primitive form "no more," which had been used most often in all the previous texts, occurred only once at Time VI. The prevailing form of the negative element that signaled *nonexistence* of objects was "no." The differentiation observed earlier between simple *nonexistence* and *nonexistence* of something that had occurred previously was no longer tenable. "No choochoo train" and "no apple" referred to nonexistence after previous existence, and "no more lollipop" was the only instance of partitive "no more."

A second important change in the negative element was the consistency of the form used in negated predicate constructions. Whereas the earlier variants "didn't" and "doesn't" occurred less often than at Time V, the three forms "can" (with negative intent), "can't," and "couldn't" were used in all the remaining predicate negations. Moreover, the forms were contrastive: "couldn't" always signaled previous events—the perfective or past tense; "can" and "can't" signaled events that occurred during the utterance or immediately previous to and during the utterance. The positive alternatives of these forms—"can" and "does"—never appeared in the text.

Syntactic expression of *rejection* continued to be productive, and the structure achieved the form that had been anticipated in the earlier texts: the negative imperative, with "don't" as the form of the negative element and the sentence-subject unexpressed but implied as the listener. The only expression of *rejection* where Eric was the agent was "I think no more"—Eric had played with a puzzle and was leaving it to play with the train.

Thus, Eric and Kathryn differed in the acquisition of the linguistic expression of *rejection*. Kathryn expressed rejection in terms of her not wanting to do or to have something, and ultimately expressed the first person subject and catenative verb in structurally differentiating these negative sentences. In contrast, Eric acquired the form of the negative imperative to express *rejection* first.

Although syntactic expression of *denial* was only marginally productive, in the five sentences that occurred with the function *denial*, the negative element was "not," and there was a demonstrative pronoun as subject in all but one of the sentences—the same structure used by Kathryn at Time III. Earlier, Eric had used "no more" or "no" as the negative element in expression of *denial*; but, whereas at Time VI "no more lollipop" occurred in expression of *nonexistence*, "that not lollipop" was used at the same time to express *denial*.

Thus, the developmental changes that characterized Phase 2 in Kathryn's development of negation had begun to emerge or were anticipated at Eric IV and V and became productive at Eric VI. The three semantic categories of negation were syntactically productive—although syntactic expression of *denial* was only marginally productive. The surface form of the negative sentences was structurally more complex, although there were still productive structures that occurred in the affirmative sentences in the text, but not in the negative sentences (for example, catenative verbs and progressive "-ing"). Sentence-subject constituents were included in expression of *nonexistence* and verb-complement predicate structures were productive in expression of *nonexistence* and *rejection*.

There was progressive differentiation in the form of the negative element, and the forms that were productive at Time VI were differentiated according to sentence function: "don't" was used exclusively to signal *rejection*; "not" was used exclusively to signal *denial*; the contrastive forms "can't" (alternating with "can") or "couldn't" and "doesn't" or "didn't" signaled predicate *nonexistence*; and "no" signaled *nonexistence* of objects most often. The sequence in which the syntactic expression of the three semantic categories of negation developed was (1) *nonexistence*, (2) *rejection*, (3) *denial*—the same developmental sequence that was observed in the negative sentences produced by Kathryn.

7.3.4. Syntactic Negation, Gia V and VI

The development of negation began most slowly in the texts obtained from Gia. In the first three texts, syntactic expression of negation was indeterminate in interpretation more often than not. In the fourth text, the number of negative sentences was so small that only tentative conclusions were possible. Because most of the sentences signaled *nonexistence*, it was concluded, tentatively, that the syntactic expression of negation was marginally productive at Time IV and signaled *nonexistence*.

Gia V. The number of negative sentences increased from 6 at Time IV to 20 at Time V, and all but one of the 20 could be interpreted. If the syntactic expression of negation had only marginal status at Time IV, it could be considered productive at Time V. All the negative sentences at Gia V have been categorized and are presented in Table 7.13.

Table 7.13. Categorization of Negative Sentences, Gia V

Nonexistence	Rejection	Denial
no more cookie	no want that	no, not
no draw ə cushion	no watch (2)	
no play ə matches	no take home	
can't doed it (3)	no MopTop	
can't open door	no pinch ə cheek (2)	
can't reach it	not that book	
can't reach pretzel	don't break it	

Note: Numbers in parentheses refer to number of occurrences in the text, discounting immediate repetitions. The underlined words are those that occurred in an immediately preceding utterance produced by someone other than the child.

There were only two syntactically productive categories—*nonexistence* and *rejection*—and a similar number of sentences occurred in each. There was only one instance of *denial*, and it was not strictly syntactic—the reinforced negative element, "no, not" (in response to the question

"Is the doll cold?"). There were also ten utterances (not presented in Table 7.13) that were interpreted as anaphoric "no" preceding an affirmative statement. In six of these, a single word followed the anaphoric "no." These utterances were elicited in an attempt to 'test' Gia's competence in expressing *denial*. For example, the investigator held up the figure of a boy and asked, "Is this the baby?" or held up the figure of a man and commented, "This is a girl." In each instance, Gia said "no" and named the figure correctly, rather than denying the identity suggested by the question or comment. It was concluded that syntactic expression of *denial* was not operative at Gia V.

The negative sentences were among the most structurally primitive sentences that occurred at Time V. For example, there was no expression of sentence-subject in any of these sentences, even though expression of sentence-subject had been productive in affirmative sentences since Time II.

There was variation in the form of the negative element; "can't" occurred only in expression of *nonexistence*, and "no" occurred in expression of *nonexistence* and *rejection*. Other forms—"no more," "don't," and "not"—each had unique occurrence.

Expression of *rejection*, as in Eric's texts, referred to the listener as agent, except for one sentence ("no want that").

The development of syntactic negation at Gia V was distinguished by two important factors: (1) there was substantial evidence that Gia had learned the cognitive-semantic notion of negation as a concept that could be expressed syntactically; and (2) there were two semantic categories of negation that were syntactically productive—*nonexistence* and *rejection*. The two classes of negative sentences were structurally differentiated only in the use of "can't" exclusively as a negative element before verbs in negation signaling *nonexistence*.

Gia VI. Any doubt about the status of negation in Gia's grammatical competence was dispelled at Time VI, when 121 negative sentences occurred and only 3 of these could not be interpreted. The proportion of sentences in the categories *nonexistence* and *rejection* was the same as at Time V, with a similar number of sentences (49 and 45) in each category at Time VI. But whereas there was only one expression of *denial* at Time V, there were 24 sentences that signaled *denial* at Time VI, so that all three categories of negation were fully productive in syntactic expression. All these sentences are presented in Table 7.14.

In addition to the 500 percent increase in the number of negative sentences, there was a substantial difference in the produced structural

Table 7.14. Categorization of Negative Sentences, Gia VI

Nonexistence	Rejection	Denial
no pockets	I no make duty in the	I didn't (2)
there's no more	potty!	no, I didn't (3)
there's ə no money	I don't ə microphone	
it's not in the bag	no! I don't want it	I not
		I'm not unhappy
I can (19)	no soap cup	I not smell
I can't (8)	no, not my button	
I can put here	don't (10)	it's not (3)
I can't put this here	don't! I say no!	it's not ready
I can put this pussy cat here	don't go (2)	it's not stop
I can't doed it	don't scare	it not all wet
I can't get out	don't stay (4)	it's not ə big spoon
I can't see it	don't say that! (2)	no, it's not raining
I can't fix it	don't take chair!	it's not cold out
I can't get it	don't take it	no, it's not the
I can't reach	don't read it!	teddy bear
I can't ə put ə lamb in	don't push two	no: it's not yours
it don't fit	don't touch this one	
no, it don't fit	don't touch ə big one	this not my stick
this don't fit in	don't touch my block! (3)	that's not mines
and this don't fit in too	don't turn the page	that not Mommy
you don't make duty in	don't hold on ə seesaw	that's not little
your diaper	don't stay in my room	/ðγ/not yours
I didn't make dirty__/	don't take your	
no duty in my diaper	microphone	
	don't stand over it	
no, I not	don't take the belt out	
no, it don't go in this box	don't take my diaper	
	don't pull my pants down	
	don't go in the room	
	don't go in here until	
	few minutes	
	no, don't here	

Note: Numbers in parentheses refer to number of occurrences in the text, discounting immediate repetitions. The underlined words are those that occurred in an immediately preceding utterance produced by someone other than the child.

complexity of the sentences at Time VI in comparison with the sentences with the same functions at Time V, when the structural differentiation of the two categories *nonexistence* and *rejection* was rudimentary.

Whereas there had been no expression of sentence-subjects in negative sentences at Time V, in expression of *nonexistence* at Time VI there was inclusion of sentence-subject in every utterance except one ("no pockets"). The form of the subject was the pronoun "I" most often, but "you," "it," "this," and "there's" also occurred.

The only instances of expressed sentence-subject in sentences that signaled *rejection* were "I no make duty in the potty!," "I don't ə microphone," and "no! I don't want it," and each referred to Gia's not wanting to do or to have something. All the remaining sentences signaled *rejection* of an event that involved the listener as actor-agent, and the sentence-subject was implied but not expressed. Thus, Gia and Eric were similar in the development of syntactic *rejection*—both children learned the structure and function of the negative imperative first. The form of *rejection* in Kathryn's texts—the negation of *desire* with expression of the catenative verb and subject "I"—was only a marginal structure in the texts of both Gia and Eric.

Most of the sentences in Gia's text that signaled *denial* included the form "it's" as subject—a form that was not used by either Kathryn or Eric. In addition, Gia used the subject forms that Kathryn and Eric used: "that," "that's," and "this." There did not appear to be a motivating difference between "it's" and other forms. Expression of *denial*, as with Eric and Kathryn, negated statements of identity most often.

Finally, as observed in the negative sentences of Kathryn and Eric at the culmination of Phase 2, there was a functionally motivated differentiation in the form of the negative element. Except for the utterance "I didn't," which expressed Gia's denial of having done something, the negative element "not" was used in all expressions of *denial*. Except for the single occurrence of each of the forms "no," "not," and "no more," the negative element in all expressions of *rejection* was "don't."

The negative element was variable in expressions of *nonexistence* with occurrence of "no," "not," and "don't," in addition to the most productive form, "can't" (which alternated with "can" produced with negative intent). There did not appear to be a meaningful difference among the forms that occurred—for example, "this don't fit in" and "I can" occurred in similar speech events. As observed also with Kathryn and Eric, the auxiliary forms *can, do,* or *did* never occurred in affirmative sentences. Rather, the forms "can't," "don't," and "didn't" appeared to have been learned as alternants of the forms "no" and "not." Although progressive "-ing" was fully productive in affirmative sentences, there was no occurrence of progressive verbs in negative sentences, so that the observation by Bellugi (1967) that the forms "don't" and "can't" were restricted to occurrence with nonprogressive main verbs in her data did not apply to the data collected from Kathryn, Eric, and Gia.

7.3.5. Comparison of the Three Children and Summary of Phase 2

The sequential appearance of syntactic expression of *rejection* and *denial*—after the appearance of *nonexistence* in Phase 1—was one important aspect of Phase 2. Although sentences signaling *nonexistence* continued to occur most frequently in most of the texts, structures signaling *rejection* and then structures signaling *denial* became productive. A schematic account of the proportional distribution of negative sentences in terms of function in Phase 1 and Phase 2 is presented in Figure 7.2.

Just as the different semantic categories appeared sequentially in the order *nonexistence, rejection, denial*—subsequent, progressive increase in the produced structural complexity of each category followed the same order. Expression of sentence-subject and the occurrence of the verb and complement constituents of predicate phrases were evident in sentences expressing *nonexistence* before these same forms were expressed in *rejection* or *denial*. When the syntactic structure of sentences expressing *rejection* subsequently increased in complexity, the most primitive syntactic form was used in the expression of *denial*.

A second important aspect of Phase 2 was the development of different but relatively homogeneous structures for the expression of the different semantic categories. The syntactic structure of expression of *denial* developed last and was similar in the sentences of the three children—the subject "this," "that's," or, in Gia's sentences, "it's" before the negative element. The complement was a single word—a noun form most often, but adjective forms also occurred ("that's not little" at Gia VI). Generally, there was no verb in these sentences. Final "-s" occurred with "that" and "it," but the inflectional paradigm of "be" was not yet productive in the affirmative sentences in the texts. There was no evidence that "it's" or "that's" represented contractions with the copula "be."

There were two forms of *rejection* (the second category in the developmental sequence), and the children differed in their use of each; either one or the other was productive in the negative sentences of each child, but not both. Kathryn expressed *rejection* of something that she didn't want to do or to have. The ultimate structure she used at Time III included expression of the sentence-subject "I" and the catenative verbs "want" or "need" before a predication that involved Kathryn as agent.

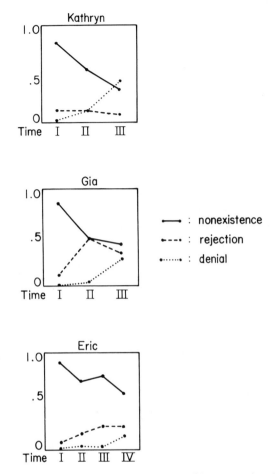

Figure 7.2. Development of negation, Phases 1 and 2: proportional distribution of negative sentences in the semantic categories nonexistence, rejection, and denial.

This was the same form of negation described by McNeill and McNeill (1967) as "internal-external"—the "lack" of "internal desire," and was also the second form of negation acquired by their Japanese subject.

However, Eric and Gia acquired an alternative form of *rejection*. Although both children produced sentences that were functionally similar to the expression of *rejection* by Kathryn, their use of these forms was marginal, and such sentences were less structurally complete than the expression of *rejection* that involved the receiver as agent. This second form of *rejection* anticipated the form of the negative imperative in the adult model. There was no catenative verb form and no expression of sentence-subject.

Two sentence types were used to signal *nonexistence*—predicate negation where the referent was the nonoccurrence of events ("I can't climb up" at Eric VI) and nominal negation where the referent was the *nonexistence* of objects ("no choochoo train," also at Eric VI). Whereas nominal negation had been the predominant expression of *nonexistence* in the earliest texts, predicate negation predominated in the later texts of all the children. Expression of nominal negation was simplest— most often the negative element "no" in juxtaposition with a noun or noun phrase. These constructions were not included in larger constructions; the one exception was "have no shoes" in response to the question "Does the little boy have shoes?" at Eric VI.

Predicate negation, for all three children, came to include expression of sentence-subject (the first person "I" most often) and elaborated predicate phrase constructions with verb and complement forms.

Finally, the third distinguishing feature of Phase 2 was the progressive differentiation in the form of the negative element motivated by the different syntactic structures that signaled the different semantic categories of negation. All three children used "not" to signal *denial*. Although the function and structure of the expression of *rejection* differed among the three children, the same form of the negative element, "don't," was used.

The negative element that was used in expression of *nonexistence* was the most variable. Both Kathryn and Gia used different forms of the negative element which appeared to be unmotivated—"can't," "don't," "not," and "no." However, the negative element in Eric's sentences was consistent; "can't" and "couldn't" occurred almost exclusively at Time VI, and the forms were temporally contrastive, even though Eric had not yet distinguished temporal reference in affirmative sentences.

It was most significant that at the time that negative sentences first began to be differentiated on the basis of function, that is, when negative sentences were used with different semantic intent, the syntactic structure used for each was the same. When the children subsequently developed more complex syntactic expression of *nonexistence*, the syntactic structure of the earliest sentences that occurred at the same time with different functions, that is, *rejection* and then *denial*, was invariably the same as the primitive form of the first sentences that had expressed *nonexistence*.

Thus, it was not necessary for the children to learn a new or different structure in order to express a new or different semantic intent. Initially, there was one meaning (m_1) of negation and one form (f_1). Subsequently, when two meanings were interpretable, (m_1) and (m_2), it was not the case that the appearance of (m_2) corresponded to the appearance of a second form (f_2), as might have been expected:

Time A: $(m_1) - (f_1)$

Time B: $(m_1) - (f_1)$

$(m_2) - (f_2)$

Rather, the appearance of a different form was associated with the first meaning (m_1), while, at the same time, the earlier form (f_1) was used to express the second meaning:

Time A: $(m_1) - (f_1)$

Time B: $(m_1) - (f_2)$

$(m_2) - (f_1)$

The acquisition of linguistic expression did not proceed hand in hand with cognitive-semantic development. Learning to express a new semantic category of negation did not involve learning a new structure for its linguistic expression at the same time. Neither was it the case that certain linguistic forms were productive in the children's speech before they knew something about the corresponding underlying cognitive notions. New, more complex structures developed and correlated with semantic categories only after expression of the categories with simpler, familiar structures had become productive in the texts.

The children differed in their rates of acquisition. Phase 1 was identified in the texts Kathryn I, Eric III, and Gia IV and Phase 2 in the texts Kathryn III, Eric VI, and Gia VI, so the transition from Phase 1 to Phase 2 was accomplished in the course of two observations of Kathryn and Gia and three observations of Eric. Although Gia's rate of development was initially the slowest, she caught up between Time V and Time VI.

In summary, even though there were differences in their rates of development and relatively minor formal and substantive differences in their linguistic development, the fact that the three children learned to differentiate the semantic categories in terms of structure in the sequence *nonexistence, rejection, denial* was the dominant feature of Phase 2 in their acquisition of syntactic expression of negation.

7.4. Early Sentence Negation: Sequential Development and Interpretation

On the basis of the relative frequency of occurrence of sentences in the different semantic categories of negation, and the progressive developments in the syntactic complexity of these sentences, the order of acquisition for all three children was specified as *nonexistence, rejection, denial.* This sequence is similar to the sequence that McNeill and McNeill (1967) anticipated in the development of negation by their Japanese subject, with two differences: a minor difference in the specification of the function of *rejection,* and a more substantial difference in their specification of the first semantic contrast. In the first contrast they observed, their subject marked the "correctness and incorrectness of statements" in addition to "nonexistence of objects and events."

Because the same sequence occurred in the acquisition of negation by the three children in this study, and there is some evidence for postulating a similar sequence of development in Japanese, it is reasonable to speculate on a rationale underlying this sequential development. Several reasons can be advanced to account for children learning certain syntactic structures before others. The factors of structural complexity and frequency of exposure or the child's experience with specific structures are two factors that are usually suggested; certainly, they play some part in the fact that use of passive sentences, for example, occurs late in the course of development.

In terms of the structural complexity of the ultimate linguistic expression of the three semantic categories, however, expression of *denial* appeared to be least complex. The shape of the negative element was constant; there was no expression of a verbal element—the complement structure on which the negative element had direct effect was a single word most often; and there was the use of a relatively constant, familiar proform as sentence-subject. In contrast, expression of *nonexistence* was ultimately most complex with expression of different sentence-subjects, variable verbal constituents with predicate complement constructions, and wide variation in the possible forms of the negative element. But expression of *denial* developed last, whereas syntactic expression of *nonexistence* developed first.

However, it was also true that in *nonexistence* the negative element had direct effect on the nominal or predicate form—for example, "no pocket" and "no fit." Expression of *rejection* involved negating the child's *wanting* to have or to do something, for example, "no (want) dirty soap"; or negating his wanting someone else to do or to have something, for example "(you) no flush" and "(you) no have it"—with an implication of more complex underlying structure.

As has been pointed out, there was no way of determining which syntactic structures were most frequent in the speech the children heard. It is a matter of speculation as to whether statements of *nonexistence* occurred more often than statements of *rejection* or statements of *denial* in the speech that the parents of the children addressed to them. In Bellugi's (1967) analysis of the negative sentences that each of the mothers of the children in her study used in a period of four hours, "basic sentence negation . . . 'you can't do that,' 'that isn't right,' 'he doesn't want it'" occurred most often, and negative imperatives occurred less frequently.

One reasonable explanation for early attention to syntactic expression of nonexistence before *rejection* was the adequacy of "no" as a single-word utterance (with appropriate behavior) in expressing *rejection*; "no" worked in expressing *rejection*, whereas "no" or even the more explicit "no more" (and appropriate behavior) communicated little information about *nonexistence*. The fact that the referent was not manifest in the context necessitated its inclusion in expression in order to transmit the information of *nonexistence*. In contrast, the fact that the referent was present—actually in *rejection* situations and symbolically in *denial* situations—made reference somewhat redundant. Thus, the children 'needed' to express *nonexistence* syntactically in order to transmit information, whereas syntactic expression of *rejection* and *denial* was less necessary.

The fact that *denial* involved a symbolic referent—the child had to perceive the referent in something said—probably accounted in part for the fact that *denial* developed last. It was observed in Chapter 2 that the children's earliest utterances tended to occur infrequently in relation to another utterance (from someone else or from themselves). Further, McNeill and McNeill (1967) observed that statements of denial usually entailed alternative affirmative statements—for example, "that's not mines. that's dolly's" at Gia VI (whether or not the alternative affirmative statement was actually expressed). Their suggestion is reasonable that "Entailment–Non-entailment" (*denial*) "requires a child to hold in mind two propositions at once" and so would be acquired after contrasts that involve only one proposition (as in *nonexistence* and *rejection*).

In summary, Kathryn, Eric, and Gia approached the task of learning negation—which, in the adult model, is a complex, explicitly differentiated grammatical subsystem—systematically and similarly. It was possible to trace their acquisition of syntactic structure in relation to the semantic correlates of negation. Further, by studying the acquisition of each of the three children individually and then comparing the obtained sequences of development, both similarities and individual differences were revealed.

The findings presented here appear to complement the description of the acquisition of syntactic structure in early sentence negation proposed by Bellugi (1967). The descriptions of the form of negative sentences in Bellugi's data were generally similar to the surface features of the sentences of Kathryn, Eric, and Gia. The negative sentences produced by the three children in the developmental stages described as Phases 1 and 2 could be described as having occurred in the earliest developmental periods that Bellugi described. However, when information about the semantic correlates of the sentences was considered, it was possible to study the syntax of negation more deeply, and to inquire into the underlying motivation of syntactic form.

8 Learning to Talk

In the course of this study, it was clear that the children's sentences were not incoherent. Semantic interpretation of utterances could be inferred in most instances so that the inherent structure of sentences could be evaluated. Thus, the failure to reach the children's 'intuition' about language was less of an obstacle to describing their language than might have been anticipated.

It has been pointed out that the study of linguistic performance must take into account the fact that children (as well as adults) make 'mistakes' in talking—that factors such as memory limitations and environmental distractions interact with underlying competence (Chomsky, 1965, pp. 3–4; Cazden, 1967). It was clear that the children made mistakes in talking; there were 'false starts,' unmotivated reduplication such as repeated syllables and words, and unfinished utterances. Representative examples included "more raisin more" and "/bei/__ Mommy milk" at Kathryn I and "I get horsie 'chine" at Eric III. However, it was significant that, first, such utterances as these did not fit any of the productive structures that could be identified in the data—each represented a unique class of 'one'; and second, the occurrence of this kind of surface error, as a result of production accident, was relatively rare in the texts. This last observation coincided with the report by Labov (1966)—that speakers of a language speak in sentences that are essentially grammatical. The speech of the children confirmed this observation; their random, accidental mistakes were inconsequential and not a dominant feature of their linguistic production.

On the other hand, there were 'errors' in the children's speech that were systematic and consistent and turned out to be errors only in their deviation from the grammaticalness of the adult model—hence, not errors at all. The structural limitations imposed on sentences by cognitive constraints on expressing syntactic complexity resulted in patterns of omission (reduction) that not only were predictable but provided evidence of productive patterns in underlying structure. Further, the creative use of certain structures—such as Gia's use of "more" in predicate constructions ("more read")—provided evidence of rule-operating behavior that deviated from the model language but was, nonetheless, grammatical. This second class of 'error' was not superficial error in production but, rather, was reflective of the child's grammatical system, and such utterances could be explained in the linguistic account of the system.

The systematic nature of the children's deviation from the model language substantiated the observation made by Jakobson (1968, p. 20) in quoting M. Grammont: "There is in the child, ... 'neither incoherence nor effects of chance.... He undoubtedly misses the goal, but he deviates from it always in the same way. ...' It is this constancy of deviation which gives importance to his language." The children did, indeed, miss the goal, and the observed constancy of their deviation from the goal was an important factor in describing and explaining their language.

8.1. Strategies for Learning Language

Stated in the simplest terms, children need to learn both substantive and relational aspects of language. In this sense, children learn substantive forms with inherent meaning ('a rose' is a rose), but they also learn the possible semantic relationships that can hold between substantive forms with variations in grammatical meaning—"Mommy push," "push Mommy," "Mommy's shoe," "my Mommy," "Mommy's a lady"—syntactic variations on essential 'Momminess.' It is not enough to learn "Mommy"—it is also necessary to learn Mommy as subject, Mommy as object, Mommy as possessor, Mommy as possessed, Mommy in identity.

Thus, certain substantive words are learned in terms of essentially constant semantic meaning, with variable grammatical meaning that depends on the relationships between category constituents in the abstract, underlying structure of a sentence. The semantic meaning of a form is defined in terms of certain inherent features ("Mommy" being $[+ \text{animate}, + \text{human}, - \text{abstract} \ldots]$), which may be added to but which probably do not change in any significant way. But the grammatical meanings of substantive words do change as a result of variable arrangements with other words in sentences.

Children also learn forms that occur with constant grammatical function, where possible variation in meaning does not depend on variable syntactic arrangement. Such forms apply a particular semantic intent to the substantive forms with which they occur—as "no" signaled nonexistence, rejection, and then denial, and "more" signaled recurrence and, it is presumed, eventually the partitive and comparative notions.

The two relational aspects of language appear to be related to the two descriptions of children's speech as 'telegraphic' and 'pivotal.' 'Telegraphic speech' appears to describe the child's attempts at manipulating substantive forms with variable grammatical meaning. 'Pivot speech' describes the child's attempts to apply a single form with invariable grammatical function in different formal contexts. Although the speech of Kathryn, Eric, and Gia reflected something about both aspects of language from the beginning, it was clear that the children used different strategies for learning language, and, moreover, that the strategies they used differed in just this dimension.

Analysis of the language of all three children revealed that there was a small number of words that occurred frequently in contexts with a larger group of words that were used infrequently. In this respect, their language confirmed Zipf's (1965, pp. 47–48) observation of the tendency of all languages to maintain an orderly balance between "frequency" and "variety" in the distribution of forms in the stream of speech. The class of frequently used words included (1) the syntactic markers (for example, "no" and "more"), and (2) substantive forms (for example, "Mommy," "Kathryn," "Gia," "raisin," "picture," "make," "read," and "fit") that occurred in contexts both with other substantive forms and with syntactic markers.

The most productive structures produced by Gia and Kathryn combined substantive forms with different grammatical relationship between them. Their earliest sentences appeared to be highly similar to the earliest two-word utterances described by Leopold (1949, Vol. III, pp. 31–32) in his daughter Hildegard's speech:

the child was now able to single out two different parts of speech for specification, . . . The words selected from the standard pattern of the sentence were two which were important for its organization. . . .
. . . In the two-word stage a verb, or a part of the predicate without the verb, was usually present. Sentences containing a subject and an object but no verb in any form occurred to the end of the second year, . . . [Both] subject . . . and

object . . . appeared during the same [the 20th] month, . . . The pattern subject-verb can be called earlier since it was fully alive and independently handled at [20 months], whereas the pattern verb-object remained imitative with regard to the words used in it until [21 months] and was not common until [23 months].

Leopold's description of the sequential order in which the grammatical relationships were learned differed from the sequence described for Kathryn, Eric, and Gia (Hildegard developed bilingually, and Leopold spoke only German to her). Verb-object and subject-object strings were more productive in the texts of Kathryn and Gia than were subject-verb strings, and Gia appeared to learn the subject-object pattern first. The early syntactic development of Leopold's daughter appeared to be more similar to the development of Kathryn and Gia than it was to the development of Eric or, for that matter, to the speech of children described in terms of pivot grammars in other investigations. Kathryn and Gia used syntax primarily to express variable relationships between substantive forms. Although certain words (such as "Mommy") appeared more frequently than others, they could not be considered simply as the fixed constituent in syntactic frames (that is, as pivots), because they occurred with variable grammatical function in relation to the other constituents with which they were juxtaposed in utterances. The early grammars of Kathryn and Gia provided for concatenation of categories with grammatical sentence functions, and classes of words were differentiated according to categorial function.

In contrast, Eric combined substantive forms only in verb-object relation; his most productive structures combined substantive forms with the smaller class of frequent operators ("more," "no," "it"). The more frequent forms in Eric's texts could be considered the fixed constituents of syntactic frames within which different forms could be substituted—but always with the same grammatical relation. In this respect, Eric's utterances were similar to those described by Braine (1963) as pivotal.

It appeared that Eric's earliest strategy for language learning involved seeking constant features in the speech he heard—forms with both constant substantive meaning and constant syntactic function. Eric organized linguistic structure around such superficial constant features with a focus on the formal patterns or shapes of constructions—for example, sentences beginning with "I" and ending with "it." Whereas Gia and Kathryn used different nominative forms as sentence-subjects and proforms subsequently, Eric used a more constant form, "I" or a variant of /ə/, in preverb positions before he used various nouns as sentence-subjects. Eric did not use the relational aspects of language to express variation in grammatical function, as did Gia and Kathryn. He relied more on the use of syntactic operators, and substantive forms occurred in relatively fixed syntactic frames. Whereas the grammars of Gia and Kathryn generated such sentences as "read book," "Gia book" (Gia's book), "bear book," and "Mommy (subject) book (object)" (where "book" occurred in variable semantic-syntactic relations in sentences), Eric's grammars specified noun forms only in relation to syntactic operators (pivots) or in object relation to verb forms.

But if Eric's grammar could be described as 'pivotal' and the grammars of Kathryn and Gia as 'categorial' in an attempt to distinguish between them, it must be observed that the two characterizations were not mutually exclusive. Eric produced utterances with verb-object and, subsequently although less productively at Time III, with subject-verb relation. Gia and Kathryn both produced constructions that combined substantive forms with syntactic operators. Leopold (1949, Vol. III, p. 29) also reported the frequent use of "this" in apparently pivotal constructions in Hildegard's speech at age 21 months.

Although there were important differences among the children, none of the grammars were incompatible with the adult model. On the contrary, it was evident that the children were learning the same language although their individual strategies in approaching the language differed. The results of this study have confirmed the observations of other investigators (Brown and Fraser, 1963; McNeill, 1966) that children's language is directly related, from the beginning, to the adult model and is not an exotic language that is eventually supplanted by a different system. Although there were important differences among them, Gia, Eric, and Kathryn each took a fairly direct and efficient route in their approaches toward the target language. However, the differences among them do raise important questions about certain theoretical issues in current psycholinguistic thinking.

For a number of reasons there is a strong tendency to approach the study of language development with the assumption that children will be more similar to each other in learning language than they will be different. Virtually all children arrive at elementary school at age 5 or 6 speaking the same language. All children pass through the same developmental motor milestones—creeping, crawling, sitting, standing, and walking—at varying rates, but in essentially the same sequence. Similarly, Lenneberg (1967, p. 133) asserted that "there is a remarkable degree of regularity in the emergence of language" although individual differences in time of onset and rate of development exist. The course of language development traditionally has been charted in terms of

developmental milestones having to do with comprehension and production of single words, phrases, and sentences: first words usually
appear at about 12 months or shortly thereafter, and the first phrases
begin to appear before the second birthday, sometime after the age of
18 or 19 months. At the end of the fourth year, children generally speak
and understand well-formed sentences.

The most important factor in minimizing the potential for individual
variation in substantive aspects of language development (as distinguished from individual differences in rate of development) has been
the search for universal grammar. "The study of universal grammar . . .
is a study of the nature of human intellectual capacities." It has thus
been assumed that specification of the universal linguistic principles for
formulating grammars—"the innate organization that determines what
counts as linguistic experience and what knowledge of language arises
on the basis of this experience"—would be an account of the innate
intuition about language that the child brings to the task of language
learning (Chomsky, 1968, p. 24).

In specifying what a linguist seeks to explain about language, Chomsky used an expository analogy in which he pointed out that a young
child learning a language must operate in much the same way as a
linguist who seeks to construct a grammar of the language. On the basis
of a limited linguistic input—what the child hears in his environment
and what is presented to the linguist as 'possible sentences in the
language'—the child and the linguist must evaluate possible grammars
so as to choose the grammar that will generate only the acceptable
sentences of the language. As a heuristic device for explicating the
processes of language learning and grammar evaluating, Chomsky
proposed an innate language acquisition device that would evaluate
potential grammars, match linguistic input (the sentences the child
hears) with structural descriptions provided by different grammars, and
choose the one grammar that is best able to account for the input
sentences (Chomsky, 1965, pp. 30–59). Chomsky's notion of a language
acquisition device has become a basic construct in the nativist position
of the origin of language.

It has since been assumed that the specifications for a language
acquisition device would include an account of the formal and substantive linguistic universals of which the child somehow has knowledge,
probably from the beginning.[1] For example, McNeill (1966, pp. 46–47)
has suggested that knowledge of the basic grammatical relations (such
as the relation between verb and object) is "part of his [the child's]

[1] For a thorough presentation and discussion of this position, see Smith and Miller,
1966.

biological endowment. . . . By assigning the basic grammatical relations a place in the child's innate linguistic endowment, we assume them to be universal." The potentiality for individual variation in language development is necessarily discounted in this view; indeed, the development of the theory of innate origin of language has relied heavily on the assumption of regularity among all children learning language.

It appears that the results of this study would cast some doubt on the view of language development as the same innately preprogrammed behavior for all children. The emerging grammars proposed for the language of the three children studied were different; a single grammar would not have accounted for the language of all three in any adequate way. Thus, in addition to differences among the children in rate of development, there were more important substantive differences among them that would not be revealed by any traditional analysis of language development in terms of utterance length or achieving the milestones—words, phrases, and sentences. The differences among them must reflect the importance of individual differences in the interaction between cognitive function and experience, which could not be assumed to be the same for any two children.

8.2. Linguistic Expression and Cognition

The basic grammatical relations were not present in the children's grammars from the beginning. At the level represented by the text and grammar of Kathryn I: (1) there was strong evidence that the predicate relationship of verb-object was fully productive for all three children, and (2) the subject-predicate relationship was fully productive for Kathryn and Gia but only beginning to emerge in Eric's speech. These grammatical relations were not manifest in the earlier texts of Eric and Gia, and the subsequent sequence of emergence was different for each. Gia learned the subject-object relation before learning the function of verb forms in predicate structures; Eric learned the verb-object relation first.

If all the early two-word utterances of the children had expressed all possible combinations of subject-verb-object (and correspondingly, if all of the early Noun + Noun constructions expressed all the possible semantic relations that can hold between two nouns in the language), it might be assumed that the children had linguistic knowledge of these basic grammatical relations from the beginning and, perhaps, used this knowledge in somehow organizing their nonlinguistic experience. But this was not the case. The children learned to use the linguistic structures selectively. There is certaintly an important difference between knowledge of language and the ability to produce it, but what a child is able to say is directly related to what he knows about language. The fact that productivity of basic grammatical relations in the speech the children used was developmentally progressive leads to the conclusion that the emergence of syntactic structures in their speech depended on the prior development of the cognitive organization of experience that is coded by language.

The children's acquisition of the semantics and syntax of negation provided further support for the assumption of prior cognitive development underlying the emergence of different syntactic structures. In the course of the development of negation there was evidence that the children's perceptual-cognitive organization was more complex than their ability to transmit information. They learned to express the different semantic categories of negation without learning different contrastive linguistic structures at the same time. When the children learned to express a new concept (rejection and then denial as categories of negation), they used a primitive structure that previously had expressed an earlier-learned concept, nonexistence.

According to the Piagetian view of the relationship between language and intellectual operations: "language is not the source of logic, but is on the contrary structured by logic" (Sinclair-de-Zwart, 1969, p. 325). Kathryn, Eric, and Gia appeared to learn to use linguistic structure for coding what they knew of the world of objects, events, and relations.

However, there were examples in the data in which linguistic expression appeared to be more 'mature' than underlying cognitive function. Just as the occurrence of "ə don't want baby" at Eric II belied Eric's competence in expressing negation (when all other negative sentences consisted of "no more" plus a noun), the earliest use of temporal adverbs was similarly misleading, as in the following examples:

(1) K:VII (Kathryn was showing her
     playschool artwork to Lois)
     Where did they come from?   oh they come from lot
                                            ə playschools.

     From playschool! And did you
     make them?   yes. all: ə them.
                                          > next Monday we'll
                                            have to go to
                                            Allan's house.
                                          > today. not today.
                                          > 'morrow.
     Tomorrow?   yes.

(Playschool met on Mondays;
this exchange took place on
Monday, but the group did
not meet at Allan's house on
this Monday, "next Monday,"
or "tomorrow.")

(2) K:VII (During the last session
of Time VI, six weeks previously,
Mommy had been ironing in the
kitchen while Lois and Kathryn
played in the living room)   > you came here last
                                                 night · when my
                                                 mother was ironing.

I came here last night?   yes.
                                              my mother my mother
                                              ironed.

Oh, your mother ironed last night?   yes.
What did she iron?   oh she ironed some
                                     clothes.

Hm. And what did Kathryn do?   oh, I played with you.
Hm. Did you play with me
tomorrow?   yes.
                        . . . . .
Yes? Will you play with me
yesterday?   > yes. last yesterday.
                                              > last night.

(Mommy had not been ironing the
previous night, and Mommy had
not talked to Kathryn about her
ironing at Time VI)

Kathryn's use of verb inflection at Time VII (when she was 30 months, 3 weeks old) was productive and appropriate in referring to past, present, progressive, and future events, but she was just beginning to use adverbial temporal reference. Such phrases as "today," "next Monday," "last night" occurred in appropriate sentence positions, and verb tense corresponded to the general temporal aspect of the adverbs— past tense occurred with "last night," future tense occurred with "next Monday." However, except for the use of "now," which was always appropriate in reference to immediate events, semantic reference was usually inaccurate or superfluous, with no inferable underlying cognitive regularity. Kathryn appeared to have learned the syntactic function before learning the semantics of these forms.

It might be said that, in the course of development, the child matches different syntactic structure to units of different semantic experience as he learns grammar. But in the course of development the matching is frequently inexact and misses the mark in certain important respects, as in the following two examples:

(3) E:IX (Eric was playing with Rob,
who was nine months younger than
he. Eric and Rob had assembled
the slide, and Eric went after the
wheels. Eric coming back to the
slide and Rob)   and ready to go.
(Rob picked up the slide and
carried it to the dining room;
Eric putting down the wheels
and then seeing Rob with the
slide; shouts)   Rob! Rob!
Bring back the slide, Rob.
Bring it back.
(Rob runs toward the bedroom
with the slide; Eric taking
off after him, shouting)   Rob!
                                                         > it's not to play with!

Here, the linguistic expression was well matched to the occasion—Eric wanted to retrieve something that he did not want Rob to have—but not 'accurate' in reference to a toy that both children had been playing with.

(4) K:VIII (Kathryn sitting at
the kitchen counter, waiting
for Mommy to give her
juice; seeing sunlight on
the counter)   Mommy, put the sun away.
Put the sun away?
(Kathryn opening counter
drawer)   > but I wanta see what this is.
(Kathryn taking out coffee
measure scoop)   ⎡oh this is mine.   ⎤
                                                         ⎢this is my one.   ⎥
                                                         ⎣this is a coffee one I want.⎦

(Kathryn holding up the
scoop for Lois to see)

$$\begin{bmatrix} \text{see see this is a coffee one} \\ \text{I use} \underline{\hspace{1cm}} \\ > \text{I 'posed to use when I was} \\ \text{a big girl you used to} \\ \text{use it.} \end{bmatrix}$$

For what?
(Kathryn putting it down,
taking juice from Mommy)   > I used to use that when I
                                       was a big girl.

In the sentence "but I wanta see what this is," Kathryn used a relational term, "but," that did not appear to relate to anything. The sentence
"I used to use that when I was a big girl" occurred in a situation in which
Kathryn was 'explaining' the coffee scoop to Lois. But the coffee scoop
had no relation to Kathryn as a "big girl" or, for that matter, as a little
girl. These examples of mismatch between linguistic expression and
semantic reference have been taken from the later samples because they
illustrate the discrepancy between form and function so directly. But
there were earlier examples as well—the overgeneralization of inflections when the children added "-s" to forms regardless of whether the
result was semantically or syntactically acceptable, for example,
"mines." Temporal adverb phrases (except "now") would have to be
assigned to the same syntactic limbo in the grammar of Kathryn VII
as the earlier, overgeneralized "-s" and the early syntactic appearance
of the negative element, without semantic contrast, in Gia I, II, and III.
Thus, describing growth in linguistic expression cannot assume that
growth in cognitive development proceeds hand in hand. Such utterances from a small child as "ə don't want baby" or "you came here last
night when my mother was ironing" or "I used to use that when I was
a big girl" were impressive in syntactic form but misleading as evidence
of linguistic competence. In the terminology of Piagetian psycholinguistics, such nonproductive aspects of the children's linguistic performance would be characterized as "prestructures" or "pseudo-
structures" which can "easily induce an overrating of [linguistic]
competence" (Sinclair-de-Zwart, 1969, p. 335).

An ideal account of language development must specify at least three
interrelated components: linguistic experience, nonlinguistic experience,
and cognitive-perceptual organization, with the three components
interacting to affect the development of linguistic competence. The
three components are represented schematically in Figure 8.1. In the

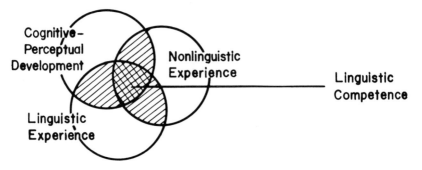

Figure 8.1. Interrelationships of hypothetical components in language development.

course of development, the three components presumably move, at varying speeds, in the direction of concentricity. Overlap of all three (the cross-hatched area in Figure 8.1) would schematically represent what the child knows about language. But there is also overlap between each of three components and one other component (lined areas in Figure 8.1) without immediate effect on linguistic competence. That is, there are interrelationships—between development of cognition and nonlinguistic experience, between development of cognition and linguistic experience, and between linguistic experience and nonlinguistic experience—that do not result, by themselves, in language competence. With movement toward concentricity of the three components, these areas of overlap are progressively superimposed. They appear to represent, in some way, the mismatch between linguistic expression and cognitive awareness observed in the course of development.

This schematic representation does not specify *how* induction of the underlying structure of language occurs—it provides only a hypothetical account of the functional components, including a cognitive component, that presumably participate in the process. It appears to be fairly clear that a process of inducing underlying structure does not stand alone as a formal, linguistic construct in the scheme of the child's total development. Rather, induction of underlying structure is intimately related to the development of cognition; accounting for the development of language competence must include an account of cognitive function.

The ultimate goal for a model of language development is the explanation of the achievement of linguistic creativity—the child's eventual ability to speak and understand an infinite number of different sentences given a finite set of linguistic facts. Moreover, "the normal use of language is not only innovative and potentially infinite in scope, but also free from the control of detectable stimuli, either external or internal" (Chomsky, 1968, p. 11). The fact that children's speech is very much tied to context and behavior was the major empirical influence on this study of emerging grammatical competence. The extent to which children's speech is stimulus-bound mitigates against the assumption of true linguistic creativity in early language. In this respect, the importance of the child's awareness and cognizance of nonlinguistic experience in relation to language in his environment, in the course of development, should not be underestimated.

It appears that children learn to identify certain grammatical relationships and syntactic structures with the environmental and behavioral contexts in which they are perceived and then progress to reproducing approximations of heard structures in similar, recurring contexts. In order to use a structure in a new situation, the child must be able to perceive critical aspects of the context of the situation. Thus, the sequence in which syntactic structures are learned by the child may be influenced as much by his ability to differentiate aspects of situational context and recognize recurrent contexts as by such factors as frequency of exposure to structures or their relative complexity. For example, the children in this study appeared to learn to perceive and discriminate, in the language they used, such aspects of a referent as its existence, nonexistence, and recurrence, before such features as relative size, color, or other identifying attributes.

Investigation of children's language must study linguistic performance—comprehension and production—in an effort to reach the child's linguistic competence. However, the study of children's language is problematical. Given the current limitations in theories of linguistics and cognition, any attempt at describing and explaining language development must be considered exploratory and tentative. This study attempted to determine *what* three children appeared to know about grammar as they began to use syntax in their speech. The crucial question of *how* this learning occurred remains unanswered.

Appendix A: Methods and Materials

A.1. Further Description of the Study

A.1.1. Kathryn, Eric, and Gia

The three children were all first-born children of families in which both parents were college graduates and native speakers of American English. The children's earlier language development was unremarkable: they had produced their first intelligible words at the time of their first birthdays, had understood simple directions and comments before that, and had begun to produce their first phrases at about 19 months. The Peabody Picture Vocabulary Test, administered to each of the children at age 3 years, produced mental age scores that ranged from 3 years 10 months to 5 years 8 months.

Eric's father was a part-time graduate student and an account executive with an advertising agency; his mother was a psychiatric social worker in a community agency and worked two evenings and one afternoon each week. Gia's father was an executive in a family-owned business, and her mother attended evening and summer art and dance classes. Kathryn's father was a physician doing research at a university medical center; her mother was a musician. Although they had regular activities that took them out of the homes an average of one full day each week, the mothers of the children were otherwise at home and caring for them. Eric's mother employed a cleaning woman from Jamaica two days a week. The other mothers did not have regular domestic help. The families of Eric and Gia were originally from New York City; Kathryn's family was from Oregon. Before the study ended Eric, at age 24 months, had a baby sister, and Gia, at age 31 months, had a baby brother.

The three families and the investigator lived in a large apartment house complex adjacent to a university in New York City, with rents that varied from $50 to $70 per room. The children played in a public park and in a playground within the apartment house complex in the mornings and afternoons. Although they knew one another in that context, they played with different peer groups. This was due in part to the differences in their ages—Kathryn was two months older than Eric, and Eric was seven months older than Gia—and in part to the fact that their mothers had different playground friends.

The children's peers were generally the children of parents affiliated with the university as faculty or graduate students. They each had friends born in other countries—England, Africa, Italy, Australia, India—but most of their peers were children of white Americans whose socioeconomic circumstances were similar to their own.

Eric was the only child who played regularly with older children— two sisters from England who were three and five years older than he. Because Eric's mother and the sisters' mother were good friends, the children were often together after school hours, and the girls played with Eric as a 'little brother'—fondling and carrying him, reading to him, or entertaining him with songs and rhymes.

The children and their families experienced no serious illnesses or accidents. The children had not been considered premature at birth, and mental and physical development were reported within normal limits. There was no suspicion of hearing impairment nor anomalies of the peripheral speech mechanism.

A.1.2. Collecting Samples of Spoken Language
The children were seen individually in their homes for approximately 8 hours within several days, every 6 weeks. The size of the samples, the frequency with which they were collected, the extent of uniformity among the samples collected for each child and among the three children, and the role of the investigator in the sessions were four important factors in the basic structure of the research design.

A judicious weighing of two factors—sample size and frequency of collection—was necessary in order to sample adequately the course of development and, at the same time, keep the amount of data within manageable proportions.

An 8-hour sample was considered reasonable in order (1) to ensure an adequate sampling of the full range of syntactic structure types used by the child at a given time, and (2) to establish the productivity of those structures—the extent to which they were used to form new or different sentences. The first two observations of Eric were 4 hours and 6 hours, respectively, because he said little, and most of his utterances were unintelligible to his parents and the investigator. At the time, these sessions were not expected to be included in the analysis.

An important result of the 6-week time lapse was that the texts generally proved to be distinct from one another with respect to the level of the children's grammatical functioning—providing a discrete basis for comparison of changes that occurred from one observation to the next.

A complete list of the toys that were used in the observation sessions, with a description of each, is presented in Appendix A.2. The toys were chosen because they could be manipulated by the children in a variety of ways and so stimulated considerable activity—both constructive and destructive. The toys proved to be attractive to all the children at least some of the time. Certain items, such as the rocking clowns, caused delight at first and then faded in popularity as the children grew older and interest in other items increased. The toys did not have the same attraction for each child. Eric spent more time with the interlocking train than Kathryn or Gia did. Gia generally played least with each of the toys, losing interest in them sooner than the others did.

The daily routines—eating, dressing, and toileting—were sampled with varying success. Gia was already dressed for most sessions. Eric and Gia did not attend to toileting as frequently as did Kathryn. As might be expected, the attempt at achieving sample uniformity was successful only part of the time. In the course of 8 hours, the children brought out their own toys, visitors rang the doorbell, mothers cleaned out closets, packed suitcases, unpacked groceries—so that variation was included in each session. The planned activities accounted for roughly one-half to two-thirds of each session.

The attempt at sampling similar situations—from session to session for each child, and among the three children—was directed at controlling variable influences on their language performance other than the factor of maturation or possible differences among the children. For example, recording only the mother-child interaction would have introduced a variable factor into comparisons of the performance of the three children. The children's utterances would have occurred in response to stimulation that differed with respect to variations in the way the three mothers communicated with their children.

Although not analyzed directly, it was observed that the mothers differed in their approaches to discipline, play, training, and attempts to restrict or stimulate behavior. For example, Eric's mother pursued toilet training with a system of rewards and emphasis on comparative parent behavior; Gia's mother introduced the subject almost casually but successfully in the course of one rainy stay-at-home week; and Kathryn's mother stressed 'self-motivation'—using the toilet when and because 'she wants to.'

In their interactions with the children the mothers tended to approve or disapprove different kinds of behavior; "please" and "thank you" were stressed by Eric's mother and never mentioned by the others. They tended to talk to the children differently and to talk about the children in different terms. Eric's and Gia's parents repeatedly 'rehearsed' descriptions of past events such as trips to the zoo, having the child complete leading sentences, "And we saw the__," or answer specific questions, "And what did Daddy buy you?"

The investigation was not directly concerned with the *process* of language learning (for which describing the mother-child interaction would have been necessary) but was directed toward describing the child's linguistic performance within the context in which it occurred. With this goal in mind, the investigator was able to control the context with respect to discourse and behavioral interaction. Interaction with the child was structured along certain guidelines that had to do with the way the investigator played and communicated with the children.

The toys that were brought were unpacked by the child, usually without delay, and the child followed his own play inclinations—doing whatever he wanted to do with the toys while the investigator sat with him on the floor. When there were signs that interest in a particular toy was waning, the investigator would introduce complications such as having the bridge collapse or the slide break. After such crises, an augmentative element was introduced, such as sliding the wheels into one of the blocks, or suggesting that the lambs might be cold or hungry. If the child was disinterested in a particular toy, the investigator would play with it and the child usually would join her.

The investigator shared the child's emotional tone—laughing with him, growing tired with him, sharing surprise, disappointment, frustration, excitement. The children were free to wander, and the investigator would follow a child's distraction to other toys or activities. The only restrictions in these sessions pertained to the safety of the child, the recording equipment, and the investigator.

Controlling the investigator's communication with the child was largely a matter of pacing. The tendency was to follow rather than lead, to talk in response to what the child did or said. It was important to watch for cues—to wait for a forthcoming utterance or the completion or expansion of an utterance. The investigator frequently repeated the child's utterances—the most innocuous response to what the child had said—and often commented in a casual aside on the activity or environment in order to record cues that would be helpful when transcribing. To obtain a repetition or expansion of an utterance by the child, the investigator would pretend not to hear or would ask for a repetition.

During each session the investigator relieved the focus on the child from time to time by walking away, looking through a magazine, or talking with the child's mother. When the child's mother or friend was present, the investigator was more of an observer than a participant in the activity.

It is important to emphasize that the investigator was well known to the children and saw them frequently between observation sessions. The children appeared to see her as a special breed of playmate who, although an adult, had unlimited time, patience, and interest in them and in what they were doing. There was never any indication of shyness or restraint—the children were open and responsive.

The extent to which these sessions and the investigator's participation might have influenced the children's language acquisition—that they might have contributed in some way to the learning process—is open to speculation. There was no empirical test to determine the influence of 8 hours of such activity every six weeks. As was seen, there were similarities in the course of development among the three children, but there were also important differences—in spite of the care with which they were selected as 'similar' children. The similarities in language acquisition probably related, at least in part, to the nature of the language they were learning, and the differences to the fact that they were three different children growing up in three homes that, although alike according to a sociological standard, differed from one another nonetheless.

A.1.3. Transcribing Recorded Tapes

As reported in Chapter 2, all the child's utterances and everything said to him were transcribed, along with information about the non-linguistic context as it was recalled and understood from linguistic and nonlinguistic cues recorded on the tape.

It was relatively easy to recall the nonlinguistic context when transcribing the children playing with certain toys: blocks falling or being nested or stacked; a car, a truck, or a train being pushed on the floor and under bridges; bridges collapsing; passengers falling off; clowns rocking; wooden furniture being arranged in the open-roofed doll house; wheels rolling—all were accompanied by characteristic noises that were clearly discernible on the tape. Other activities and play with other toys—finger animal puppets, woolly lambs, bendable family figures, puzzles—often left minimal or no audible traces. However, it was possible to record pertinent and unobtrusive comments during the activity—for example, "yes, there are two" when (1) the child commented "lamb in house" and (2) there were two lambs in the house. The children's reports of distant past or future events were checked with their mothers.

A certain expertise was developed in re-creating the observation session for transcription. Total recall could not be claimed, and there were certainly difficulties, but a good amount of the important information was available. Although the utterance and situation recorded on the tape were sometimes equivocal, in the course of the 8-hour sample these unidentified utterances represented a small minority of the total number of utterances available for analysis.

A.2. Description of the Toys Used in Collecting Language Samples [1]

Nesting wood boxes (Q810)—"blocks"; four graduated, hollow blocks with five sides and a solid fifth block as the smallest; could be stacked or nested; round peek holes in two sides of each hollow block; alternately natural wood and orange paint.

Mirror box (Q786)—hollow block lined with metal reflectors on the bottom and two sides; 2-inch round holes in other two sides; natural wood.

Balancer (B634)—"seesaw" or "teeter totter"; natural wood with six removable riders, "boys"; riders fit into three holes on either side of balancer; balancer, natural wood; "boys," painted orange with natural heads, no features.

Roll-a-wheel (R011) – "slide"; wooden runway with center groove on one side; separate wooden upright support attached at 50-degree angle; four wooden wheels, red, blue, green, yellow.

Rubber stand-up puzzle (T504)—rubber family figures that fit loosely into a wooden form board; father, mother, girl, boy, baby; alternately blue and yellow.

Interlocking freight train (R009; R098)—solid natural wood block; engine, tank car with removable tank, dumpcar with revolving dumper, and seven flat cars; no wheels.

[1] The names of the toys, catalog numbers, and descriptions were taken from the 1965 and 1966 catalogs published by Creative Playthings, Princeton, New Jersey—the source for all the items. The words in quotation marks are the terms that the children used to refer to the toys.

Dress-me doll (D312)—boy rag doll; orange hair; embroidered eyes and mouth; no nose; removable blue pants with zipper and buckled belt, laced orange shirt.

Mr. Tot's auto (B065)—"car"; solid wood; removable driver; black wheels; car painted red; natural wood driver.

Thin arch (B996)—"bridge"; molded plywood.

Bendable rubber people: white family (B292)—realistically molded and painted rubber over bendable wire frames; figures sit, stand, and assume different positions; father, mother, girl, boy, baby; scaled for use with doll house.

Folding doll house (D100M)—open-roofed; 30 by 30 inches; 8 inches high; four movable walls; walls divide the house into five different sized rooms; painted blue with white walls; windows and doors cut out.

Solid block doll house furniture (D108M)—scaled for the folding house; kitchen: stove, refrigerator, sink; living room: couch, armchair, chair; dining room: table, four chairs; bedroom: double bed, chest with four removable drawers; playroom: cradle, single bed, rocker; all of the above in natural wood; bathroom: sink, toilet, bathtub, painted white.

Wood head finger puppets (G447)—each fits a child's finger; five animals: dog, cat, bear, donkey, wolf; painted features; attached, movable ears; cloth bodies.

Flexible standpatter (B581)—"man"; two; wire arms and legs; natural wood body and head with no features; weighted metal feet; no hands; man sits or stands.

Rocking clowns (not listed)—two natural wood, weighted clowns that rock and make a rattling sound when shaken.

Truck (not listed)—same size as car; natural wood; black wheels; removable driver painted green and shaped differently from the car driver.

Lambs and farmer (not listed)—four wool-covered lambs; one black, three white; no legs or tails; ears and nose features on natural wood head; farmer made of natural wood, wearing hat; no arms or features.

Books—(1) *Pat the bunny* ("rabbit book"), Dorothy Kunhardt, Golden Press; (2) *Baby's first counting book* ("animal book"), Platt and Munk; stiff board pages, used as a "bridge"; (3) *The toy book* ("bear book"), Joe Kaufman, Golden Press; (4) *Anybody at home?*, H. A. Rey, Houghton Mifflin; (5) *Papa Small*, Lois Lenski, Henry Z. Walck, Inc.

Appendix B: Data Analysis Form

B.1. Sample of the Form

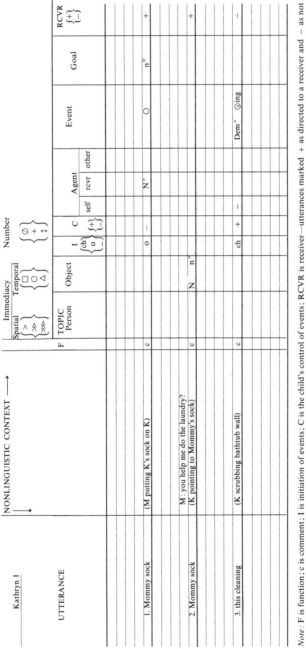

Note: F is function; c is comment; I is initiation of events; C is the child's control of events; RCVR is receiver—utterances marked + as directed to a receiver and − as not directed; N is a proper name; n is any other noun; v is a verb.

B.2. Notations for Entering Nonlinguistic Information on Data Analysis Form

The following notations were used to record aspects of nonlinguistic context.

Spatial Immediacy of Objects

>	Proximal
≫	Distal
⋙	Removed

Temporal Immediacy of Events, event occurring

□	Immediately previous to the utterance
○	During the utterance
△	Immediately subsequent to the utterance
⧇	During the utterance and repetitive
□′	Distant past
△′	Distant future

Number of Objects

+	Dual
‡	Plural

Initiation of Events

ch	Child
o	Other

The child's control of events was indicated as [+] or [−].

Utterances were marked as directed to a receiver [+] or not [−].

Appendix C: Lexicon, Kathryn I Grammar

C.1. Lexical Items in Syntactic Contexts

[+N]	f	[+anim]	[+Nom]	+[__Prep]
appetite	2			
apple	2			
baby	13	+	+	
ball(s)	6			
beanbag	1	+	+	
bear	4	+	+	
block	2			
book	8			
boot	1			
boy	2	+	+	
button	1			
cake	1			
car	4			
carrot	1			
(pussy)cat	6	+	+	
cereal	3			
cheek	2			
chicken	1			
children	6			
'chine	2		+	
cottage cheese	5			
cup	1			
Daddy	1	+	+	.
diaper	1			

[+N]	f	[+anim]	[+Nom]	+[__Prep]
dog (s,ie)	2			
drawer	1			
dress	1			
ear	1			
elevator	1			
file	1			
fire	1			
flower	2			
foot(s)	4			
girl	2		+	
Grandma	1	+	+	
hair	2			
haircurl	5			
hand	8			
hangnail	1			
hat	4			
heater	1			+
heel	1			
hole	1			
home	1			
horse	2			
house	2			
HunkeyDorey	2			
Jeremy	1			
Jocelyn	1	+	+	
juice	1			
Kathryn	12	+	+	+
kiss	2			
lap	1			
laundry	1			
leg	1			
Lois	6	+	+	
man	3			
marshmallow	3			
meat	4			
milk	3			
mirror	1			
Mommy	26	+	+	
Muffin Man	1			
necklace	2			+
noise	2			
noodle(s)	2			
nut(s)	2			
orange	1			
paper	1			+
page	2			

[+ N]	f	[+ anim]	[+ Nom]	+[__Prep]
pants	1			
pigtail	8			
pin	5			
pocket	3			
polkadot	1			
raisin	14			
rubber band	1			
shadow	2			
sheep	3	+	+	
shirts	1			
shoe	1			
shovel	2			
slipper	6			+
soap	3			
sock	10			
spoon	2			
spider	3			
sweater	1			
tail	2			
tape	2			
tiger	2	+	+	
toe	1			
toenail	1			
toy	8			
umbrella	1			
vegetable	1			
watch	1			
wall	4			
Wendy	4	+	+	
window	3			

[+ ADJ]	f	
all	5	+[__ADJ]
baby	1	
big	3	
bread	1	
coffee	2	
cold	2	
dirty	7	
funny	5	
fuzzy	2	
heavy	1	
jewelry	1	

[+ADJ]	f
little	1
more	19
'nother	4
party	1
pink	1
sharp	2
sticky	3
tiny	7
tire'	4
two	5

[+VB]	f	+[__NP]	+[__Part]	[+VB]	f	+[__NP]	+[__Part]
ate	1	+		look	2	+	
away	5	+		make	8	+	
bounce	1			open	1	+	
busy	3		+	play	2	+	
catch	1			pull	3	+	
cleaning	4	+		push	2		
close	2			put	3	+	
comb	3	+		read	1	+	
coming	2			ride(ing)	3	+	
cough	1	+		see	3	+	+
dance	1			sit down	7	+	+
do	3	+		stretch	1		
find	1	+		stuck	3	+	
fit	2			show	1	+	
get	2	+		squish	2		
go	5	+	+	throw	2	+	+
have	1	+		touch	2	+	
help(ing)	6	+		turn	4		
here	2	+		want	6	+	
hurt	1			wash	2	+	
in	1	+		watch	1	+	
iron	1			zip	1		
jump	1		+				

Note: The number, f, refers to the number of different syntactic contexts in which the lexical item occurred in the text. The lexicons presented in this and the subsequent Appendices are intended as representative, inasmuch as they include only the words that occurred in the language samples. If the samples had been extended, it is assumed that other words would have occurred, and words in the lexicons would have occurred in contexts with features that are not specified here. The form in which the lexicons are presented may be considered unorthodox, but there does not appear to be a consensus regarding the form for lexical entries in a dictionary. Moreover, the form of the lexicon is not the issue; attention has been given to the children's use of words—in syntactic contexts and in isolation.

C.2. Single-Word Utterances and their Frequencies of Occurrence

all better
all gone, 4
all through
all right
arm
ate
away, 2

baby, 10
ball
bang!
bathtub, 2
beanbag, 3
bear
bicycle
big, 3
bird(s), 3
block, 2
book, 9
boom, 2
boots, 2
box, 2
boy
brush
bunny, 2
busy, 3
butterfly
button, 3
byebye, 3

cake
candle
car, 3
careful
cat, 10
cereal
chair
chap
chicken, 3
children, 2
'chine, 21
choochoo
clean(ing), 4
clock
close, 3
cold, 4

comb
cookie
cottage cheese, 2
cry
cup

Daddy
dance
dirty, 4
dogg(ie), 4
door
down
dress, 3
duck, 2

elephants

feet
fish, 4
fit, 4
flower, 2
foot(s), 3
footstool
fork
frog, 2
funny, 3
fuzz, 2
fuzzy, 2

girl, 4
gobble
Grandma, 2
grasshopper
grocery
   store, 2

hair, 3
hair curl, 4
hand, 9
hat(s), 11
heater
heel
Hello, 2
help, 2
here, 2
Hi, 6

hold, 2
horse(ie), 5
hot, 3
house, 15
hungry
HunkeyDorey, 2
hurt, 4

Jack
Jeremy
jingle bell
Jocelyn
juice, 2
jump
just right, 2

Kathryn
kiss
knee

lamb
lap
letter, 2
Lois, 8
London fall
   down

mail chute
man, 6
marshmallow
meat, 5
'member
milk, 3
mirror, 6
Mommy, 20
moomoo
more, 4
mouth
Muffin Man, 2
music

napkin
necklace, 4
nice
no, 55
noodle, 4

off, 6
O.K., 42
on top, 3
open, 2
orange
ouch, 6
outside

paper
picture, 2
pig, 3
pigtail, 3
pink, 2
polkadot(s), 2
pudding, 3
pull, 2
push

raisin, 3
ribbon
right now
ring, 2
rubber band, 2

sack
Santa Claus, 2
scarf
scrub, 2
shadow
shake
sharp, 3
sheep, 5
shirts
shoe, 5
shovel
sit down, 4
sit(s), 9
slipper, 4
soap, 3
sock
squirrel, 4
stretch
stuck, 14
suit
sun, 3

tape, 2	touch	vegetable	yes
thank you, 23	toy(s), 11		
thats, 3	truck, 4	walk	zip, 2
this, 3	turn, 5	watch, 5	
tiny, 2	turtle	water	
tire', 2		Wendy, 3	
toe	umbrella, 4	wheel, 2	
toilet seat	up, 4	woof woof, 3	

Appendix D: Lexicon, Gia I Grammar

D.1. Lexical Items in Syntactic Contexts

[+N]	f	[+anim]	[+N]	f	[+anim]	[+VB]	f	
baby	3		Daddy	1		away	4	
bag	1		ear	1		blow	1	
ball	1		eyes	1		close	1	
balloon	1		Eric	1		go	4	+[__Part]
band	2		fish	1		gone	2	
bang	1		fly	3	+	lean back	1	
bed	1		Gia	2	+	make	1	
blanket	4		girl	5	+	out	1	
block	3	+	gum	1		ride	1	
Blueyes	2		Jocelyn	1		throw	1	
boat	1		Justin	1		tie bow	1	
book	1		lady	1		up	1	
box	1		lamb	1	+	write	5	
bugug	1		Mommy	6				
button	1		pen	2				
car	2		piece	1				
clown	2		pocket	1				
cookies	1		rabbit	1				
crackers	1		rock	1				

[+N]	f [+anim]	[+N]	f [+anim]	[+VB]	f
slide	1				
tree	1				
truck	2				
wheel	2				
wowwow	2				

Note: The number, f, refers to the number of different syntactic contexts in which the lexical item occurred in the text.

D.2. Single-Word Utterances and their Frequencies of Occurrence

again	camera	Gia, 6	melon
ah, 3	car	girl, 3	milk
ahah	Caroline	go, 11	mine
animal, 4	carriage	goat	more, 51
away, 26	cat, 2	gone	music
	cheese, 2		
baby, 6	cigarette, 3	hair	neck
back, 4	close	here	nice, 6
bag	clown, 3	Hi, 11	no, 16
ball, 5	come	horn	nose, 2
balloon	cookie(s), 2	horse, 5	
bang	cow	house	off
barrette	crackers		oh, 3
bath	crayon	ice cream, 2	out
bear	cry	iron	owl
beard		it	
bib, 2	Daddy, 3		page, 3
birds	dolly	Jocelyn	peekaboo
blanket	down, 10		piece, 4
block, 12	dress	keys, 6	pig
blow	duck	knee, 2	pocket, 10
Blueye(s), 4			
boat, 2	ear	lamb, 4	
book, 7	elephant	leg	rabbit, 6
bottle, 2	Eric	light	raccoon
bow, 5	eye(s), 3	look	radio
bus			rain
butter, 2	finger	Mommy, 19	read, 2
button, 8	fish, 2	magazine, 2	ring
bye, 5	flower	mailbox	rock, 3
byebye, 5	fly, 7	man, 5	round

slide, 9	ticktock	wash	wowwow, 5
slipper	tongue	watch	write, 25
suitcase	top, 5	water	
	toys	whale	
telephone, 3	train, 2	wheel, 4	yes, 13
throw	truck, 6	woop	

Appendix E: Lexicon, Gia II Grammar

E.1. Lexical Items in Syntactic Contexts

[+N]	f	[+anim]	[+N]	f	[+anim]	[+N]	f	[+anim]
animal	2		cow	2	+	lion	1	
apple	3		Daddy(s)	7	+	Lois	6	+
baby	13		dinner	1		magazine	1	+
bag	3		dolly	2		man	14	+
band	2		Dumbo	1		me	1	
bank	1		Eric	1		microphone	2	
barrette	1		eyeglasses	1		milk	2	
bath	5		face	1		mine	2	
beard	1		fish	3		mobile	2	
bee	1		garage	1		Mommy(s)	36	+
block	5	+	Gia	15	+	monkey	1	
boat	1		girl	6	+	music	3	
book	13		Grandma	1		Papa	1	+
bottle	3		gum	1		paper	4	
box	1		hand	1	+	pattycake	1	
bridge	2		hat	1		peaches	2	
butterfly	1		horse	1		peekboo	2	
car	3		jacket	1		picture(s)	10	
Caroline	1		Jeffrey	1		piece	1	
carriage	1		key(s)	2		pinwheel	3	+[__up]
cat	1		kite	1		plum	1	
chicken	1		label	3	+[__off]	potty	1	
clown	1		lamb	1		pretty	3	
cookie(s)	5		light	3		rabbit(s)	8	

[+N]	f [+anim]	[+N]	f [+anim]	[+N]	f [+anim]
rain	1	shopping bag	1	truck	5	
record	6	Teddy Bear	1	wheel	2	+
Roger	2	stroller	1	window	2	
shoe	3	toy(s)	7	wowwow	2	
slide	3	train	5		

Note: The number, f, refers to the number of different syntactic contexts in which the lexical item occurred in the text.

[+VB]	f	+[__NP]		Unaccounted for	f
away(s)	12	+		broke	2
come	1			hot	1
crying	1			right	1
do	1	+			
draw	1	+			
eat	2	+			
fix	1				
go	8	+	+[__Part]		
got	1	+			
in	6				
nice	3	+			
on	9	+			
out	2	+			
play	1	+			
push	1	+			
read	9	+			
ride	9	+			
ringing	1				
see	4	+			
sit	3				
sleep(ing)	2				
stand(up)	5				
stuck	1				
turned	1	+			
upidown	4				
weewee	1				
wipe	1				
write	7	+			

E.2. Single-Word Utterances and their Frequencies of Occurrence

all right	back, 4	bank	bee
apple, 2	bag, 3	barrette, 2	bird
away, 37	ball, 3	bath, 11	block, 5
	balloon, 4	beads	Blueyes
baby, 14	band	beard, 3	book, 20

bottle, 4
bridge, 4
broke, 3
bum, 2
butterfly
button, 3
byebye, 5

camera
car, 3
Caroline, 2
carriage, 2
carrot
cat, 2
clean, 2
clown
cookie, 10
cow
crash
crying, 3

Daddy(s), 8
diaper
dinner, 2
down, 5
draw
drink, 2
dry

ear
elephant, 8
Eric, 5
eyes

fish, 2

garage, 3
gas

get
Gia, 24
giraffe, 2
girl, 3
go, 7
grass

happen
hat
help
Hi, 7
highchair, 2
honeycomb
horse, 4
hot, 2

ice cream, 2
in, 14
iron, 4
is
it

jacket, 3
jump, 3

key(s), 5
kite, 4

label, 8
lamb, 3
laundry
light, 7
Lois, 7
look

maid
mama
man, 40

man's
meat
meatball, 3
microphone
milk, 3
mine, 4
mirror
Mommy(s), 54
monkey, 2
moon
more, 78

nice, 3
no, 24
noise
noodle, 2

off, 6
oh, 74
on, 21
out, 2
outside, 3

papa
pattycake, 2
peaches, 3
peekboo, 2
picture, 7
piece, 5
pinwheel, 4
phone
pocket, 4
potty

rabbit(s), 14
read, 10
record, 4
red

ride, 15
right
ringing
Roger, 2
rub
rubber

shoe
sit, 9
sleep(ing), 6
smoke
spoon
stand, 6
stroller
stuck, 4

thank you
tire
tissue
top
touch
toy(s), 20
train, 10
truck, 8

uh oh, 9
up, 10

wagon
watch, 2
wet, 3
whee, 3
wheel
window, 13
wipe, 4
wowwow, 4
write, 7

yes, 145

Appendix F: Lexicon, Eric II Grammar

F.1. Lexical Items in Syntactic Contexts

[+N]	f	[+VB]	f	
air conditioner	1	broke	1	
apple	1	build	1	
baby(s)	5	comes	1	
blocks	1	cry	1	
boat	1	down	2	
cereal	1	eating	1	
'chine	4	find	1	
cleaner	1	get	1	
clown	3	go	1	
door	1	help	1	
Eric	1	hit	1	
goose	1	make	1	
hands	1	in	1	
hats	1	play	2	
home	1	see	1	
house	2	show	1	
juice	1	sit	1	
light	1	sleep	1	
me	1	turn	2	+[__Part]
Mommy	3	want	1	
noise	4			
toy	2			
turn	1			

Note: The number, f, refers to the number of different syntactic contexts in which the lexical item occurred in the text.

F.2. Single-Word Utterances and their Frequencies of Occurrence

airplane	Daddy, 5	horse	off, 3
Allison	diaper	hot, 2	O.K.
all right, 2	dirty, 2	house	on, 2
	dog, 3	hungry	one, 2
baby, 12	door		out, 4
bad	down	juice, 10	
bath	drop		pee
battery, 3	drum	kiss, 4	phone, 2
bed	ducky		please, 3
blocks, 3		light, 7	push
boy, 2	eat		
broke, 4		me	round, 2
bunny, 2	find	mine, 4	
bye, 4	fix	Mommy, 12	see, 5
	food	money	shoe
car, 5	funny, 2	more	sit, 11
castle, 3		mousie	
cat	good		Teddy, 4
'chine, 25		naughty	teeth
choochoo, 5	hand	nice, 9	thank you, 2
cleaner, 6	hat	no, 76	this, 2
climb up	heavy	no more, 4	truck
clown, 4	Hello, 4	noise, 15	turn
cocoa	here, 9	'nother	
cookie, 8	Hi, 10		up, 2
cry, 4	hold		

Appendix G: Lexicon, Eric III Grammar

G.1. Lexical Items in Syntactic Contexts

[+N]	f	[+N]	f	[+VB]	f
airplane	1	juice	6	cry(ing)	2
apple	8	lamb	2	do	1
baby(s)	6	light	3	down	3
birdie	2	lollipop	1	eat	2
blanket	1	man(s)	7	find	4
blocks	2	medicine	1	fit	13
book	1	Mommys	1	fix	6
boy	1	naughty(s)	2	found	1
bunny	1	noise	4	get	3
car	2	one	7	go(s)	9 +[__Part]
cheese	1	phone	1	hold	1
'chine	3	puzzle	1	look	2
cleaner	5	seal	1	made	1
clown	1	sand	1	move	1
'coon	1	shoe(s)	3	need	4
Daddy	1	slide	1	off	3
doggie	2	toy(s)	5	out	1
dumpcar	1	train	1	ready go	3
Eric	1	truck	1	round	1
foots	1	wheel	1	see	3
horsie	1	whistle	1	sit(s)	7
				stand up	1
				throw	1
				want	4
				watch	1

Note: The number, f, refers to the number of different syntactic contexts in which the lexical item occurred in the text.

G.2. Single-Word Utterances and their Frequencies of Occurrence

---

airplane, 6	dirtys	lamb, 8	sharp
apple, 17	dog, 3	light, 6	sheep, 3
around	doll	lion	shoe(s), 13
away, 3	door, 2	little, 3	Simon, 2
	down	lollipop	sing
baby, 7	duck	look, 3	sit(s), 8
balloon	dumpcar, 2		sleep
bead		machine	slide
beep	ear	man, 9	snail
beep beep	eat, 7	mans	sock(s), 2
bees	eating	meat	soup
belly	Eric, 2	Mommy, 10	spin, 2
birdy(s), 4		Mommys	squirrel
blanket		monkey	stars
bless you	fair	moo	sun
blocks, 6	feet	moon, 2	sunny
boom	fish	more, 11	supper
bottle	fit, 3	mouse, 4	
box, 3	flush		tank
boy, 6	food, 2	naughty, 8	tank car
brush	foot, 6	naughtys	Teddy
bunny, 4	foots	nice, 5	that, 2
bye, 8	fox	night	there
	funny, 4	no, 42	this, 2
candy, 2		no more, 8	Thor
car, 9	get	noise, 11	tiger, 2
carriage	go, 3		tink toy
cat(s), 4	good, 3	off, 3	toot, 10
cheese, 2		one, 8	toot toot, 10
'chine, 12	hat	out, 15	toy(s), 8
choo	Hello, 6		train, 2
choochoo train	help, 2	peep, 4	truck, 3
clean	here, 42	phone, 7	Tubby, 2
cleaner, 10	Hi, 3	pie	
clown, 4	hit	piece	under
cocoa, 2	horsie, 2	pin(s), 2	up
cold	hot	'possum	
'coon	hurry	puppies	
cow			water, 3
crown	in, 2	ready, 10	way
cry(ing), 16		ride	whistle
cup	juice, 11	round	wool
Daddy, 2	kangaroo	sand, 3	yellow
dark	key, 2	seal, 3	
dirty, 8	kiss	see, 2	zip(s), 4

Glossary of Notation and Terms

A. Notations used in presenting speech events

Parentheses enclose descriptions of context and behavior. Utterances on the left side of an example, not in parentheses, were spoken by someone else in the environment. Utterances on the right side of the example were spoken by the child.

. . . . .	indicates lapse of time.
:	indicates lapse of time with intervening activity or speech.
----	indicates unintelligible or inaudible utterance.
"girl__"	"__" indicates abrupt juncture: either a self-correction or false start.
·	(raised period) indicates pause within an utterance without terminal contour.
:	indicates elongation of the immediately preceding element—for example, "no:".
[ ]	enclose more than one utterance occurring in succession, except as indicated in Table 7.7, Chapter 7.
>	indicates a particular utterance (in a sequence of utterances) that represents the example referred to in the text or in the title of the table in which it appears.
↑	indicates rising pitch contour.
↓	indicates falling pitch contour.
//	enclose phonetic representation.

In the tables, the names of persons are abbreviated as follows: G is Gia, K is Kathryn, E is Eric, M is Mommy, D is Daddy, and L is Lois (the investigator).

259

B. Notations used in rules of grammar

An explanation of rules and symbols is presented in Chapter 2 in the discussion of generative transformational grammar.

→	indicates that the string on the left 'is rewritten' as the string on the right in a phrase structure rewrite rule.
⇒	indicates that the structural representation on the left 'is rewritten' as the structural representation on the right in a transformation rule.
( )	indicate an optional choice; the element enclosed may or may not occur.
{ }	indicate a choice among elements, one of which must occur.
[ ]	enclose features of lexical items.
#	indicates sentence boundary.
S.D.	represents 'structural description' (of an underlying string).
S.C.	represents 'structural change' (the transformation of the underlying string).
NP	noun phrase.
VP	verb phrase.
Nom	nominal.
N	noun.
Pron	pronoun.
Dem	demonstrative pronoun.
V	verb.
ADJ	adjective.
Ng	negative element, for example, "no" or "not".
Q	quantifier, usually "more".
Pred P	predicate phrase.
Prep P	prepositional phrase.

C. Terms used in discussion

Reference to particular chapters indicates where the term was originally defined for the purpose of this investigation.

ambiguous: a description of an utterance having two (or more) possible interpretations that can be distinguished or resolved—for example, "Mommy sock" meaning "Mommy's sock" or, alternatively, "Mommy (verb) sock." (Chapter 3)

anomalous: a description of an utterance that appears to have no interpretation; the occurrence of an utterance in a situation to which the linguistic expression bears no apparent relation—for example, Gia eating peaches and saying "no more." (Chapter 3) *category symbol:* a symbol in phrase structure rewrite rules, such as N and V, from which lexical items (for example, "raisin" and "fit," but not /ə/) are derived. (Chapter 2)

comment: a function of a speech event in which the referent is manifest. Comments accompany ongoing behavior or announce immediately subsequent or previous behavior. They are either directed to a receiver or not but do not attempt to influence the behavior of the receiver. (Chapter 2)

competence: the knowledge of language.

corpus: the group of utterances selected from the speech sample for linguistic analysis; that is, all the utterances containing more than one tentative morpheme and excluding repetitions, imitations, and fragments of songs, rhymes, or stories.

derivation: the result of successive application of phrase structure rules, rewriting one element at a time, in generating a sentence. (Chapter 2)

direction: a function of a speech event in which the child seeks a change in the context that he is unable or unwilling to effect himself, involving the behavior of someone else. (Chapter 2)

discourse: interdependent utterances spoken in succession by one or more persons in a single speech event. (Chapter 2)

equivocal: a description of an utterance having two (or more) possible interpretations that cannot be distinguished, either one or the other interpretation being acceptable in the particular situation—for example, "Mommy iron," where "iron" is an homophonous form as either a noun or a verb. (Chapter 3)

generative: the notion that specifies the interrelation of the rules of a grammar.

grammar: in the traditional, taxonomic view, an account of the principles of arrangement of linguistic elements and their relations, in terms of morphology and syntax. In the generative view, the system of rules that assigns structural descriptions to sentences to account for sound-meaning relationships.

grammatical category: such notions as noun phrase or verb phrase in phrase structure rules (see *category symbol* and *major category symbol*). (Chapter 2)

grammatical function: the inherent relations that hold between categories in a sentence, such as those defining subject of the sentence, object of the verb, predicate of the sentence. (Chapter 2)

indeterminate: a description of an utterance for which an interpretation cannot be made, most often because of insufficient evidence. (Chapter 3)

lexicon: a dictionary—the words (and their inherent semantic and syntactic features) that can be substituted as lexical items in the last line of the derivation of a sentence through the operation of a substitution transformation (Chapter 2)

major category symbol: a symbol in phrase structure rewrite rules such as NP and VP, from which category symbols (N or V) are derived. (Chapter 2)

morpheme: the smallest meaningful unit of language that can occur alone, as "run," or only in bound relation to other morphemes, as "-ing" in "running."

morphology: the combination of morphemes into words.

observation: the entire period of time, usually about 8 hours, in which ongoing activity was tape-recorded to obtain a speech sample.

performance: actual use of language (understanding or speaking) as internal and environmental factors interact with underlying language competence.

phrase-marker (or branching tree-diagram): a schematic representation of the derivation or underlying structure of a sentence. (Chapter 2) *phrase structure :* the base or categorial subcomponent of the syntactic component of a generative grammar that contains a sequence of rewriting rules that, when applied successively, generates the underlying structure of a sentence. (Chapter 2)

productivity : the use of a syntactic structure with different formatives in different situations in a corpus. A structure was judged *unique* if it occurred only once in the corpus of a speech sample, *marginal* if it occurred fewer than five times, and *productive* if it occurred five times or more. (Chapter 2)

report : a function of a speech event in which the referent is not manifest. Reports are informative utterances directed to a receiver, without an attempt to influence behavior. (Chapter 2)

rewrite rules : rules in the phrase structure that specify the underlying order of elements in a sentence and the grammatical relations that hold among them. (Chapter 2)

speech event : the unit in which an utterance occurs, including such factors as can be specified in terms of behavior, context, and other participants. (Chapter 2)

speech sample : the child's total output of utterances in the course of a particular observation.

surface structure : the structural specification for the actual physical and acoustic event of the spoken sentence—the linear sequence of elements produced by the sender and heard by the receiver. (Chapter 1)

syntax : the arrangements of morphological units and words in larger constructions, such as phrases and sentences.

text : the linguistic transcription of a speech sample.

transformation : a rule of grammar that effects a structural change on the underlying structure of a sentence by adding, deleting, or reordering elements to derive the specification for the surface structure. (Chapter 2)

underlying structure : the structural specification for the underlying semantic interpretation of a sentence—as intended by the speaker and understood by the receiver. (Chapter 1)

References

Bach, Emmon, and Robert T. Harms (Eds.) (1968). *Universals in Linguistic Theory* (New York: Holt, Rinehart and Winston).

Bellugi, Ursula (1967). "The Acquisition of Negation." Doctoral dissertation, Harvard University.

Braine, Martin D. S. (1963). "The ontogeny of English phrase structure: The first phase," *Language, 39*, 1–13.

——— (1965). "Three suggestions regarding grammatical analyses of children's language." Paper presented to the Annual Conference on Linguistics of the Linguistic Circle of New York.

Brown, Roger, and Ursula Bellugi (1964). "Three processes in the child's acquisition of syntax," *Harvard Educational Review, 34*, 133–151.

———, Courtney B. Cazden, and Ursula Bellugi (1969). "The child's grammar from I to III." In J. P. Hill (Ed.), *1967 Minnesota Symposia on Child Psychology* (Minneapolis: University of Minnesota Press).

———, and Colin Fraser (1963). "The acquisition of syntax." In Charles N. Cofer and Barbara S. Musgrave (Eds.), *Verbal Behavior and Learning* (New York: McGraw-Hill), pp. 158–197.

Cazden, Courtney B. (1967). "On individual differences in language competence and performance," *Journal of Special Education, 1*, 135–150.

——— (1968). "The acquisition of noun and verb inflections," *Child Development, 39*, 433–448.

Chomsky, Noam (1957). *Syntactic Structures* (The Hague: Mouton & Co.).

——— (1964a). "Current issues in linguistic theory." In Jerry A. Fodor and Jerrold J. Katz (Eds.), *The Structure of Language* (Englewood Cliffs, N.J.: Prentice-Hall), pp. 50–118.

——— (1964b). Formal discussion. In Ursula Bellugi and Roger Brown (Eds.), *The Acquisition of Language* (Monograph of the Society for Research in Child Development, 29), pp. 35–39.

——— (1965). *Aspects of the Theory of Syntax* (Cambridge, Mass.: The M.I.T. Press).

——— (1968). *Language and Mind* (New York: Harcourt, Brace and World).

——— (1969). "Deep structure, surface structure, and semantic interpretation." Unpublished paper reproduced by the Indiana University, Bloomington, Ind.

Ervin, Susan M. (1966). "Imitation and structural change in children's language." In Eric H. Lenneberg (Ed.), *New Directions in the Study of Language* (Cambridge, Mass.: The M.I.T. Press), pp. 163–189.

Greenberg, Joseph H. (1963). "Some universals of grammar with particular reference to meaningful elements." In Joseph H. Greenberg (Ed.), *Universals of Language* (Cambridge, Mass.: The M.I.T. Press), pp. 73–113.

Gruber, Jeffrey S. (1967). "Topicalization in child language," *Foundations of Language, 3,* 37–65.

Harris, Zellig S. (1964). "Discourse analysis." In Jerry A. Fodor and Jerrold J. Katz (Eds.), *The Structure of Language* (Englewood Cliffs, N.J.: Prentice-Hall), pp. 355–383.

Hymes, Dell (1964). *Language in Culture and Society* (New York: Harper and Row).

Jakobson, Roman (1968). *Child Language Aphasia and Phonological Universals* (The Hague: Mouton & Co.).

Jespersen, Otto (1917). *Negation in English and Other Languages* (København).

———— (1961). *A Modern English Grammar*. Part V (London: George Allen and Unwin).

Klima, Edward S. (1964). "Negation in English." In Jerry A. Fodor and Jerrold J. Katz (Eds.), *The Structure of Language* (Englewood Cliffs, N.J.: Prentice-Hall), pp. 246–323.

———— and Ursula Bellugi (1966), "Syntactic regularities in the speech of children." In J. L. Lyons and R. J. Wales (Eds.), *Psycholinguistic Papers* (Edinburgh: Edinburgh University Aldine Press), pp. 183–208.

Labov, William (1966). "Grammaticality of everyday speech." Paper presented to the Linguistic Society of America.

Lenneberg, Eric H. (1967). *Biological Foundations of Language* (New York: Wiley).

Leopold, Werner F. (1939–1949). *Speech Development of a Bilingual Child* (Evanston, Ill.: Northwestern University Press), 4 vols.

———— (1961). "Patterning in children's language learning." In Sol Saporta (Ed.), *Psycholinguistics* (New York: Holt, Rinehart and Winston), pp. 350–358.

Lewis, M. M. (1951). *Infant Speech, a Study of the Beginnings of Language* (New York: Humanities Press).

Lieberman, Philip (1967). *Intonation, Perception, and Language* (Cambridge, Mass.: The M.I.T. Press).

McCarthy, Dorothea (1954). "Language development in children." In Leonard Carmichael (Ed.), *Manual of Child Psychology* (New York: Wiley), pp. 492–630.

McNeill, David (1966). "Developmental psycholinguistics." In Frank Smith and George A. Miller (Eds.), *The Genesis of Language* (Cambridge, Mass.: The M.I.T. Press), pp. 15–84.

———— and Nobuko B. McNeill (1967). "A question in semantic development: What does a child mean when he says 'no'?" Paper presented to the Society for Research in Child Development.

Miller, Wick, and Susan Ervin (1964). "The development of grammar in child language." In Ursula Bellugi and Roger Brown (Eds.), *The Acquisition of Language* (Monograph of the Society for Research in Child Development, 29), pp. 9–34.

Murata, Koji (1961). "The development of verbal behavior: III. Early developmental processes of the linguistic forms and functions of requests," *Japanese Journal of Education Psychology, 9,* 220–229.

Postal, Paul M. (1964). "Underlying and superficial linguistic structure," *Harvard Educational Review, 34,* 246–266.

Sapir, Edward (1921). *Language* (New York: Harcourt, Brace and World).

Shipley, Elizabeth F., Carlota S. Smith, and Lila R. Gleitman (1969). "A study in the acquisition of language: Free responses to commands," *Language, 45,* 322–342.

Sinclair-de-Zwart, Hermina (1969). "Developmental psycholinguistics." In David Elkind and John H. Flavell (Eds.), *Studies in Cognitive Development* (New York: Oxford University Press), pp. 315–336.

Slobin, Dan I. (1966). "Comments on 'developmental psycholinguistics'." In Frank Smith and George A. Miller (Eds.), *The Genesis of Language* (Cambridge, Mass.: The M.I.T. Press), pp. 85–91.

—— (Ed.) (1967). *A Field Manual for Cross-Cultural Study of the Acquisition of Communicative Competence* (Berkeley: University of California Press).

Smith, Frank, and George A. Miller (Eds.) (1966). *The Genesis of Language* (Cambridge, Mass.: The M.I.T. Press).

Weir, Ruth H. (1966). "Some questions on the child's learning of phonology." In Frank Smith and George A. Miller (Eds.), *The Genesis of Language* (Cambridge, Mass.: The M.I.T. Press), pp. 153–168.

Wells, Rulon S. (1963). "Immediate constituents." In Martin Joos (Ed.), *Readings in Linguistics* (New York: American Council of Learned Societies), pp. 186–207.

Zipf, George K. (1965). *The Psycho-Biology of Language: An Introduction to Dynamic Philology* (1st ed., Boston: Houghton Mifflin, 1935; 2nd ed., Cambridge, Mass.: The M.I.T. Press).

Index

267